# Mens et Manus

A Pictorial History of North Carolina
Agricultural and Technical State University

# *Mens et Manus*

## A Pictorial History of North Carolina Agricultural and Technical State University

by Teresa Jo Styles
and Valerie Nieman

DUST JACKET FRONT COVER: The Dudley Memorial Building was built in 1931 to replace the previous administration building.

FRONT ENDSHEET: The campus of A&M College is taking shape in this early photograph. Dudley Hall can be seen at back right. Agriculture was the emphasis throughout the early years, and remains vital to the university's mission in its second century.

TITLE PAGE: Proctor Hall (foreground) and the New Academic Classroom Building. JESSIE GLADDEK/UNIVERSITY RELATIONS.

BACK ENDSHEET: Students hone their techniques in an animal science laboratory. JESSIE GLADDEK/UNIVERSITY RELATIONS.

DUST JACKET BACK COVER: The new Student Health Center was built in 2014 to replace the Sebastian Health Center. JESSIE GLADDEK/UNIVERSITY RELATIONS.

THE
DONNING COMPANY
PUBLISHERS

The Donning Company Publishers
184 Business Park Drive, Suite 206
Virginia Beach, VA 23462

Lex Cavanah, *General Manager*
Barbara Buchanan, *Office Manager*
Heather L. Floyd, *Editor*
Stephanie Danko, *Graphic Designer*
Monika Ebertz, *Imaging Artist*
Jennifer Elam, *Project Research Coordinator*
Nathan Stufflebean, *Marketing and Research Supervisor*
Katie Gardner, *Marketing Assistant*

Lynn Walton, *Project Director*

**Library of Congress Cataloging-in-Publication Data**
Styles, Teresa Jo.
  Mens et manus : A pictorial history of North Carolina A&T State University / by Teresa Jo Styles and Valerie Nieman.
    pages cm
  Includes bibliographical references and index.
  ISBN 978-1-57864-967-9 (hardcover : alkaline paper)
1. North Carolina Agricultural and Technical State University—History. 2. North Carolina Agricultural and Technical State University—History—Pictorial works. I. Nieman, Valerie, 1955- II. Title. III. Title: Pictorial history of North Carolina Agricultural & Technical State University. IV. Title: Pictorial history of North Carolina A and T State University. V. Title: Pictorial history of North Carolina Agricultural and Technical State University.
  S537.N8S78 2015
  630.71'1756—dc23
                                                                                      2015006024

Printed in the United States of America at Walsworth

# Contents

# Foreword from the Chancellor

North Carolina Agricultural and Technical State University is endowed with a remarkable history and great traditions. In 1891, the university began as the Agricultural and Mechanical Arts College for the Colored Race at Shaw University. As one of the 1890 land-grant institutions—historically black colleges that were established under the Second Morrill Act—the university's purpose was to provide education in agriculture, home economics, mechanical arts, and professions relative to the era. Today, N.C. A&T remains committed to fulfilling the fundamental purposes of the land-grant university through exemplary undergraduate and graduate instruction, scholarly and creative research, and effective public service and engagement.

From our humble beginnings until now, the university has adopted an uncompromising expectation of integrity and excellence among our students, faculty, staff, and alumni. A&T has historically produced socially conscious, globally prepared, and competent leaders. Aggies were on the front lines in the sit-in movement, attended rallies, and protested silently from the hallowed halls on campus, and they continue to serve as ambassadors and champions for equality all over the world. We serve today in leadership positions throughout a variety of industries, agencies, and organizations worldwide as well as positions of influence in communities throughout our nation.

As chancellor of this great institution, I am as impressed today as I was years ago as an eager, young freshman. A&T's heritage is well-defined through an unforgettable collection of stories of courage, perseverance, innovation, and achievement. The university's legacy and traditions over the last 125 years, from the formative years of the 19th century, to the war years of the 20th century, to the contemporary ideals and technological innovations of the 21st century, have been chronicled in the following pages and photographs. A&T's presence continues to be critically important in shaping the lives of thousands, including our students, faculty, staff, administrators, alumni, and supporters.

Uniquely presented by the Pictorial History Book Advisory Council, this project reflects an impressive illustration of the broad teaching, research, and service aspects of the university. The council's hard work and dedication are greatly appreciated.

Thank you for joining us in commemorating this special anniversary.

Harold L. Martin, Sr.
*Chancellor*

# Acknowledgments

The pictorial history book of North Carolina Agricultural and Technical State University could not have been accomplished without the contributions of the Book Advisory Council under the leadership of Bluford Library's dean, Vicki Coleman. Members past and present include David Arneke, Lewis Brandon III, Lenora Bryant, Olen Cole, Jacqueline Greenlee, Richard Herring, Wanda Lester, Conchita Ndege, Marian Rogers-Lindsay, Philip Rubio, Patricia Shelton, Arwin Smallwood, Velma Speight-Buford, Allahquan Tate, Sharon Waldrum, and Sandrea Williamson.

Special thanks are extended to library faculty members Arneice Bowen, Euthena Newman, and John Teleha. Archivist Gloria Pitts, undergraduate student Michael Thomas, former provost Winser Alexander, current provost Joe B. Whitehead, Sandra Brown, Nicole Pride, Judy Rashid, the *A&T Register*, past and present Board of Trustees members, the Greensboro Historical Society, the *Greensboro News & Record*, the North Carolina Digital Heritage Center, Alex Albright, and A&T's Office of University Relations are also appreciated for their assistance on the many sections of this book.

The project could not have been achieved without the participation of alumni, faculty, staff, and students who shared their documents, knowledge, and photographs. More information on the university and its 125th anniversary may be located on a special website, www.ncat.edu/125, and at the F. D. Bluford Library Archives, www.library.ncat.edu/resourcesarchives. To those who gave of their energy and time, but have not been cited, thank you.

# CHAPTER ONE

# Laying Foundations

## 1890–1918

Students work intently at their instruments in the biological laboratory in 1899. This was one of a series of photos taken for W.E.B. Du Bois to present at the 1900 Paris Exhibition.

Biological Laboratory

oney was in short supply in the war-ravaged South, so when the Second Morrill Act, in 1890, offered $15,000 per year for states to set up colleges for "instruction in agriculture, the mechanical arts, the English language and the various branches of mathematical, physical, natural and economical science,"[1] North Carolina was eager to apply. But the Morrill Acts, named for Sen. Justin Morrill of Vermont, who sponsored them, had a catch.

"No money shall be paid out under this act to any state or territory for the support and maintenance of a college where a distinction of race or color is made in the admission of students ...." However, it did allow for the "establishment and maintenance of such colleges "separately for white and colored ..." so long as funds were "equitably divided."[2]

Just three years before, North Carolina had set up a College of Agriculture and Mechanic Arts (NC A. and M.) for the white race—now NC State—and was ready for those funds. Although efforts had been made as far back as 1879 to found a college for African Americans "fostered and controlled by the state, of equal dignity to the state university of Chapel Hill,"[3] those calls had been ignored. Now, faced with the necessity to create a separate land-grant institution, the Board of Trustees of NC A. and M. worked out an arrangement with Shaw University in Raleigh to offer a course of studies for Negro students desiring to be admitted to the land-grant program. In the fall of 1890, 37 students began their studies in the "Shaw Annex" under the instruction of four professors.[4]

On March 9, 1891, the North Carolina Legislature approved the creation of the Agricultural and Mechanical College for the Colored Race (A&M), today's North Carolina Agricultural and Technical State University (A&T). A board of trustees was organized with members drawn from every corner of the state. First order of business: find a home for this new college. Proposals from Raleigh, Wilmington, Greensboro, Durham, Winston-Salem, and Mebane came before the board in June 1891. Greensboro, represented by future vice president and professor Charles H. Moore, offered $11,000 cash and 14 acres of land. It would prove to be the winning offer—and a solid investment.[5]

The fledging college was the inheritor of a tradition that began immediately after the Civil War, with training schools set up by the Freedman's Bureau, along with black churches and white philanthropies. Among the colleges founded were Cheyney, Howard, and Fisk, and in North Carolina, St. Augustine's and Johnson C. Smith. These first HBCUs (historically black colleges and universities) were private and nonprofit. The Morrill Acts would create a new class of colleges, land-grant institutions, to provide education for lower- and middle-class

An Act to Establish an Agricultural and Mechanical College for the Colored Race.

The General Assembly of North Carolina do enact:

Section 1. That a college of agriculture and mechanical arts be and the same is hereby established for the colored race, to be located at some eligible site within this state, to be hereafter selected by the Board of Trustees hereinafter provided for.

Sec. 2. That the said institution shall be denominated "The Agricultural and Mechanical College for the Colored Race".

Sec. 3. That the leading object of the institution shall be to teach practical agriculture and the mechanic arts and such branches of learning as relate thereto, not excluding academical and classical instruction.

Sec. 4. That the management and control of the said college and the care and preservation of all its property shall be vested in a Board of Trustees, who shall be selected by the General Assembly at each term thereof consisting of nine members, one from each of the several congressional districts of the State, three of whom shall be selected for a term of two years, three for four years and three for six years, and at the expiration of the term of each class their successors shall be elected for a term of six years. Any vacancy which may occur for any cause shall be filled by the Governor for the unexpired term. That the said Board shall elect one of their number to be President of the Board of Trustees.

Sec. 5. That the said Board of Trustees shall have power to prescribe rules for the management and preservation of good order and morals at the said college as are usually made in such institutions. Shall have power to appoint its President, instructors, and as many other officers or servants as to them shall appear necessary and proper, and shall fix their salaries, and shall have charge of the disbursement of the funds, and have general and entire supervision of the establishment and maintenance of the said college, and the President and instructors in the said college by and with the consent of the Board of Trustees shall have the power of conferring such certificates of proficiency or marks of merit and diplomas as are usually conferred by such colleges.

Sec. 6. That the said Board of Trustees are empowered to receive any donation of property, real or personal, which may be made to the said College of Agriculture and Mechanic Arts, and shall have power to invest or expend the same for the benefit of said college, and shall have power to accept on behalf of this college such proportion of the fund granted by the Congress of the United States to the State of North Carolina for industrial and agricultural training as is apportioned to the colored race.

Sec. 7. That in addition to the powers herein before granted, the Board of Trustees shall have power to make such rules and regulations with respect to the admission of pupils to said college for the various congressional districts of this state

The act to establish the Agricultural and Mechanical College for the Colored Race.

John O. Crosby, the first president.

Americans, starting with Alcorn State in 1871 and continuing with 19 more black colleges set up under the Second Morrill Act, including A&T.[6]

The first president, Professor John O. Crosby of Salisbury, was elected by the board in May 1892. By the next summer, the first building had been constructed with bricks made by the college. At the same time, Crosby unveiled the first program of study.

Of the seven major divisions, the first was "language and literature embracing English grammar, elocution, composition and rhetoric; history, economics, and general literature."[7] Penmanship and industrial drawing, tool instruction, mathematics, science, agriculture, and military science rounded out the program. A preparatory school also was inaugurated, and the first bills set: $6 per month for board, fuel, and room rent for state students, $7 for others.[8]

Founded as A&M, North Carolina's new land-grant college faced a dilemma from its very founding: provide practical skills for African Americans from primarily agrarian

Postcard of the old administration building (later Dudley Hall), a multipurpose facility that was the largest building on campus until 1930.

13838—A. M. College, GREENSBORO, N. C.

backgrounds, or prepare them to reach intellectual heights through a classical education? The first reflected the views of Booker T. Washington, who was willing to restrain the Negro's quest for political power, civil rights, and higher education in order to achieve economic advances and conciliation with the South.[9] The second was an endorsement of W.E.B. Du Bois, a graduate of Fisk University and Harvard, who countered, "Is it possible, and probable, that nine millions of men can make effective progress in economic lines if they are deprived of political rights, made a servile caste, and allowed only the most meagre chance for developing their exceptional men? If history and reason give any distinct answer to these questions, it is an emphatic No."[10]

The answer to A&M's dilemma began to appear in those very first years. The college found it difficult to attract students. True, few North Carolina public high schools were preparing Negro students, indeed students of any race, for college admission. "To this must be added the further fact that parents simply did not see the importance of going to college to learn farming and mechanics, vocations which they

The Sessions of 1892. Note the bowler hats and waistcoats with watch fobs.

had heretofore learned without spending time in college. They thought of a college as an institution in which the liberal arts were taught, and most parents, [sic] ambitions for their children seized upon the liberal arts as a means of social, if not economic advancement, for their sons and daughters."[11] By 1895, the college had altered its program to include a four-year course in agriculture along with technical training, a two-year course focused on a specific vocation, as well as "a winter short course for farm boys who were unable to get into school until after harvesting their crop." A one-week course also was offered.[12]

The 1897 college report states, "The Agricultural and Mechanical College is destined to be the door by which the youth of the country shall pass from the public schools into industrial

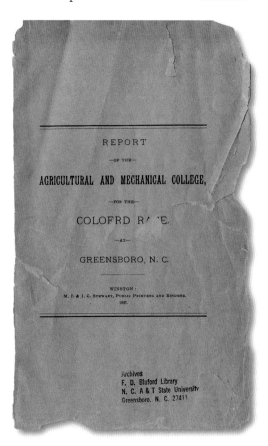

Report from 1897.

fields." Freshmen students studied arithmetic, algebra, English, physical geography, physiology and hygiene, history, chemistry, botany, agriculture, shop work, and farm work.[13]

Each county of the state was allowed a limited number of students on free tuition, provided they passed an examination equivalent to that of a second-grade teacher. Those who paid faced tuition of $1 per month, plus $5 for board, and $1 for use of room per month. Students followed a strict schedule, with the "signal for rising" given at 6 a.m., prayers at 6:30, breakfast at 8:15 after morning study, and then classes until 4 p.m. Time was set aside for recreation from 4 to 6 p.m., with "lights out" at 10 p.m.[14]

North Carolina families sending their children off to A&T had witnessed the collapse of Reconstruction and the rise of segregation, "an arrangement whereby Black Americans, as a minority were systematically treated in a separate, but constitutionally sanctioned way."[15] The injustice was codified, year by year. In 1890, the year before the college's birth, the Mississippi Plan used literacy tests to disenfranchise Negro men, while a North Carolina "suffrage amendment" in 1900 had a grandfather clause allowing illiterate white men to vote but effectively disenfranchising black men.[16]

The Louisiana State Supreme Court upheld "equal but separate accommodations for the white and colored races."[17] This would go before

the U.S. Supreme Court in 1896 as *Plessy v. Ferguson.* The justices' decision to uphold the Louisiana court, making Jim Crow the law of the land, "enabled public facilities, such as schools, accommodations, transportation, parks, swimming pools, restaurants, cemeteries, hospitals, asylums, and prisons to be organized on a 'separate but equal' basis, a precept quickly and widely implemented."[18] Justice John Marshall Harlan, in his lone dissent, maintained that the "Constitution is color-blind, and neither knows nor tolerates classes among citizens."[19]

African Americans in North Carolina were subjected to discrimination and segregation. When the white Democrats lost control of state politics in 1896 to white Populists and African American Republicans, the stage was set for violence. In 1898, riots flared in Wilmington, North Carolina, after an election in which Democrats were reported to have stuffed the ballot boxes. A small army of white men set fire to an African American newspaper office. "African Americans armed themselves and whites began to hunt and gun them down .... When the riot

The Class of 1900.

ended the next day, it was reported that twenty-five African Americans had been killed. However, it was strongly suspected that hundreds of African Americans had been killed and their bodies dumped into the river."[20]

The college's biennial reports in those early years repeatedly noted the urgent need for buildings, dormitories, equipment—even things as seemingly routine as heating and sewage systems.

Faced with growing hostility and reduced opportunities, A&T from early on sought a middle way. The 1906 catalog states that "brains and hands are here educated together."[21] Students could work in the college dairy or the kitchen by day, and take classes in the evening. Lectures in the arts were supplemented with practical skills learned at the lathe. The reality those early students knew was a society of discrimination, disenfranchisement, and segregation—one they would have

to adapt to, with the college generally following the views of Booker T. Washington's "Atlanta Compromise" speech of 1895: "In all things that are purely social we can be as separate as the fingers, yet one as the hand in all things essential to mutual progress."[22]

Lucille Johnson Piggott '54 recalled a different childhood growing up in Alton, Illinois. "We were the only blacks in the school, the rest were Caucasian. We had good relationships. We had spelling bees every Friday, games that were primitive as I look at games today." She asked her mother, "Am I a little colored girl?" Years later, she returned to her hometown. "Many of my classmates came and hugged us. They were in awe that someone from that little school had a doctorate."[23]

Agriculture was first in the title of this growing school, with good reason. The 1906 catalog notes that "fully eighty percent of the Colored people in the state live in the country

The 1905 baseball team.

and subsist on agriculture. The future of the Colored Race in the south depends upon the ownership of farm lands and their intelligent, and skillful treatment by colored farmers. This field is free from competition and race feeling."[24]

A 100-acre farm was developed in 1904 on East Market Street. Field crops were emphasized in the first years, but in 1907 a dairy was added, and in 1910 a poultry department. Recruitment was important: Farmers' Institutes were held around the state to assist farmers with new information and to promote the new agricultural college. A State Farmers' Week held at the college in 1915 featured short courses in agriculture and prizes for the best corn, cotton, and tobacco.

Haywood Eugene Webb graduated in 1909 with a bachelor's degree in agriculture—his diploma from The Agricultural and Mechanical College for the Colored Race is headed by an elaborate illustration of farm workers. He would farm and teach for 10 years before entering the Agricultural Extension Service, serving as the black farm agent for Guilford County for 15 years. His career took him into insurance, back to agriculture—and 21 years as the desk clerk at the Hayes Taylor YMCA after retirement. His sons would continue the legacy at A&T (see related photo in Chapter Five): Harold Webb became the first black to serve as director of personnel for the state. Burleigh Webb became dean of A&T's School

A barn and dairy are shown from the early years in agricultural education.

A view of the campus from the back, including the administration building and old Crosby Hall.

of Agriculture. Reginald Webb was with the Department of Housing and Community Development, and Haywood Webb Jr. was a physical research scientist at the U.S. Air Force base in Rome, New York.[25]

The Smith-Lever Act of 1914 provided new support for agricultural education, funding outreach programs that would become the Cooperative Extension Service and building on the work of Booker T. Washington and others. Funding flowed through the U.S. Department of Agriculture to the land-grant institutions, to be matched by states and counties. No less than 6 percent of the total appropriation was set aside for programs at 1890 land-grant colleges such as A&M.[26] Three years later, the Smith-Hughes Act of 1917 would provide yet more impetus for education in vocational and industrial skills.[27]

While farming remained primary in North Carolina, the pace of industrialization was quickening, and A&M sought to expand its offerings. Students had been learning practical applications such as masonry and cabinet-making, while being introduced to more technical fields. In 1911, the mechanical engineering department added courses in electrical engineering, hydraulics, power plant design, and house planning. In 1915, the shift was recognized with a new name: A&M became The Negro Agricultural and Technical College of North Carolina.[28]

The year 1915 would also mark the death of Booker T. Washington.

The early 1900s ushered in the Progressive Era, a time when America was experiencing rapid economic growth. A&M was represented in Europe as an institution of higher learning in 1900, when W.E.B. Du Bois included photographs of A&M students in the Paris Exhibition.[29] Against the backdrop of lynchings, voter suppression, and violence, black intellectuals were organizing. In 1905, Du Bois began the Niagara Movement, which brought together black intellectuals dedicated to racial equality,[30] and a few years later he helped to establish the National Association for the Advancement of Colored People. By 1910, Du Bois had founded the NAACP journal, *Crisis*.[31] The National Urban League was founded a year later.

African Americans sought relocation to places where they were less likely to encounter the social ills of the South. Since 1900, "over a million Negroes have migrated to the Southern cities where they felt freer and safer; while a million and a half have gone to urban areas of the North."[32] The reality of moving from the country to the city, even in the South, gave African Americans better schools. In the North, African American children received educational accommodations substantially equal to whites. "There were approximately 250,000 white students in colleges in the South, as compared with less than 25,000 Negro students,

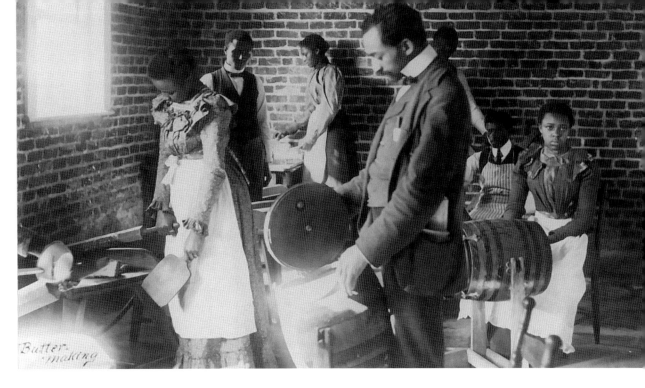

Butter-making

Sewing

Blacksmithing

A&M was represented in Europe when W.E.B. Du Bois included photographs of A&M students in the Paris Exhibition in 1900. Photographs show students taking classes in a variety of subjects including blacksmithing, sewing, and butter-making. These images are among 23 taken in 1899 for Du Bois and Thomas J. Callaway for the "American Negro Exhibit" at the Paris Exposition. *LIBRARY OF CONGRESS, LOT 11296.*

Even in a segregated world, career options and professional opportunities for African Americans grew as a result of obtaining college degrees. This photo was taken at A&T sometime in the early years.

although the ratio of whites to Negroes in this area was only 3 or 4 to 1. On the average, the states provided for 16 white students in higher institutions supported by state funds to each Negro provided for in other supported institutions—ranging from 6 to 1 in North Carolina to 39 to 1 in Texas. The majority of all white college students in this area … are receiving their education in state-supported colleges and universities, while only two-fifths of the Negro students enrolled in similar institutions …. There was not a single state-supported institution where a Negro could pursue graduate or professional education."[33]

Beginning about 1910, The Great Migration saw African Americans of the rural South flood to northern industrial cities. The *Chicago Defender*, with widespread readership outside of Chicago, urged migration:

"*The Defender* invites all to come north. Plenty of room for the good, sober industrious man. Plenty of work … Anywhere in God's country is far better than the Southland … Come join the ranks of the free. Cast the yoke from around your neck. See the light. When you have crossed the Ohio river, breathe the fresh air and say, 'Why didn't I come before?'"[34]

Noted alumni such as John W. Mitchell '09 began to make their mark. An educator and agricultural extension specialist, he was appointed field agent in 1917, district agent in 1929, and state agent in 1939 for the Federal Extension Service in

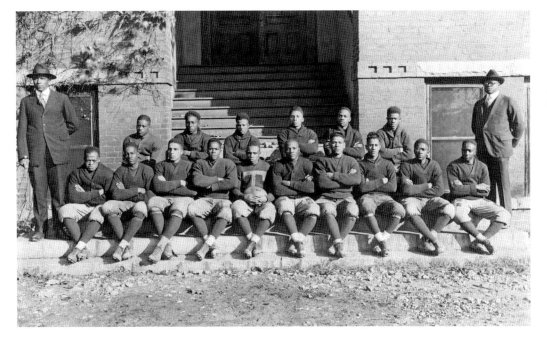

A football team from the early 1900s.

The 1911 championship baseball team is shown, with the S. W. R. Slade Class of 1911 pictured in the back row. *HAROLD H. WEBB.*

the Upper South. Four years later, he would become national extension leader for the Federal Extension Service.[35] Students came in from small southern towns to study at A&T, then begin careers in education, dentistry, law, theology, medicine, pharmacology, and nursing.

The first 10 years saw a steady accumulation of milestones: 1894, the first college newspaper; 1895, the first college catalog. In 1897, women were admitted to all but agricultural courses (though enrollment would be restricted to men only from 1902 to 1928),[36] a Bachelor of Science degree was authorized, and a Summer School program to train public school teachers was inaugurated. In 1899, the first degrees were awarded, with students gathered under the motto of "No Steps Backward."[37] Two years later, the first woman would graduate, Frances T. Grimes of Asheville.[38]

Student life wasn't all study and work, however. Intercollegiate athletics began right after the turn of the century, and there was a heated rivalry in baseball and football between A&M and Bennett College, then co-educational. Hundreds of spectators watched A&M and Bennett College play to a scoreless tie in the 1914 Thanksgiving game. "The game was of much interest, yet it was evident the A. and M. outclassed Bennett from start to finish."[39] The college played baseball where Bluford Library now stands, with the biggest games moved to Cone Athletic Field on Summit Avenue.[40]

The Class of 1910 is pictured here. The motto inscribed on the back of this photograph is, "By our efforts we rise." Class members are listed as C. H. Best; J. H. Green, real estate; R. D. Moore, postal clerk; J. P. Neal; E. S. Plummer, mechanic; J. R. Guick; and Chas. Robinson. President Dudley is in the back row at right.

This period also saw the college's first change in leadership, as President Crosby resigned in 1896 to be replaced by James B. Dudley. A longtime high school principal and member of the Board of Trustees, the Wilmington native was a delegate to the 1896 Republican National Convention and an organizer and early president of the North Carolina Teachers Association.[41]

When Dudley became president, the college had 58 students living in one brick dormitory, eight teachers, and one classroom building. Water was drawn from a single well on the 25-acre campus. The president

reported to Gov. Charles B. Aycock, "We found the College heavily in debt, its unpaid bills amounting to $10,000 … We found the curriculum of the College much too high for the colored race in its present state of advancement … We found that it had no farm where practical agriculture could be taught."[42] Dudley focused on paying off bills, revamping the curriculum, and buying a farm as well as building up the various industrial training areas.

By 1910, the president could report that the college encompassed an administration building, "two dormitories, a Mechanical building, a barn and dairy upon a campus of

A view of the A&T farm.

twenty-five acres and a farm of 100 acres a mile from the college. The entire plant—land, buildings and equipments—is worth $144,180.00." He was also pleased at the recent addition of bathing and sanitary facilities, writing that "students and teachers are alike warm in expressions of appreciation for these additional conveniences which have added so much to comfort and also to the preservation of health."[43]

A major curriculum change came in 1904, better delineating the courses for students leading to a Bachelor of Agriculture or a Bachelor of Science degree. A rationale written by the Department of Mechanics stated, "The work of this department is to obtain the two most valuable possessions which no search warrant can take away, no reverse of fortune destroy. They are what is put into the brain: knowledge; and what is put into the hand: skill."[44] There would be an increasing emphasis on practical agriculture and mechanics. By 1917, the college required students to do 70 hours of practical work each quarter—135 hours for trade students.

The 20th century heralded a steadily increasing list of technological accomplishments. The first wireless message across the Atlantic was sent in 1901. The Wright Brothers flew their motorized airplane off the dunes at Kitty Hawk, North Carolina, in 1903. The vacuum tube was developed in 1906, making radio and then television possible. President Theodore Roosevelt sent the Navy's new steel battleships, called the "Great White Fleet," around the Pacific Ocean in 1907–1909. Henry Ford brought out his Model T in 1908 for a price of $850. The greatest passenger ship ever built, the *Titanic*, was launched in 1912 and sank in the ice of the North Atlantic.[45]

Education was the key to a future in this new world of electric lights and "Tin Lizzies." The motto on the masthead of *The Register* in 1915 was "Lifting as We Climb." Better students

President Dudley (front, second from left) and college administrators are shown in 1909-10.

The High School Department helped students bridge the gap between high school and college. The department was organized early on, but this shot is from the 1920s.

were needed, and better teachers. The university added a teacher-training program in 1907, to prepare teachers for agricultural instruction and classes in the trades for the public schools. Loose requirements for admission in the early years reflected the nature of the schools from which students were drawn. The 1906 catalog states, "Applicants must be in good health and not under sixteen years of age; must understand fairly well the forms and rules of the English language; must be familiar with arithmetic, and have a knowledge of geography and history."[46]

A "High School Department" had been in place since the beginning. As President Dudley noted in a 1908 report to the Board of Trustees, "the students enter with very little preparation."[47] The preparatory program was demanding: in 1911, it required two years of English, arithmetic, music, geography, reading, writing, and drawing, as well as a year each of state and national history. Prep school students also were required to participate in the shop, dairy, or greenhouse.

Charles E. Stewart in the classroom. He became the director of music in 1909.

By 1918, applicants to A&T had to submit 10 units of secondary school work—six of them in English, history, and algebra. Graduates of A&T received degrees in agriculture and mechanic arts, and certificates if they completed trade programs.

Among the noted faculty of the time was an Antiguan, Samuel Benjamin Jones, who taught English. He was known for his "string of degrees," and was a licentiate of the Royal Fellows of Physicians and Surgeons from Glasgow, the Royal College of Surgeons in Edinburgh, and the Royal College of Physicians of London. He would earn a Doctor of Medicine (M.D.) degree from Loyola in Chicago while teaching at A&M. Returning to his native land, he would become a renowned doctor and a member of the Order of the British Empire.[48]

In 1895, Margaret Faulkener was credited with beginning the music

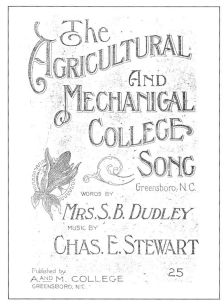

The school song was created by President Dudley's wife Susan and the music director, Charles Stewart. It uses the terminology of the time to refer to "Dear A&M, dear A&M, a monument indeed." Generations of Aggies have sung the chorus and pledged to "spread thy trophies year by year from Dare to Cherokee."

program. Charles E. Stewart became director of music in 1909. He would provide the tune for the college's "Alma Mater," with words by Susan Dudley, the president's wife. Dudley was likewise recognized for her skill in playwriting, and over the years would work closely with Richard B.

Summer School, 1909.

The Class of 1913 is shown with books in hand.

Harrison to promote dramatic arts on campus and across the state. In 1916, the music program welcomed W. E. Lew as director. He said of music, "Our mothers need it in the family. Our manhood needs its refining and hallowed power. Our churches demand it. Our very nature by Divine Providence craves it and no education is complete without it."[49] The band was recognized prior to World War I and its concerts reportedly rivaled those put on by Tuskegee.[50] Music was required for all students, with opportunities in the choral club, band, and orchestra. Literary societies likewise were important, and attendance at chapel monitored.

Military drill was part of campus life, and year by year, the students marching in formation could see a gathering storm. The United States intervened in Nicaragua in 1911. In 1914, our troops were in Vera Cruz, and it seemed that there might be war with Mexico. The Great War began to spread across Europe in 1914. Gen. John J. Pershing crossed into Mexico in 1916 to pursue Pancho Villa.

The nation did not want to enter the European conflict—the Civil War and the Spanish American War

D. K. Cherry, professor of mathematics, who taught from 1911 to 1928. He served in the Army from 1917 to 1919.

had taken their toll. Yet, President Woodrow Wilson summoned Americans to support our entry in 1917, saying, "But the right is more precious than peace, and we shall fight for the things which we have always carried nearest our hearts— for democracy, for the right of those who submit to authority to have a voice in their own governments, for the rights and liberties of small nations, for a universal dominion of right by such a concert of free peoples as shall bring peace and safety

The horns predominate in this shot of the A&M Greensboro College Band. The man at center holds a drum major baton, but does not wear the elaborate uniform that would become popular.

to all nations and make the world itself at last free."[51]

The United States was going to war on foreign soil. Preparations included the creation of Fort Bragg in 1918. African American men were drafted alongside whites and made up 13 percent of the draftees. By the end of the war, some 380,000 African Americans had served in the American Expeditionary Forces.[52] However, they were assigned to segregated units commanded by white officers and were often shifted into unskilled labor rather than employed as combat troops. The French military, sapped by the war, asked for and received several regiments of black combat troops.

As America entered World War I, President Dudley spoke to the college: "Nowhere in the world has any race of people under similar circumstances shown such loyalty to its country as has the Negro race."[53] No other Negro land-grant college would train more soldiers than A&T.[54] The service of the students was matched by their instructors: by 1918, one-fifth of the teachers and administrative staff were in the service.[55]

**ENDNOTES**

In regard to the citations for each chapter, all entries with a date only are from *The Register*, A&T's student newspaper.

1. "Second Morrill Act"
2. "Agricultural Colleges," 418
3. Gibbs, *History*, 4
4. Gibbs, *History*, 5
5. Kelley, 9-10
6. Redd, 34
7. Kelley, 15
8. Gibbs, *History*, 11
9. Kearns, 331
10. Du Bois, *Souls*, 51-52
11. Gibbs, *History*, 10
12. Kelley, 15
13. *Report*, 1897, 6
14. *Report*, 1897, 23
15. King, D.S., 9
16. North Carolina Museum
17. *Plessy*, 537
18. King, D.S., 18
19. *Plessy*, 559
20. North Carolina Freedom
21. Gibbs, *History*, 103
22. Du Bois, *Souls*, 42
23. Piggott
24. Gibbs, *History*, 103
25. "Haywood"
26. "Agricultural Extension," 372
27. "Vocational Education," 929
28. Spruill, 3
29. Du Bois, "Paris"
30. Lewis, 315-16
31. Lewis, 409
32. Thompson, C.H., 943
33. Thompson, C.H., 939-40
34. "Invites"
35. Spruill, 111
36. Kelley, 16
37. Spruill, 2
38. Gibbs, *History*, 130
39. January 1915
40. Moore, "Sports"
41. Kelley, 19
42. Kelley, 20
43. *Biennial Report*, 8-9
44. Gibbs, *History*, 41
45. Sloan et al.
46. Gibbs, *History*, 45
47. Gibbs, *History*, 42
48. Spruill, 69
49. Gibbs, *History*, 44
50. Gibbs, *History*, 25
51. Wilson
52. Hine et al., 381
53. Gibbs, *History*, 60
54. Kelley, 24-25
55. Gibbs, *History*, 45

CHAPTER TWO

# Migration, Renaissance, and Depression

## 1919–1939

Students work on their sketches during an art class. *Greensboro Historical Museum Archives.*

The Great War had changed the map of the world. Four empires had dissolved and change was in the air: in Russia, in a reordered Europe, and back home in the United States.

Temperance movements that had been around since the American Revolution shifted their focus to complete abolition of alcohol. The 18th Amendment was ratified in 1919, prohibiting the sale and manufacture of alcohol. Women saw the dream of Susan B. Anthony and Elizabeth Cady Stanton likewise realized in 1919, when Congress submitted the women's suffrage amendment to the states for ratification, 41 years after it was introduced. That ratification was completed in 1920.

But 1919 was also a year of reaction and violence known as the year of the "Red Summer,"[1] with 26 race riots between May and October.[2] Also during this time, anti-Communist sentiment and fear of immigrants grew, culminating in quotas to encourage Northern Europeans but excluding people from Asia and Eastern Europe.

African Americans who had served with distinction in Europe came home to a country that considered them still second-class citizens. Among A&T's heroes was Capt. Robert Campbell, who had started in 1911 as head of the machine shop and power plant. He served in the Spanish American War and then World War I, serving in the 368th U.S. Infantry Regiment. He received the Croix de Guerre and the Distinguished Service Cross for bravery under fire, then came back to teach military science and assist with the college's drum and bugle corps.[3] A&T had supported the war effort by training soldiers and then welcomed the returning "doughboys"

Capt. R. L. Campbell was among the faculty members who fought in World War I.

who flooded into colleges with the aid of veterans' training programs. Still, prominent African Americans who had supported the war effort were dismayed that returning vets were not adequately supported with education and housing.

Organizations such as the National Association for the Advancement of Colored People (NAACP) and the National Urban League began to grow, and thousands of African Americans protested racial violence and discrimination. In 1919, as Du Bois grew "disillusioned with what he saw as the NAACP's 'mere appeal based on the old liberalism,' his interest in black consciousness increased, and he helped organize the Pan African Congress that met in Paris."[4] Dr. Carter G. Woodson, founder of the Association for the Study of Negro Life and History, came to campus in 1932 to deliver the commencement address.[5]

This was the Jazz Age. Affordable automobiles gave Americans new freedom, and radios brought entertainment into homes both rich and poor. However, many Americans were uncomfortable with the new urban "mass culture" that included a large black presence, from music to literature to film. The Ku Klux Klan expanded in the South and the Midwest. Prohibition had unintended consequences, including the glamorization of gangster culture. Even the laboratories of A&T's Chemistry Department became part of the story, as local police relied on college labs to

test seized products for alcohol content.[6] On the heels of Red Summer, the 1920s saw more conflict and the rise of Marcus Garvey's African nationalist movement, considered the first black American mass movement.

Black representation was slow in returning to American government. In 1931, A&T hosted a visit by Oscar DePriest, a Republican congressman who was the first African American representative from Illinois.[7] In 1938, Arthur W. Mitchell visited, the first African American Democrat to be elected to Congress after defeating DePriest in 1934.[8, 9]

The Progressive Era that had launched the century continued, with more of the U.S. population experiencing economic growth. Before the start of the Civil War, America could count three millionaires. "Forty years later the number of millionaires had increased to about 3,800. About one-tenth of the population owned nine-tenths of the wealth of the nation."[10]

Under President Calvin Coolidge, prosperity continued and the nation moved to a consumer economy. Madam C. J. Walker, who died in 1919, left a legacy of entrepreneurship. The hair care preparation she invented made her America's wealthiest African American woman. Later, her company not only manufactured the products but sold them door to door in St. Louis—her model was later adopted by Avon and Mary Kay.[11]

Black-owned companies began to grow in North Carolina, such as

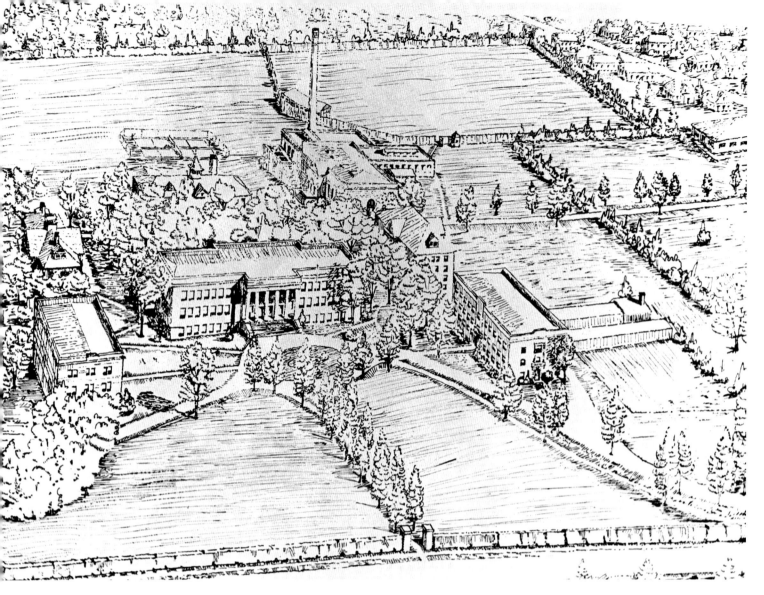

Aerial view of campus, 1933.

North Carolina Mutual Life Insurance Company, whose executive Asa Spaulding visited the campus to speak. Students were interested in new opportunities—a Kollege Business Klub was operating in 1929, while the 1939 *Ayantee* had a photo of The Business Seminar, a student organization created "to encourage a social spirit among commercial students, [and] to promote interest in the business world."[12] Students could look up from their classrooms and see the 17-story Jefferson Standard Building rising on the Greensboro skyline, the tallest building between Atlanta and Washington, D.C.[13]

As business prospered, labor wanted its share. African Americans began to join labor unions, especially in the industrial cities. A. Phillip Randolph organized the Brotherhood of Sleeping Car Porters, the first African American trade union, in 1925, although the union did not receive full recognition until 1937.[14] By 1856, Greensboro was located on the east-west railroad line from Goldsboro to Charlotte. By the 1890s, the city "became known as the Gate City for its busy train station (60 running daily),"[15, 16] and A&T graduates and their fathers were among those who worked as porters.

To meet the challenges of the industrial age, A&T set graduation requirements of 120 credits, again in that pivotal year of 1919.[17] The pace of change picked up throughout the 1920s. A bachelor's degree in physics was initiated, a Department of Military Science was started in 1920, and H. Clinton Taylor formed the Art Department in 1927.[18]

The College of Arts and Sciences became a reality in 1929, joining the School of Agriculture and the School of Mechanic Arts.[19] Jerald M. Marteena came to the college in 1929 to teach mechanical engineering, and would become dean of the School of Mechanic Arts four years later. During his time a chapter of the American Society of Tool and Manufacturing Engineers was set up, the first on a predominantly black campus.[20] On the vocational side, new courses were started in hotel and lunchroom management and laundering. The first-ever vocational

and technical conference at A&T was held in 1927.

During the decade of the 1920s, $1 million was appropriated for capital improvements at the college, the largest state appropriation for higher education of African Americans at that time in the South. Noble Hall, Morrison Hall, and Vanstory Hall all went up in 1924.[21, 22] The 1922

Vanstory Hall.

A gathering of the A&T faculty in 1925.

Fire destroyed the original administration building, renamed Dudley Hall, in 1930. *Greensboro Historical Museum Archives.*

commencement exercises program is a small, brown leather booklet with pictures of President Dudley and campus landmarks. The Baccalaureate Sermon on Sunday was followed by an address on Monday, Class Day on Tuesday, and Alumni Day on Wednesday. Commencement Day on Thursday featured the "Negro National Anthem," an address by Gov. Cameron Morrison, and agricultural and mechanical demonstrations.[23]

In 1930, fire destroyed the original administration building that had been renamed Dudley Hall.[24] A newspaper article reported, "The fire, of unknown origin but attributed to defective wiring, was discovered by the night watchman at 5:20 a.m., and in ten minutes the three story brick structure was an inferno with the heart-pine woodwork making a grand

fire." The clipping goes on to state that 7,000 volumes were lost in the library, along with supplies of the ROTC. "Over 10,000 round of rifle ammunition kept the big crowds back for 30 minutes."[25]

The building would be replaced by the new Dudley Memorial Hall in 1931 at a cost of $160,000,[26] and four years later, Alma I. Morrow was appointed assistant librarian, becoming head librarian in 1937, although "the President had her to understand that he wanted a man to head all departments at the College when such a candidate could be found ...." She would be vital to the expansion of A&T's library—during her three decades, "appropriations grew from $1,500 a year to $86,000 in 1957."[27]

The college was led by James B. Dudley from 1896 until 1925 and then for 30 years by Ferdinand Bluford. "The vigor and hard work given by Dudley to the growth and development of Alma Mater is unquestionable. From fifty-eight students, a one-room brick dormitory, eight teachers, and one classroom building all valued at fifty thousand dollars in 1896 the enrollment increased to 476 during the regular sessions and around 500 during the summer session. The physical plant increased to 13 buildings valued at over $1,000,000 by 1925, the College had purchased 74 more acres of land to add to its 26 acres, and the curriculum had improved immensely."[28]

The front page of The Register in May 1925 was devoted to Dudley's obituary, with sympathy notes, floral tributes received, and resolutions filling the inside pages. "His ever-wise counsel and noble example shall ever be our guiding star and though he sleeps, he yet lives in the hearts of the thousands of young men and women who have come under his guidance and direction," read one such tribute from D. W. Lee and Jas. M. Watlington of Coyle, Oklahoma.[29] Clyde DeHughley, property custodian and instructor in shoe repair, recalled Dudley as "a lover of students, a great leader, and a grand teacher of yesteryear ..."[30]

As Bluford took over leadership of the college, the South Dorm had been remodeled, the mechanical building renovated, and an old dairy barn torn down and a new one completed at a cost of $25,000.[31] Later in the Bluford years, the original farm on East Market Street (where the Lorillard tobacco factory was later built) was sold and a larger farm purchased on McConnell Street Extension. The emphasis on agriculture was strengthened by this expansion,

President Dudley's body lies in state following his death in 1925.

The Negro Land-Grant College delegation to the White House in 1926.

Two students work with dairy equipment.

which fell in line with the prevailing spirit of the times.[32]

A 1928 report on colleges in the southern and border states listed three assumptions: 1) "The economic salvation of the Negro is dependent to a great degree upon his training in the fields of agriculture, mechanic arts, and crafts," 2) "The national social and economic life demands the training of many more Negro professional and technical leaders. This is also a question of higher education," and 3) "The Negro people are an integral part of the American Citizenry. Numbering 11,600,000, they represent nine percent of the total population of the United States."[33]

Alumnus Henry E. Frye '53 recalled, "I worked in the mill and on the farm. I worked from can't to can't … can't see when you rise and can't see when you leave at night." The Jim Crow laws were just a way of life in the South. "Blacks and whites lived across the road from each other. Blacks and whites worked together curing tobacco, then by Saturday afternoon, we separated in different groups. I always wondered if we could have done something different."[34]

The Cooperative Extension Service, authorized in 1914, set out to improve the productivity of farmers and the lives of farm families. It wasn't an easy task. The young college had to depend on appropriations funneled through its sister institution, NC State, through the 1970s. As the extension agents worked with minority farmers—in some cases with their salaries paid by donations from the farmers themselves—some white farmers resented this help.

"Agents here were seen as community activists. One agent, L. R. Johnson, was actually beaten for being an activist," said Valorie McAlpin, director of communications for A&T Extension and Research.[35] This agent would go on to organize the Smithfield Ham and Egg Show and become known as the father of the North Carolina ham industry.

Among the agricultural leaders who visited A&T were George Washington Carver, who gave the speech at the vesper service in 1933,[36] and Henry Wallace, secretary of the Department of Agriculture, who visited in 1933 and 1937. The college hosted yearly gatherings of the New Farmers of America.

In the 1920s, tobacco became a major crop in North Carolina. At A&T, a new leader in animal husbandry helped move that branch of agriculture forward. When Dr. W. L. Kennedy arrived in 1936, the college had "13 dairy animals, 16 beef animals, and one heifer calf ... the daily productions of milk could be carried to the College in a ten gallon can."[37] Kennedy focused on improving and increasing this herd. The cattle shows were both class work and a major social event.

Dr. W. L. Kennedy (center) of the Agriculture program is shown with one of the college's herd of prize-winning Jersey cattle.

But while A&T was helping shift agriculture toward a more scientific undertaking, life on the farm remained hard. Black people had good reason to move north, including the lack of opportunity at home in the South outside of agriculture. The Great Migration had been pushed by World War I, as immigrants from Europe either stopped coming or returned to their homelands—leaving vacant jobs that African Americans were eager to fill. Furthermore, the employment opportunities increased for those who had migrated north due to the 1920s legislation restricting the number of immigrants allowed into the country.[38]

Sports gained prominence at A&T. Baseball began as early as 1902, followed by football and then basketball. The college's first track team traveled to Raleigh in April 1927, and took home five first places.[39] The college joined the Colored Intercollegiate Athletic Association (CIAA) (later the Central Intercollegiate Athletic Association) in the mid-1920s.[40]

Among the great athletes of the 1920s was Clifton Howell, "a bruising 220-pound fullback who helped A&T win the 1923 football game which earned the Aggies membership in the CIAA."[41] He went on to become a professional educator and president of the Alumni Association.[42]

In 1927, A&T's football team compiled a 7-0 season and won its first CIAA championship with a team that featured the legendary J. F. "Horse" Lane, a powerful fullback who was called "a good student, a good man, and a man of the highest character."[43] Among the other stars of the period was Charles DeBerry, a small (135 pounds) man who excelled in five sports and was considered A&T's greatest all-round athlete. He would play professional baseball with the Homestead Grays and return to A&T as a coach.[44] Another outstanding athlete was John Daniels, an All-American center in 1938.

Sometime in the 1920s, the Aggies gained a mascot—the bulldog.

Two 1936 football players pose at the field. *Greensboro Historical Museum Archives.*

Stories vary, but two accounts agree that a bulldog was at the field during a close football game, perhaps with Virginia Union. After a hotly disputed call by the referee, a scuffle broke out. According to one version, "Just at that moment someone untied the bulldog and he tore into the referee. Down on the ground he went and bulldog began to work him overtime." A&T was severely reprimanded by the CIAA.[45]

In 1937, the basketball team added to the college's laurels by taking home the CIAA crown. "Dr. Ralph L. Wooden, a retired A&T professor, was a member of that team. 'We played our games in the cafeteria,' he said. 'They stacked the tables on top of each other after we finished eating.'"[46] Women were also playing intramural basketball, and tennis was being played—the college hosted the third Annual North Carolina Intercollegiate Tennis Tournament in 1937.

Women played intramural basketball against other HBCUs in the state. This photo is from 1937. *Greensboro Historical Museum Archives.*

The 1937 CIAA championship basketball team. Front row (from left): S. A. Barksdale, assistant coach; James Neeley; "Pecky" Conway; "Slim" Riddick; Bill McLain, captain; Sanford Roan; James Mitchell; and H. K. Parker, coach. Second row: A. Lynch; Maceo Glenn; D. Snuggs; S. Hudgins; "Ghost" Coles; and Ralph Wooten. Back row: M. Shute, scorer; L. Davenport, student manager; and G. Laws, trainer. Nathaniel Webster, the mascot, holds the ball at front.

Then as now, students participated in a wide variety of activities. The social events scheduled for 1926–27 were: "new student social, trade school social, high school social, Marian Anderson recital, Phi Beta Sigma conclave, Klodd Hopper, Triangle Debates, High School Debates, annual track meet."[47] The Klodd Hopper had begun early in the college's history as a special agricultural-themed activity for students who could not go home for the holidays. Before World War II, the annual observance of Mother's Day was a major event on campus, including a Mother of the Year Award. Homecoming was the highlight of the year, with a parade, pep rally, and bonfire.

Debating was extremely popular in the 1920s through the 1940s, and A&T competed at the intercollegiate level. The 1927 team was undefeated, winning both sides of the question in contests with schools in Virginia and South Carolina.[48] The Debating Society was winner of the Tri-State Cup every year from 1934 to 1939. The 1939 *Ayantee* yearbook pictures not one but two French clubs—Le Cercle Francais included ballet and French foil fencing in its activities.[49] *The Register*, A&T's student newspaper, had been around since the early 1900s, when it was a small four-page paper that "published only agricultural news …. Today the *Register* publishes news for all of the departments and the size of the paper is 12x17 inches with 8 pages."[50]

The first fraternity established on campus was Phi Beta Sigma, in

Students work out problems in the science classroom.

1918, opening the way for a series of Greek organizations for men and women. The year 1931 brought Kappa Alpha Psi fraternity, and in 1932, the creation of Alpha Kappa Alpha and Delta Sigma Theta sororities.[51] "Thus, the young ladies are venturing out into the mysterious realm of the Greeks. … These organizations will enrich them in college life, and add to the prestige of the college."[52] Photographs of the 1938 Homecoming Day parade showed floats from Zeta, Omega, Glee Club, Alpha, Hort Club, and AKA with its emblematic ivy leaf.[53]

Commercial radio had dawned in 1920, when KDKA went on the air in Pittsburgh, and its contribution to the homogenization of American society was immense and rapid. More than 500 stations were broadcasting by 1923, and radios were in 12 million households by the end of the decade. Because of radio and movies, people knew the same dances, told the same jokes, and used the same slang.[54]

President Bluford's goals for the college sound quite contemporary: "developing in students an intelligent understanding of world conditions" and preparing students for "well-rounded citizenship of the highest type and for more creative and intelligent leadership in a world of social change."[55] The college gained "A" ratings from the North Carolina Department of Education, New York Department of Education, American Medical Association, and the

The Eta Chapter of **Phi Beta Sigma Fraternity Inc.** (1918)

The Mu Psi Chapter of **Omega Psi Phi Fraternity Inc.** (1927)

The Beta Epsilon Chapter of **Alpha Phi Alpha Fraternity Inc.** (1929)

The Alpha Mu Chapter of **Delta Sigma Theta Sorority Inc.** (1932)

The Alpha Phi Chapter of **Alpha Kappa Alpha Sorority Inc.** (1932)

The Zeta Alpha Chapter of **Zeta Phi Beta Sorority Inc.** (1934)

The Gamma Chapter of **Sigma Gamma Rho Sorority Inc.** (1951)

The Kappa Psi Chapter of **Alpha Phi Omega National Service Fraternity Inc.** (1953)

The Aggie Chapter of **Groove Phi Groove Fraternity Inc.** (1966)

The Zulu Zeta Chapter of **Iota Phi Theta Fraternity Inc.** (1969)

The Aggie Chapter of **Swing Phi Swing Social Fellowship Inc.** (1971)

The Iota Beta Chapter of **Phi Mu Alpha Sinfonia Fraternity Of America Inc.** (1972)

The Sigma Chi Beta Chapter of **Chi Eta Phi Sorority Inc.** (1975)

The Iota Zeta Chapter of **Kappa Kappa Psi National Honorary Band Fraternity Inc.** (1990)

The Theta Zeta Chapter of **Tau Beta Sigma National Band Service Sorority Inc.** (1990)

Southern Association of Colleges and Secondary Schools.[56]

The automobile did the most to reshape American life. "Low prices (the Ford Model T cost just $260 in 1924) and generous credit made cars affordable luxuries at the beginning of the decade; by the end, they were practically necessities. In 1929 there was one car on the road for every five Americans."[57]

The initial migration of unskilled Southern laborers to work in shops and factories across the North helped fuel postwar prosperity and development of the black bourgeoisie. Cultural and intellectual growth occurred for both blacks and whites

Founding dates for Greek organizations active on campus in 2014. *NCATSU STUDENT AFFAIRS.*

Langston Hughes gave this signed photograph to President Bluford.

in the 1920s and 1930s, and America embraced the works of the Harlem Renaissance and writers such as Jean Toomer, Zora Neale Hurston, Claude McKay, Nella Larsen, Countee Cullen, and Langston Hughes. *The New Negro: An Interpretation*, edited by Alain Locke, appeared in 1925 and Du Bois was publishing *The Crisis* and *Opportunity: Journal of Negro Life*. Both publications were closely linked with the civil rights movement, and received prizes for creative expression. Other publications of the time included *The Messenger* and *Negro World*, the organ of Garvey's Universal Negro Improvement Association.[58]

A&T students were interested in local, national, and international issues. Phi Beta Sigma hosted a national conclave where "large contributions had been made through subscriptions toward sending a commission to Haiti to investigate problems, both political and social."[59] American Negro History Week was celebrated

with appearances by the Fisk University president, the Fisk Jubilee Quartet, and Richard B. Harrison. An editorial in *The Register* took note of a recent Supreme Court decision on voting rights. "Progress is gradually being made by the Negroes in politics, but this progress can be speeded up if the thousands of students who do not use their privileges would vote."[60]

If F. Scott Fitzgerald's novels were the script to the Roaring Twenties, jazz musicians Louis Armstrong, Duke Ellington, and Cab Calloway provided the soundtrack. The Cotton Club where Ellington got his start in 1926 gave more visibility to Harlem and the creative work of black Americans. "The rise of the 'race records' industry, beginning with OKeh's recording of Mamie Smith's 'Crazy Blues' in 1920, spread the blues to audiences previously unfamiliar with the form. Alberta Hunter, Clara Smith, Bessie Smith, and Ma Rainey—who had been performing for years in circuses, clubs, and tent shows—found themselves famous."[61] A&T's band, attired in "snappy blue and white new uniforms," toured 32 cities and 35 high schools in the state in 1932.[62]

The film industry prospered as well, moving from silent to sound pictures. Pioneer filmmaker Oscar Micheaux produced his first film, *The Homesteader*. Eubie Blake and Noble Sissle created the musical revue *Shuffle Along*, which hit Broadway in 1921. *Harlem* brought the language of the streets to the New York stage.

African Americans were also making their mark abroad, most notably, dancer and actress Josephine Baker. She became a celebrity when *La Revue nègre* opened in 1925 in Paris.[63]

In 1923, Richard B. Harrison joined the A&T Summer School, teaching the state's teachers until 1931. He reached his greatest national fame as "De Lawd" in the Broadway hit *The Green Pastures*. The Depression-era play portrayed the Old Testament as seen through the eyes of an African American child.[64]

A&T's Summer School program, begun in 1897, helped schoolteachers improve their classroom skills.[65] Enrollment in the summer of 1926 was the largest of any Negro college in the state.[66] By 1934, that number would reach 400,[67] and then 600 by 1936. Charlotte Hawkins Brown, president of Palmer Memorial Institute, spoke to this group in 1936.[68]

Southern blacks who had found a new economic and intellectual life in the cities of the North were not the only ones being liberated. Women shed long dresses, long hair, and societal norms that kept them homebound. They took over office jobs, and had the money to make their own purchases. Women had help with new devices such as the washing machine. Women wanted education. Absent from the campus since 1902, they would be admitted to the general program in 1928, most often gravitating to teacher training programs.[69] In 1931, the A&T Student Council was

Richard B. Harrison (center), eminent actor and teacher, receives an honorary degree in 1934 from President Bluford while Dean Warmoth Gibbs looks on.

The A&T College band leads the way for the members of the 1935 graduating class as they march through campus. *Greensboro Historical Museum Archives.*

Students and faculty assemble in 1931 in front of the new Dudley Memorial Building.

expanded with co-ed members and Ruth Hull was elected co-chairman.[70]

On the other side of town, the North Carolina College for Women had opened in 1892 with a faculty of 15 and a student body of 198. First called the State Normal and Industrial School, it offered women instruction in commercial, domestic science, and pedagogy.[71] Bennett College, now a female-only institution, and Woman's College, along with Guilford and Greensboro colleges, stood beside A&T and the Palmer Memorial Institute in the first Inter-racial Week program in 1939.[72]

The vibrant life of the 1920s would collapse as the 1929 stock market crash launched the Great Depression. President Herbert Hoover did not act decisively, but when Roosevelt took office, he began to "wage a war against the emergency" just as though "we were in fact invaded by a foreign foe."[73]

The economic crisis is reflected in the fall 1929 issue of *The Register*, which was mimeographed rather than printed. The editors apologized,

noting that the college had formerly paid for the newspaper, but it was now to be student-financed.[74] An ad in a 1931 edition by the Elmer Inn Café on East Market Street offered Thanksgiving dinner for 50 cents and 75 cents.[75]

Everyone tightened their belts. "In spite of the depression and the thirty per cent cut in the budget, through rigid economy and loyal and faithful cooperation of our workers, we were able to balance the budget."[76] The college took care of its own needs through its mechanical department: "The students under the direction of the dean and teachers of the department have just completed the erection of a tool shed and a barn at the college farm. Cement walks have also been laid on the campus … All repairs to the College buildings are made by the students of this division."[77] The agricultural side of the college continued to expand its classes and its outreach to the state's farmers, and excel in farm production. President Bluford could report in 1939 that "our Dairy herd won four

Dudley Memorial Building was built in 1931 to replace the destroyed administration building.

Grand Champion prizes, six First Prizes, and five Second Prizes at the Guilford County Fair. Our herd is considered one of the best Jersey herds in the State. It is now producing about 100 gallons of milk per day, which is used in the college cafeteria."[78]

By June 1933, Congress had passed 15 pieces of major legislation, but of all the New Deal agencies, the Agricultural Adjustment Administration was the most important in North Carolina, where farming remained primary. "During the early years of the Depression, tobacco prices plummeted from around 20.0 cents per pound during the end of the 1920s to 8.4 cents in 1931. Cotton prices fell from 22 cents a pound in 1925 to 6 cents in 1931."[79] The agency put in farm production controls, requiring farmers to sometimes plow under their crop, and offering payments to reduce production and raise prices. County Extension Service agents worked with farmer committees on this plan.

Many African Americans who had migrated north lost employment in the economic disaster and found themselves traveling back to the South. In the face of the persistent economic slump, Roosevelt introduced the Second New Deal in 1935. Legislation created the National Labor Relations Act, the Social Security Act, and for the first time, a system of unemployment insurance and aid for dependent children and the disabled. Federal programs helped sustain families in the worst years of the Depression.[80] The Works Progress Administration (WPA) had a large impact. In North Carolina, some 125,000 were employed by the WPA between 1935 and 1940, completing 3,984 projects. "Although North Carolina ranked last in the country in per capita WPA spending, the agency had improved life during the Great Depression for many in the state."[81]

A woman and her children snap peanuts at Roanoke Farms in North Carolina. Photo by John Vachon. *LIBRARY OF CONGRESS, LC-DIG-FSA-8A03107.*

On the A&T campus, the short-lived federal Civil Works Administration approved a new steam tunnel system, plus renovation of the mechanical building and improvement of recreation centers. A&T graduates were selected as instructors in the Civilian Conservation Corps.

*The Pittsburgh Courier* expressed the general black American view in 1939: "For the Negro the New Deal has been the Old Deal in new clothes … Worse it has helped spread Jim Crowism over the country where it had not before existed." The NAACP complained to Eleanor Roosevelt: "There is hardly a phase of the New Deal program which has not brought some hardship to colored people."[82]

While public works were the heart of the New Deal programs, such as the new post office (federal) building on West Market Street, Greensboro, that was dedicated in July 1933, employment was also offered to writers, artists, theatre folk, and musicians.

"In the middle and late 1930s, federal arts projects under the New Deal provided an unprecedented level of encouragement to the development of black artists and helped start the careers of a new generation of artists that included Romare Bearden, Jacob Lawrence, and Norman Lewis."[83] In North Carolina, the Federal Writers' Project hired unemployed journalists, historians, poets, novelists, and librarians—some 300—and published a *Guide to the Old North State* and an anthology of interviews with average working people.[84]

People sought distraction from bad news of the Depression at home and war-gathering in Europe. African American artists and athletes were more and more a part of the national conversation. From 1935 to 1937, Count Basie formed his orchestra, and students spent many nights dancing to the big band sounds. Jesse Owens won four gold medals at the Olympics in Germany, and Joe Louis became the heavyweight boxing champion of the world. Among the many poems printed in *The Register* was one in July 1937 by Little Jas. Rawlinson, "Joe Louis—Rah! Rah! Rah!"[85] Hattie McDaniel became the first black actor to win an Academy Award for her role in *Gone With the Wind*. By the end of the 1930s, Americans were devouring more literature as the result of paperback editions from Penguin and Pocket Books.

Etta Moten, a star of radio, stage, and screen, came to A&T in 1935,[86] and singer Roland Hayes appeared in 1937.[87] Marian Anderson, already a noted singer when she visited A&T in 1927, returned for a

Nat Williamson was the first Negro in the United States to receive a loan under the tenant purchase program. He is shown in Guilford County with FSA official E. H. Anderson. Photo by John Vachon. *LIBRARY OF CONGRESS, LC-DIG-FSA-8A03110.*

President and Mrs. Bluford are shown with contralto Marian Anderson (center) in 1931, when she performed in the Lyceum Series. She had already appeared at Carnegie Hall.

Lyceum performance in 1931.[88] She would make history in 1939, when the Daughters of the American Revolution refused to let her sing to an integrated audience in Constitution Hall. First Lady Eleanor Roosevelt and President Franklin D. Roosevelt stepped in, and on Easter Sunday, she performed on the steps of the Lincoln Memorial to an audience of more than 75,000 and a radio audience in the millions.

Former professor Richard B. Harrison returned to give the commencement speech in 1934. Ceremonies were moved to World War Memorial Stadium to handle the crowd expected for the Broadway star—A&T's first open-air commencement.[89]

Among the graduates of the 1930s was Conrad L. Raiford, in 1936. He was one of the city's first African American certified lifeguards and a Negro League ballplayer. He would go on to become one of the first black

police officers in Greensboro, a bail bondsman who put up the bond for student protest leaders, and a member of Greensboro City Council.[90, 91]

Despite the economic hard times, A&T continued to expand its offerings. In both 1938 and 1939, the newspaper reported record freshmen enrollment.[92, 93] The college was reaching out to potential students—1,644 high school seniors visited for the first all-state gathering in the fall of 1939.[94] They would have more academic options: a major in art was started in 1930, housed in the Engineering Department, and physics was moved there from Agriculture.[95] Home economics was added as a discipline in 1933. Before that, women had gone to Bennett for training. Director Carolyn Crawford, college dietitian for 10 years, "had a hand" in obtaining the Garrett House that was built by the WPA.[96] The High School Department was discontinued. In 1931, the College

Miss A&T 1936, Ruth Green. *Greensboro Historical Museum Archives.*

of Arts and Sciences became the School of Education and Sciences. The Alpha Kappa Mu Honor Society was one of the original chapters present at the organization of the nationwide group in 1937.[97]

A court case, *Gaines v. Missouri*,[98] led to the creation of a graduate program at A&T in 1939, with degrees initially offered in agriculture, technology, and applied sciences.[99] Self-help was important during this period. Faculty created the Educational Workers Federal Credit Union in 1938. The Hicks-Mosely Student Loan Fund started in 1939,[100] and help also came from the National Youth Administration (NYA), a student aid program organized in 1935. "For the 1935–36 school year, the NYA provided $572,571 to assist an average of 5,907 students per month in 53 North Carolina colleges and 885 public schools. Students received part-time jobs, scholarships, and loans based on need."[101]

The freshman Class of 1938 set a record.

A group of students perform a dance in costume on the lawn at A&T in 1937. *Greensboro Historical Museum Archives*.

The 1937 May Queen is seated outdoors on some steps and surrounded by her court of six young ladies. *Greensboro Historical Museum Archives*.

Students take part in a theatrical production onstage in 1937. *Greensboro Historical Museum Archives*.

Well-dressed men and women are seated around an open square table in the college dining room for a formal occasion in 1938. *Greensboro Historical Museum Archives.*

Members of the A&T University Glee Club pose onstage in 1938. *Greensboro Historical Museum Archives.*

The A&T Marching Band and a few floats parade through a stadium. This shot was taken in 1938. *Greensboro Historical Museum Archives.*

At A&T, students went on strike in 1936 over food service, then for theatre desegregation in 1937.[102] A peace group was organized. In 1939, a student strike brought attention from the state government—and an investigation. Pastor and activist the Rev. Adam Clayton Powell Sr. attracted a large crowd to a 1939 vesper service.[103]

"People always talking about civil rights beginning on campus with the A&T Four. But students were activist forever. Back in 1937, the students used the band to communicate. One instrument being played meant to meet at one place. The other instrument meant they met somewhere else," said Velma Speight-Buford '53. "They ran the Board of Trustees out of Harrison Auditorium … that was the beginning of activism on this campus when they were not treated right."[104]

A drum major in 1938. *GREENSBORO HISTORICAL MUSEUM ARCHIVES.*

Calls for change at home would soon be overwhelmed by world events. In 1939, Adolph Hitler's Third Reich annexed Czechoslovakia and invaded Poland. France and Great Britain and Canada declared war on Germany. While the student newspaper did not carry national news, the editorial cartoons and letters make it very clear that students were watching with interest and apprehension.

"As war broke out in Europe, American sentiment heavily favored isolationism. With the nation still skeptical of Allied propaganda after it had lured the U.S. into the first World War, the United States declares its neutrality in the European War."[105] That was September 5, 1939. The slogan, "A War to End All Wars," was now a bitter taste in the mouth of Americans. War was coming, and it would bring massive changes for all Americans, and for A&T.

*The Register* carried locally drawn cartoons, including this one showing the prewar mood in the fall of 1939.

PRESIDENTS OF LAND GRANT COLLEGES

Presidents of the land-grant colleges gather for their ninth annual convention at the YMCA in Chicago, November 1931.

**ENDNOTES**

1. Johnson, J.W., 341
2. "Time Line"
3. Spruill, 76
4. Kearns, 331
5. May 1932
6. Gibbs, *History*, 46
7. May 1931
8. May 1938
9. Hornsby, A., 139
10. Weinberg and Weinberg, xiii
11. "Walker"
12. *Ayantee*, 48
13. "Greensboro: History"
14. Franklin, 486
15. "Greensboro: History"
16. O'Keefe, 47
17. Gibbs, *History*, 46-47
18. Gibbs, *History*, 87
19. Gibbs, *History*, 64
20. Spruill, 70
21. Kelley, 25
22. Spruill, 3, 33
23. "Invitation"
24. Gibbs, *History*, 9, 170
25. "Insurance"
26. March 1931
27. Spruill, 65-66
28. Spruill, 33
29. May 1925
30. Spruill, 33
31. July/August 1926
32. Gibbs, *History*, 67
33. Gibbs, *History*, 176-77
34. Frye, H.

35. Barr
36. May 1933
37. Spruill, 48
38. Johnson and Campbell, 80
39. April/May 1927
40. Spruill, 91-92
41. Moore, "Sports," 8
42. Spruill, 90
43. Spruill, 93-94
44. Spruill, 95
45. Spruill, 88-89
46. Moore, "Sports," 8
47. July/August 1926
48. April/May 1927
49. *Ayantee*, 45, 50
50. *Ayantee*, 44
51. Gibbs, *History*, 107-09
52. February 1932
53. *Ayantee*, 64-65
54. History.com, "Roaring"
55. Kelley, 34-35
56. Gibbs, *History*, 179-80
57. History.com, "Roaring"
58. Hine et al., 413-20
59. January 1927
60. February 1927
61. "Harlem"
62. May 1932
63. Hine et al., 413-20
64. Gibbs, *History*, 85
65. Gibbs, *History*, 94
66. July/August 1926
67. July 1934
68. July 1936
69. Kelley, 16
70. December 1931

71. "History of UNCG"
72. February 20, 1939
73. History.com, "New"
74. September 1929
75. November 1931
76. Bluford, "Annual," 1932, 1
77. Bluford, "Annual," 1937, 5
78. Bluford, "Quarterly," 1940, 3
79. Abrams et al.
80. "Chronology," 1076
81. Abrams
82. King, D.S., 31, 264
83. "Harlem"
84. Hill
85. July 1937
86. December 1935
87. February 1937
88. March 1931
89. May 1934
90. "Conrad"
91. Schlosser
92. October 1938
93. October 1939
94. December 1939
95. Gibbs, History, 48
96. Spruill, *72-73*
97. Gibbs, 111
98. *Missouri*
99. Gibbs, *History*, 48, 64-65
100. Gibbs, *History*, 92
101. Abrams et al.
102. Kelley, 38
103. May 1939
104. Speight-Buford
105. "Timeline of World War II"

# CHAPTER THREE

# The War Years

## 1940–1949

Army second lieutenants celebrate on the parade grounds in this undated photograph.

Richard Wright's best-selling novel *Native Son* was published in 1940. Its depiction of racial oppression that leads a poor black man to murder would be an intellectual backdrop to the struggle African Americans would continue to face through the war years. The need for men on the fighting line—and men and women in the factories—would bring new opportunities, but "Jim Crow" seemed entrenched across the South.[1] Still, there were signs of change. At the dedication of the Richard B. Harrison Auditorium and Alexander Graham Vocational Building in early 1940, UNC President Frank P. Graham said, "Both races join hands here this afternoon as one more step toward the larger fulfillment of the American democratic dream and the kingdom of God."[2]

President Roosevelt won reelection in 1940, while the Axis was coalescing in Europe under Mussolini and Hitler. Technically neutral, the United States had begun mobilizing with a peacetime draft and fivefold expansion of the defense budget. In October 1941, a British lord visited campus, raising funds for an ambulance plane—A&T donated $100, while the Guilford County Colored Committee gave $660.[3]

As in World War I, A&T trained the troops. "During World War II, a U.S. Army specialized training assignment and reclassification unit was operated at A&T, the only such unit at a historically black college."[4] Hundreds of young soldiers settled into classrooms, not to study literature or biology, but to learn how to fight a war. The college operated an aviation school in 1941, with 10 students receiving their

The college participated in the Army Specialized Training Program and Signal Corps Training Program.

pilot's licenses. The march toward war could also be seen with courses in airplane mechanics and participation by trades students in the National Defense program.[5] In addition, the Fourth Service Command Signal School and its ROTC program were housed at A&T. The college was widely recognized for its military drill team—the only one at a black institution in North Carolina. This drill team became a Senior ROTC for infantry officers in 1942;[6] by the end of the decade, A&T was said to have the largest ROTC unit in the nation.

The student newspaper, filled with familiar news from Greek organizations and columns of jokes and poetry, also took note of the situation in Europe. Students were asked their opinions of Hitler and Mussolini, and letter-writers debated defending democracy versus promoting peace. In 1941, the college celebrated the Men's Glee Club and A Capella Choir being heard "over a nation wide

Men sit onstage during a CBS radio/ WBIG program at A&T College in 1940. © *Carol W. Martin/Greensboro Historical Museum Collection.*

Students take part in an NBC radio program. A&T's choral groups participated in national broadcasts, including the groundbreaking black cultural program of the 1930s and 1940s, *Wings Over Jordan*.

hookup on the morning of January 2nd from 9:15 to 9:45, through the facilities of WBIG."[7] This was the choir's second coast-to-coast broadcast, having earlier presented one over the NBC networks.

Roosevelt's win meant the continuation of the New Deal. It also revealed the hopes and dreams of black Americans yet to be fulfilled. The United States became FDR's "Arsenal of Democracy," and expansion of defense industries and government agencies offered opportunities that African Americans were determined to access. Even as Benjamin O. Davis Sr. became the highest-ranking black officer in the Army with his promotion to brigadier general, institutional racism in the American military prompted black leaders such as A. Phillip Randolph, the founder of the Brotherhood of

T. D. Williamson, the Negro extension agent for Caswell County, chairs a 1940 meeting at the schoolhouse in Yanceyville. The colored county land-use planning committee is working on county maps. Photo by Marion Post Wollcott. *LIBRARY OF CONGRESS, LC-USF34-056364-D.*

Sleeping Car Porters, to "organize the March on Washington Movement in 1941 to demand the end of segregation in the armed forces."[8] Long-simmering racial grievances were brought to a boil by the case of *Mitchell v. United States*, where a black man who had paid a first-class fare to travel interstate had been told to move to a second-class car. The Supreme Court ruled in 1941 that racial discrimination violated the Interstate Commerce Act.[9]

Roosevelt, warned of the growing number of African Americans expected to participate in the March on Washington, feared the protest would provide fodder for German propaganda. He sent First Lady Eleanor Roosevelt and New York Mayor Fiorello LaGuardia to dissuade Randolph, but to no avail. FDR responded: In Executive Order 8802 of June 25, 1941, he affirmed "the policy of the United States that there shall be no discrimination in the employment of workers in the defense industry or government because of race, creed, color, or national origin."[10, 11] Randolph called off the march. In his autobiography, NAACP leader Roy Wilkins wrote, "To this day, I don't know if he would have been able to turn out enough marchers to make his point stick … but, what a bluff it was."[12]

The executive order, the first presidential action to counter discrimination since Reconstruction, established the Fair Employment Practices Committee to monitor discrimination in the defense industries. The number of black Americans working in government rose from approximately 40,000 in 1938 to over 300,000 during the war.[13] Work in the post office and the classroom provided an avenue for advancement. In connection with A&T's 50th anniversary celebration, under the banner of "The Negro Land Grant College in a Changing Social Order," about 500 participants in concurrent agricultural and technical science conferences concluded that "further integration depends upon the efficiency of … training, in spite of racial or economic barriers."[14] The 50th anniversary also included a speech by Gov. J. M. Broughton, a performance by tenor Roland Hayes, and presentation of an honorary doctor of laws degree to Charles H. Moore, who had been instrumental in the creation of the college.[15] A poem by Dolores E. Dunlap celebrated A&T's half-century: "You've served in war and sent beacon lights / To become great warriors in the Negroes' fight."[16] In April 1941, the college hosted the largest convention ever by the North Carolina Negro Teachers Association, with some 3,000 teachers.[17]

A&T awarded master's degrees for the first time in 1941, to Woodland Ellroy Hall and Mamie Cooper.[18] That year also had a diverse lineup of visitors, highlighted by Dr. Mary McLeod Bethune, "The First Lady of the Struggle," president of the college she had founded, Bethune-Cookman

University.[19] Jazz singer Ella Fitzgerald was featured in concert in May.[20] A&T hosted Cortez W. Peters, world speed-typing champion. Both father and son held that title and operated the first black-owned business schools.[21, 22]

On December 7, 1941, Japan attacked Pearl Harbor and America was at war again. Twenty-two-year-old Dorie Miller downed four Japanese planes with a machine gun after moving his wounded captain to a safer place. The African American hero of Pearl Harbor received the Navy Cross and was cited for "distinguished devotion to duty, extraordinary courage and disregard for his own personal safety," then was sent back to mess duty without a promotion.[23, 24]

The December 1941 issue of *The Register* noted that students were "hit hard" by the draft.[25] Another front-page story stated that the Military Department had the largest class of student cadets ever—freshmen and sophomore men numbering 585, with 33 commissioned and non-commissioned officers.[26] In 1942, the college began an accelerated program to let students finish in three years, and offered new defense-related courses. "The college is opening all the agricultural and technical courses to women, and urging them to take these courses, so that they can fill many of the jobs now held by men."[27] With food becoming more difficult to secure, a cannery was opened, an ice cream facility added, and pork and poultry production expanded.[28] Land

on Bessemer used by the college was purchased for an Army camp, so the college bought new acreage near the McConnell Road farm, boosting its holdings to 455 acres.[29]

A little-known part of the war effort in North Carolina was the "B-1 Band," organized primarily from A&T and Dudley High School students.[30] "The B-1 bandsmen were among 2.5 million African Americans who registered for the draft; over a million served. North Carolina managed these important distinctions: at Montford Point, near Camp Lejeune, the first African Americans to serve in the Marines were trained, as was the first black Marine band. And the U.S. Navy B-1 Band,

organized in Greensboro at North Carolina Agricultural and Mechanical College—now N.C. A&T University— was comprised of the first African Americans to serve in the modern Navy at rank other than messman."[31]

These steps toward integration focused on A&T for a reason: the Navy was seeking top-notch, college-educated musicians who could live and work under the stressful conditions of "separate but equal."[32] The A&T Band was already known by its travels through the South and East.[33] A&T bandsmen and B-1 veterans would go on to lead bands themselves: Walter F. Carlson Jr. would become a longtime leader of the A&T Band, and Lou Donaldson led his own orchestra.[34]

The first 13 men to join the band were announced on May 10, 1942. Among them was the son of an A&T administrator, Warmoth T. Gibbs Jr., who played clarinet.[35] The recruits took part in a mass swearing-in at Raleigh, then headed to Norfolk, Virginia, for training.[36] They would be stationed in Chapel Hill, North Carolina, to play for ceremonies, meals, and social events at the pre-flight school.

"We were aware of what was happening, of what we were doing by going into the Navy. Everyone was aware that we were the first to break the barrier," recalled French horn player Calvin Morrow.[37]

They had been handpicked by a committee made up of Gov. J. M. Broughton, C. C. Spaulding, President Bluford of A&T, and the presidents of North Carolina College and Fayetteville State. Although this unit was well-respected from its leader, James Parsons, throughout its ranks, the B-1 had to live three miles from the white officers who were being trained in Chapel Hill, and march back and forth to barracks at a community center in the black

Preserving food was an important part of the war effort. Filling cans at the Fuquay Springs High School in Wake County in 1944 are (from left): vocational agriculture teacher L. M. Burton, Olivia Redi, Roberta Burton, and Ora McCullers.

B1 NAVY Bandroom 1944

B1 NAVY Band Members 2012

A photo of the B-1 Band in 1944 (background) and surviving members in 2012 (foreground). *Charles E. Watkins/University Relations.*

The B-1 Band plays for the raising of colors at Alexander Hall, pre-flight school headquarters at UNC. *U.S. Navy, courtesy James B. Parsons/Alex Albright.*

area.[38] "But even though we were fully well-conditioned to segregation, we'd accepted it as a way of life, many times we wondered why we couldn't eat in that big dining hall on the campus," said William Skinner.[39]

This story underscored the reality that separate seldom meant equal. "Racial conflict in the South was apparent among the military when on August 6, 1941, a number of serious racial disturbances involving white and black soldiers occurred aboard a bus in North Carolina."[40] Black soldiers in Army camps were housed in undesirable locations and black officers were denied use of officers' clubs. It was a common complaint that German prisoners of war were treated better than African American soldiers.

At least two of the B-1 members had participated in the college's pilot training program, hoping to join the Army's school for black pilots. The students flew planes at the Greensboro-High Point Airport to supplement classroom instruction. At the Turkey Day Classic in 1940, one of the aeronautics students "put on a demonstration over the stadium in a cub monoplane. He went through tailspins, loops and side-slips—all of which were breathtaking."[41]

The Army pilots, the 99th Squadron or "Tuskegee Airmen," would be in the air by the end of 1941. About 600 black pilots received their wings during World War II.[42] But the Army's efforts at integration, while sometimes halting, were not matched in other branches of the

This chemistry class includes quite a few women.

service. "Banned altogether from the Marines and Air Force, confined to jobs as longshoremen and cooks in the Navy, only in the Army could blacks join combat units. But their life there was an endless stream of humiliations, from being herded to the back of military buses on U.S. bases to being refused food by white units on the beach in Normandy."[43]

Despite the war, the largest freshman class ever was reported for the fall of 1942.[44] Also that year, the college welcomed back Charles DeBerry, a member of the 1927 football championship team, as head coach and athletic director. The A Capella Choir performed a half-hour Christmas concert that was broadcast coast to coast on the Columbia Broadcasting System.[45]

The Rev. Adam Clayton Powell Jr., pastor of Abyssinian Baptist Church in New York and the first black man elected to the New York City Council, spoke at the spring 1941 commencement,[46] and again in February 1942, saying, "Democracy will lose its place as a world power unless the negro and other dark races are given equal rights in the peace."[47]

The student newspaper was filled with war news, including "homefront issues" such as sugar rationing, the "silk stocking problem," and pleas to buy war bonds. Yet the war's dislocations did not dislodge segregation in the South. Some worked to break down those barriers—a 1942 event in Greensboro united the choirs of A&T, the Palmer Institute, and Bennett with white choirs from Woman's College, Greensboro College, and Guilford College.[48, 49] These lights were bright but small in the prevailing gloom of Jim Crow.

President Ferdinand Bluford (left) with Dr. M. C. S. Noble, for 45 years the chair of the Board of Trustees, and H. Clinton Taylor, artist and founder of the Art Department. Noble was honored with this portrait in 1942, on his 87th birthday.

In a letter to the editor of the *Pittsburgh Courier*, James G. Thompson wrote, "Being an American of dark complexion and some 26 years, these questions flash through my mind: 'Should I sacrifice my life to live half American?' 'Will things be better for the next generation in the peace to follow?' 'Would it be demanding too much to demand full citizenship rights in exchange for the sacrificing of my life?' 'Is the kind of America I know worth defending?' 'Will America be a true and pure democracy after this war?' 'Will colored Americans suffer still the indignities that have been heaped upon them in the past?' These and other questions need answering." Then he proposed what he called "the double V V for a double victory … The V for victory sign is being displayed prominently in all so-called democratic countries which are fighting for victory over aggression, slavery, and tyranny. If this V sign means that to those now engaged in this great conflict, then let we colored Americans adopt the double V V for a double victory. The first V for victory over our enemies from without, the second V for victory over our enemies from within. For surely those who perpetuate these ugly prejudices here are seeking to destroy our democratic form of government just as surely as the Axis forces."[50]

*The Courier*, reaching more than 200,000 homes nationwide, was the most widely read black newspaper. This letter drew such a strong response that a week later, *The Courier* printed an insignia on its front page for "Democracy: Double Victory at Home-Abroad" and would run it through 1943.[51] In this same period, the Congress of Racial Equality (CORE) was founded by Bayard Rustin and James Farmer in Chicago.[52]

Racism extended its reach in other directions. In 1942, the United States interned 100,000 Japanese Americans in camps.[53] North Carolina continued its segregationist policies by recasting the Cherokee Indian Normal School of Robeson County as Pembroke State College for Indians (now UNC-Pembroke) in 1941, the nation's first public four-year college for Native Americans.[54]

The continued push of protest groups and the military need for manpower saw all armed forces relax their restrictions on African Americans. On July 20, 1942, the Women's Army Auxiliary Corps was formed. Black women were accepted with whites. Charity Adams became the first black woman commissioned officer in the WAC. Black women served as Army nurses and, like black men, served in all-black units in the U.S. military.[55]

Alice Majorie Johnson, a 1942 graduate, was posted to India to serve as an American Red Cross staff assistant.[56] The following year, Jean M. Bright was in a similar posting in New Guinea.[57] Leading nurse Carolyn Crosby appeared at local campuses on behalf of the National Nursing Council

Jean Bright graduated from A&T in 1939 and served with the Red Cross from 1944 to 1946. She went on to get a master's degree in English from Columbia University, and taught for many years at A&T, co-authoring books with Darwin T. Turner and Richard Wright. *Lewis A. Brandon III.*

for War Service to inform women about opportunities in nursing. The U.S. Cadet Nurse Corps offered free education at more than 1,000 schools for those who pledged to remain in essential military or civilian nursing for the duration of the war.[58]

A&T students would find their careers entwined with the military in other ways. Thelma Marina Hauser, a 1947 graduate in biology and social science, went to Howard University and then joined the Veterans Administration Medical Center in Washington, D.C.,

as a social worker. She also chaired the D.C. Social Work Board and D.C. Commission on Aging.[59, 60]

In the spring of 1943, the enlisted Reserve Corps at A&T—including most upper-class campus leaders—was called into service.[61] The call-up of these and others—more than 300 Aggie men were in the fighting service—left gaps across the campus that were quickly filled by female students.[62] Barbara Canada was elected the first woman student body president.[63]

Aggies far from home remembered their alma mater. Pvt. Joseph McKinney wrote, "I have just received a copy of *The Register* today and it

The May Queen and her court, May 1945.

Bill Robinson, known as "Bojangles," was among the stars visiting A&T.

made me think of the days when I was back at A. and T. I am awful sorry that I was not able to attend school this year and take up my duties as a reporter on *The Register* staff." He also mentioned the value of his military science classes, and said that Ft. Huachuca had "many colored officers—some from A. and T."[64]

The early 1940s marked many creative achievements for African Americans. Paul Robeson opened on Broadway in *Othello* and singer Lena Horne and dancer Bill "Bojangles" Robinson appeared in the all-black musical film *Stormy Weather*, all in 1943.[65] Robinson would visit A&T early the next year to perform at the Alpha Kappa Alpha music concert and sell war bonds.[66] Other luminaries who visited included writer Margaret Walker, winner of the Yale

Troops in formation at Basic Training Camp No. 10, better known as ORD (Overseas Replacement Depot), where soldiers were trained, processed, and shipped out, mainly to Europe.

Younger Poets Prize,[67] and Todd Duncan, who was in "his third triumphal season as Porgy in the Gershwin Negro folk opera, 'Porgy and Bess.'"[68]

Phairlever Pearson, a captain in the ROTC, was perhaps best known for a particularly showy and demanding type of leadership. His obituary program from 1999 states that, "while at A&T, he became the University's first drum major."[69] He went on to be a teacher, principal, and community leader, facing poor facilities and segregationist policies

that kept students from educational opportunities. His daughter Pauletta was a musician and actress who met her future husband, actor and film-maker Denzel Washington on the set of the television film *Wilma*.[70]

As the black military fought in the European and Pacific theatres, along with discrimination they encountered a new sense of purpose. As noted sociologists of that time wrote: "Negroes were different this time—for the thirty years between the First and Second World War has seen a great expansion of school facilities in the South and distribution of newspapers and radios."[71] Soldiers returned from the front with a commitment to fight inequality. Racial unrest occurred in May and August 1943—40 people were killed and U.S. troops were called out in Mobile, Alabama, and Detroit, where the clashes threatened defense production.[72] Other confrontations occurred in Harlem and Beaumont, Texas. The ineffectiveness of the Fair Employment

Practices Committee of 1941 prompted President Roosevelt to issue Executive Order 9346 in 1943,[73] and a new FEPC committee was formed to hear cases concerning discrimination in the shipbuilding and railroad industries.

"The machines hum, the motors purr and the welder's torch hisses and flares night and day, as the College carries on its work of training men and women for the war program and the supporting civilian activities," wrote President Bluford.[74]

Defense industries were important in North Carolina. The

A section of a class in brick-making works at the rear of Crosby Hall in 1943.

Soldiers are shown eating in the fields.

Soldiers gather in the mess line.

Two soldiers take shelter under a tent.

An ROTC commissioning ceremony on the lawn.

Wilmington Shipyards employed more than 5,300 African Americans, and in 1943, the B-1 had one of its biggest performances there at the launching of the USS *Merrick*. John Merrick, a founder of North Carolina Mutual Insurance in Durham, had been suggested for that honor by Mutual President C. C. Spaulding.[75] A&T engineering and science graduates who had struggled to find appropriate employment before the war were suddenly in high demand. The new opportunities were noted in *The Register*, with a letter to Professor Bowling from a New York radio station recruiting his students.[76]

In 1944, Dean Warmoth Gibbs prepared a monograph, "A Program for Research for A. and T. College," stating that "because of the large number of departments and courses dealing with practical problems of everyday life, research should become a regular part of the college program as soon as possible."[77] Bluford had commented, "The Negro land grant colleges have not done much in this important field because of the lack of funds and trained personnel to carry on such work. Practically no money that has been appropriated by the State and Federal Governments for research in land grant colleges [has] been allotted to Negro Land Grant Colleges. Most of our land grant colleges have well trained teachers, and are striving to make research an essential part of their programs."[78]

On June 6, 1944, the Allied invasion of German-occupied France began. The D-Day landings became the largest amphibious invasion in history, with over 160,000 soldiers. "Some 2,000 black troops hit Omaha and Utah beaches in Normandy on June 6, 1944, though you've probably never heard of them. 'You see these movies and stuff like *The Longest Day*—you don't see African Americans,' says one black veteran interviewed in (the documentary) *A Distant Shore*."[79]

Troops fought their way across France and into Germany. *The Register* carried a front-page photo and story on a 1939 alumnus lost on the Italian front. "Sgt. James Edward Reid, former student and instructor in the field of Horticulture, died as he had lived, for the good of his fellowman."[80] 2nd Lt. Leonard C. Rohr was awarded the Silver Star for gallantry in action in Italy.[81]

Service members were asked to send in their photos and information. Not all were at the front. Pfc. Ruben G. Burrell, a 1941 Fine Arts graduate, reported that he had received his Master of Arts degree from Columbia and exhibited at the Museum of Modern Art before entering the Army. He became post artist at Chico Army Air Field.[82]

President Roosevelt died on April 12, 1945. As the train carrying his remains from Arkansas to Washington passed through Greensboro at night, townsfolk and students gathered at the rail station to pay their respects.[83] A month earlier, First Lady Eleanor Roosevelt, a champion of human rights and a staunch ally of African Americans, had spoken to A&T students.[84, 85]

Vice President Harry Truman was sworn in as the nation's 33rd president. On May 7, the Germans signed an unconditional surrender. At an Allied conference in Potsdam, Germany, an ultimatum was issued for Japan: it must agree to an unconditional surrender or face "prompt and utter destruction."[86] President Truman's decision days later to strike Hiroshima and then Nagasaki with atomic weapons is still debated. The Japanese formal surrender occurred on September 2, 1945, aboard the USS *Missouri*.[87]

Troops swarmed home to take advantage of the GI Bill, a 1944 measure to further the education and employment of veterans.[88] President Bluford noted that because the founding act cited agriculture and mechanic arts, "an erroneous impression has prevailed that the land grant college is only a technical institution." But liberal arts and sciences made the land-grant college "uniquely adapted to meet the needs of the postwar period in the education of civilian students and that large number of veterans who will return."[89]

A&T welcomed the students—but where to house them? The college had 541 veterans in 1945–46, with 300 more turned away for lack of space.[90] In 1946, the college acquired the hospital area of the former Overseas

Replacement Depot and converted its buildings into dorms, classrooms, offices.[91] A&T had a threefold increase in enrollment and staff in three years. "We have permanent dormitories for only 600 students, while more than 1,300 students are now living in dilapidated army barracks and temporary buildings supplied wholly by the Federal Government and the college," wrote Bluford in a plea for dormitory construction.[92] "In one biennium, the State Legislature had appropriated over $5,000,000 in capital improvements. This came at the peak of the enrollment of G.I.'s on the campus when the officials had enrolled over 3,000 students, a figure that was far too high for the facilities and equipment

First Lady Eleanor Roosevelt is escorted on campus by President Bluford in 1945.

The A&T band on parade
in 1944 in Raleigh.

Students learn typing.

available for education."[93] Classes operated from 7 a.m. to 7:30 p.m.[94]

Shirley Taylor Frye '53 said that "there were many more men on campus than women. I immediately got involved on the debate team. That is where I met my husband. I had my English class in the barracks. A lot of students were on the GI Bill. Most of those I came in contact with were in engineering, science and electronics."[95]

Agricultural production, emphasized throughout the war, would become a focus for returning vets as well. Sidney B. Simmons of Agricultural Education was a leader throughout the period. From 1935 to 1955, he served as the national executive secretary of the New Farmers of America, a program to develop agricultural students in high school. Following the war, he directed the Veteran on the Farm Training Program.[96]

While the GI Bill was vital to the education of the veterans, other students were in need of help, and the college also needed assistance to grow and develop. The University Foundation was chartered in March 1946, as a mechanism for the college to receive and administer gifts and donations. This would be an

Noble Huntly and his project of 550 turkeys, shown in 1946 as part of the veterans training class. He earned a Modern Farmer degree in 1941 and served in the Army for more than three years, two of them overseas.

important adjunct to state funding, which could be changeable.[97]

The Double V campaign was far from over, as the gains of black men and women were erased as the armed forces dismantled and factories began to reinstate discriminatory hiring practices.[98] A White House memorandum at the close of the war warned that "the prospect of decreasing employment and the return of troops raises the same danger signals that preceded the riots of 1919."[99]

Adam Clayton Powell Jr. was elected to the House of Representatives from Harlem in 1945 and would serve 11 consecutive terms. He visited A&T again that year.[100] *Ebony*, a magazine about African American life, was an instant success upon its founding in 1945, and instrumental in chronicling black achievement.[101]

President Truman's investigation sought to examine the status of African Americans in society and in government, prompted by a heart-rending experience in 1946 brought to his attention by the NAACP. Truman wrote to his attorney general Tom Clark: "They told me about an incident which happened in South Carolina where a Negro Sergeant, who had been discharged from the Army just three hours, was taken off the bus and not only seriously beaten, but his eyes were deliberately put out and the Mayor of the town had bragged about committing this outrage."[102]

Aggie men learn the fine art of tailoring.

Unrest continued in Alabama and Pennsylvania in 1946. The Supreme Court had banned segregation in interstate bus travel,[103] but that ruling had little effect in the South. Discontent among veterans, continued issues of discrimination, and the growth of protest groups set the agenda for the African American community to renew the journey for equality in education, employment, and housing. On April 9, 1947, Freedom Riders were sent by the Congress of Racial Equality to test the Supreme Court's ruling on bus desegregation.[104]

While Freedom Riders put their lives on the line to further racial progress, advancements were being made in a far different field: athletics. On April 10, 1947, Jackie Robinson was admitted to Major League Baseball when he joined the Brooklyn Dodgers, followed a year later by Roy Campanella.[105] Classes were excused in 1949 when a cavalcade of African American baseball stars visited the campus: Robinson, Campanella, and Big Don Newcombe from the Dodgers, 1949 National League champs, and Larry Doby of the Cleveland Indians, 1948 world champions.[106]

Sports teams at A&T bloomed at war's end with the arrival of a new athletic director and head football coach, Dr. William Bell, in 1946.[107] The second black to play football at Ohio State, he had been an Air Force officer, then coached at Clafin and Florida A&M.[108] An Armistice Day game at the Polo Grounds in New York City featured A&T taking on the U.S. Navy Under Sea Raiders. It was the third in a series of interracial football games sponsored by the Associated Football Charities and Douglas G. Hertz, who found

Roy Campanella.

that sporting events such as the Olympics could be "the soundest possible basis for international and interracial amity."[109]

The Aggies appeared twice in the Flower Bowl, winning over Southern on January 1, 1943, then losing to Tyler Junior College on January 1, 1945. The Aggies played in the "Black Rose Bowl," the Vulcan Bowl, for the 1948 season, losing to Kentucky State in the game played on January 1, 1949, in Birmingham, Alabama. Late that year, they would appear in another postseason classic, defeating Florida A&M in the Orange Blossom Classic in Jacksonville, Florida, on December 10, 1949.[110]

A&T produced several All-American football players: William "Red" Jackson, Bill Boyers, Walter Hunter, Charlie Weaver, and Art Statum, who also won an NCAA heavyweight title.[111] During the 1940s, the college also had a boxing team. Eldridge Williams, a Tuskegee Airman, became A&T's head basketball coach but was recalled in 1948 during the Berlin Airlift.[112]

Running back Robert H. "Stonewall" Jackson was the first HBCU player drafted into the NFL, taken in 1950 by the New York Giants. He first drew notice in that 1946 interracial football game against submariners. Jackson, a member of the A&T and CIAA halls of fame, would go on to coach at NC Central. "A&T gave me foundation for life, and it's my alma mater,

NORTH CAROLINA
A & T COLLEGE
VS.
U.S.
NAVY
UNDER SEA RAIDERS

OFFICIAL
PROGRAM
25 CENTS

POLO GROUNDS
ARMISTICE DAY — NOVEMBER 11, 1946

which I love and I would do anything for except when they play [NCCU] in football," he said.[113] In baseball, Tom Alston was an outstanding Aggie player of the 1940s. The six-foot-five Alston had served in the Navy before coming to A&T, and "would come up on April 13, 1954, as the player who integrated the Cardinals."[114]

Homecoming came into prominence again. "More alumni members were present for this event than in the last ten years. Huge numbers of visitors and citizens of the city viewed the parade," and an audience of over 10,000 saw the game against West Virginia State.[115] For the 1948 parade, a

Souvenir program for the interracial football game at the Polo Grounds. The A&T roster notes that 11 players served in World War II.

A cheering squad from the 1940s. Kneeling (from left): Sarah Catherine Stubbs, Teresa Robinson, Deloris Colonial Wilson, and Barbara Spence. Standing at right is Francis Spruill.

Home economics students gather at Garrett House in the late 1940s. *DEBORAH PETERSON UNDERWOOD.*

"chariot" crafted by Omega Psi Phi was chosen as the best.[116]

In 1947, veterans at A&T learned that they were entitled to various service medals, and a presentation ceremony was set for Dudley Lawn on Armistice Day, November 11, 1947. Veterans formed their own organization, the Veterans Association.[117]

Also that year, A&T hosted the national convention of the New Farmers of America, the black equivalent to the Future Farmers of America. In 1948–49, more than 15,000 people would come to the campus for meetings and conferences, a significant increase over the 1947–48 totals of 9,600 attendees.[118, 119]

As the decade ended, students at A&T were engaged with intellectual and artistic development. Campus artists were inspired by the visit

ABOVE: The Marshville, North Carolina, New Farmers of America embark on a trip to Raleigh in 1947.

LEFT: NFA pledge.

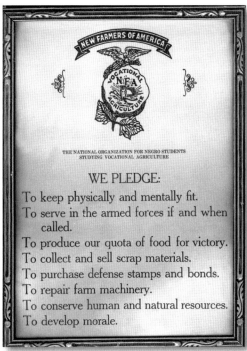

the next twenty or twenty-five years without a war, then there will not be a great possibility of war, but numerous conflicts will continue to exist among the people throughout the world."[122]

The closing years of the decade saw a return to normalcy and an emphasis on consumer culture. The student newspaper sported ads for Chesterfield Cigarettes and Freeman Shoes. A&T raised $1,000 for a local polio drive, the most of any school in the city.[123] One of the largest college dormitories in the country was built, along with a trades building and a gymnasium.[124]

President Truman's victory in the 1948 election was due largely to the black vote in key Northern states. The conflict within the Democratic Party over civil rights was so severe, a split occurred at the 1948 convention.[125]

of Zelma Burke, who designed the portrait of FDR used on the dime.[120] The International Relations Club met and debated the pros and cons of the Marshall Plan.[121] Anthropologist Margaret Mead visited campus in 1948, saying, "If we can get through

The Rhythm Kids plus All Stars perform in the late 1940s. "Saturday Night at Harrison Auditorium" was a popular performance venue during the period. Some of the members of the Rhythm Kids plus All-Stars Band are shown here. Among those associated with the band were Lindsay Davis, Wilfred "Wimp" Robinson, Melvin Smith, Willis Green, and William Lax. Not pictured are Rufus "Big Petty" Pettiford and Charlie Morrison. *CARL FOSTER*.

In February 1948, President Truman "instructed the secretary of defense to take steps to have the remaining instances of discrimination in the armed services eliminated as rapidly as possible."[126] That July, he signed Executive Order 9981, creating the President's Committee on Equality of Treatment and Opportunity in the Armed Services.[127] Executive Order 9980 was aimed at eliminating racial bias in federal employment through a Fair Employment Board.[128] Truman's efforts would align the Democrats with civil rights and begin the process for legislation that continued through the 1950s and '60s, but would be carried out most effectively by a Southern Democrat, President Lyndon Baines Johnson.[129]

**ENDNOTES**

1. Hornsby, A., 145
2. February 1940
3. October 1941
4. Moore, "Military"
5. Bluford, "Quarterly," 1941, 1
6. July 1942
7. February 1941
8. Hornsby, A., 145-46
9. Mitchell
10. Hine et al., 484
11. Roosevelt, 8802
12. Hine et al., 485
13. King, D.S., 25
14. March 1941
15. March 1941
16. March 1941
17. April 1941
18. Gibbs, *History*, 65
19. Gibbs, *History*, 148
20. April 1941
21. February 1941
22. "Cortez"
23. Hornsby, A., 146
24. Hine et al., 485-86
25. December 1941
26. December 1941
27. Bluford, "Quarterly," 1942, 1
28. Bluford, "Quarterly," 1942, 3
29. Bluford, "Annual," 1943, 7
30. Gibbs, *History*, 117
31. Albright, 11
32. Albright, 17
33. Albright, 51
34. *Jubilee*, [8, 27]
35. Albright, 56
36. Albright, 63
37. Albright, 59
38. Albright, 86
39. Albright, 76
40. Hine et al., 485
41. December 1940
42. Hornsby, A., 146

43. Garvin
44. October 1942
45. January 1943
46. May 1941
47. Albright, 53
48. February 1942
49. Albright, 53-54
50. Thompson, J.G.
51. Roberts and Klibanoff, 16, 22
52. Hornsby, A., 146-48
53. Hine et al., 496
54. "History of UNCP"
55. Hine et al., 489
56. October 1944
57. January/February 1945
58. October 1944
59. Spivak
60. Hauser
61. Gibbs, *History*, 49
62. March 1943
63. May 1943
64. January 1943
65. PBS, "Timeline: Building"
66. February 1944
67. November 1943
68. February 1944
69. "Phairlever"
70. Bost
71. Hine et al., 492
72. Hornsby, A., 149
73. Roosevelt, 9346
74. Bluford, "Annual," 1943, 3
75. Albright, 91
76. July 1941
77. Jones et al., 13
78. Jones et al., 13
79. Garvin
80. October 1944
81. Bluford, Annual, 1945, 5-6
82. August 1945
83. O'Keefe, 47
84. Spruill, 5
85. Bluford, "Annual," 1945, 7
86. Naval, "Potsdam"

87. Naval, "Japan"
88. "G.I. Bill"
89. Bluford, "Annual," 1945, 10
90. Bluford, "Annual," 1946, 1
91. Bluford, "Annual," 1947, 1
92. Bluford, "Annual," 1948, 5
93. Spruill, 39
94. Bluford, "Annual," 1946, 2
95. Frye, S.
96. Spruill, 52
97. Wesley et al., 3-4
98. Hine et al., 497
99. King, D.S., 34
100. Hornsby, A., 150
101. PBS, "Timeline: Building"
102. King, D.S., 34-35
103. *Morgan*
104. Hornsby, A., 150-52
105. Hornsby, A., 152-53
106. November 1949
107. Spruill, 5
108. Haire
109. *Armistice*
110. DeLassus
111. Williams
112. Scheckner
113. Armstrong
114. Harris, J.
115. November 1947
116. October 1948
117. November 1947
118. Bluford, "Annual," 1949, 3
119. Bluford, "Annual," 1948, 2
120. March 1948
121. March 1948
122. October 1948
123. March 1949
124. November 1949
125. King, D.S., 35
126. Hine et al., 500
127. Truman, 9981
128. Truman, 9980
129. King, D.S., 35

A visit to the A&T dairy farm.

Beonia Mae Edwards, soon to be Mrs. Leonard Dunn, is pictured in 1949. *PATRICE DUNN.*

President Bluford and the faculty from the 1940s or 1950s.

LEFT: The B-1 Band marches in Honolulu's V-J Day parade. *U.S. NAVY, COURTESY JAMES B. PARSONS/ALEX ALBRIGHT.*

BELOW: Negro deputies in the Treasury Department, appointed to work among farmers and rural families selling war bonds, are shown in Washington at a special intensive training course in October 1942. At far right is J. C. McLaughlin of A&T College. *LIBRARY OF CONGRESS, LC-DIG-FSA-8B07518.*

# CHAPTER FOUR

*The Civil Rights Era*

1950–1965

The A&T Four are shown on the street after the first sit-in, the only photo of that first day's event. *News & Record*.

The upheaval of the Depression and two world wars had left African Americans with a new view of the world—and a stronger voice to demand change. As Warmoth T. Gibbs was inaugurated president of A&T in the mid-1950s, he said, "In America, to each rising generation, the door of opportunity has always opened wider; and once opened, it never closes."[1] From 1950 to 1965, while A&T continued to turn out farmers, scholars, teachers, and tradesmen—500 diplomas were granted in 1950—it would also become a focus for the civil rights movement.

The decade opened with notable achievements by African Americans. Ralph Bunche won the Nobel Peace Prize for mediating the Arab-Israeli conflict in the Middle East in 1950, and Gwendolyn Brooks, a leading figure in the "Chicago Renaissance," became the first African American to win a Pulitzer Prize. Three years later, Ralph Ellison's *Invisible Man* received the National Book Award.[2]

But progress was uneven. Although President Harry Truman had mandated equality in the armed services, not until the Korean War was his executive order fully implemented.[3] President Eisenhower finally ordered the end of segregation in the armed services, which in August 1954 was predicted to "be completely eliminated within a matter of months."[4]

Education would launch the modern civil rights movement in the 1950s, both through student activism and legislative action. Southern universities began the slow process of desegregation: The University of North Carolina at Chapel Hill admitted its first black student on April 24, 1951.[5]

At A&T, the decade opened with the construction of The Oaks as the presidential home,[6] and a new trophy, as the football team—which had won its first championship in 1927—again took the conference title.[7] The accelerating pace of technological change was reflected in a new emphasis on science and research. The earliest recorded externally funded research at A&T was in the early 1950s, when Dr. Booker T. White received U.S. Department of Agriculture funding.[8] William L. Bedford, a 1950 honors graduate in electrical engineering, faced initial difficulties obtaining engineering jobs because of his race, but went on to work for the U.S. Army

President and Mrs. Bluford meet with civil rights leader and international negotiator Ralph Bunche (at right).

Corps of Engineers, General Electric, the School District of Philadelphia, the University of Pennsylvania, and as president at Electrical Power Systems Engineering, Inc.[9]

A&T brought technical skills into the community. A photo in *The Register* shows A&T Radio School certificate holders Charles D. Bolden '48 and James Clark in their new radio shop on East Market Street.[10] The Technical Institute became a separate school located in the new Trades Building (Price Hall) in 1952.[11] In 1952, the School of Mechanic Arts became the School of Engineering,[12] and an Air Force ROTC unit was established.[13]

The college hosted the statewide conference of the State Farm Bureau Federation's Negro members, 1,000 farmers from across the state.[14] The Cooperative Extension, directed

by Aggie alumnus R. E. Jones, was working in 50 counties with a staff of 107.[15] As a result of the efforts of the new public relations director, Ellis Corbett, the college was "having the best publicity that it has ever enjoyed and we feel that it will be reflected in an increase in our student body."[16]

TOP: President F. D. Bluford (third from left) is shown touring the USS *Franklin D. Roosevelt* in 1951.

BOTTOM: Rules are prominently posted on the back wall of the A&T library in 1950.

In 1952, Tuskegee Institute reported that for the first time in the 71 years it had kept records, there were no lynchings.[17] The NAACP's long fight against Jim Crow, from its founding through Thurgood Marshall's work as lead attorney in the 1930s and the creation of the

Legal Defense Fund in 1940s, would come to fruition with the 1954 Supreme Court decision in *Brown v. Board of Education of Topeka*,[18] described as "the most important American government act of any kind since the Emancipation Proclamation."[19] The unanimous decision brought to an end the "separate but equal" doctrine in public education.[20] In response, segregationist Citizens' Councils emerged in the South.[21]

The School of Nursing was authorized in 1953 as a four-year program with stringent admission and curriculum requirements. A portion of Noble Hall formerly used for the Department of Home Economics was remodeled for the nursing program.[22]

The year 1954 brought two storms: the North Carolina coast was battered by deadly Hurricane Hazel,

A drawing class at work in Crosby Hall in 1950.

The A&T Concert Band, 1950–51.

Members of the first nursing class at A&T, shown at their graduation in 1957. *Ethel Crooks.*

and Edward R. Murrow, a Guilford County native, took on powerful Sen. Joseph McCarthy on his television program *See It Now.* From 1950 to 1954, McCarthy had exploited anticommunist fears—now the tables were turned in the Army-McCarthy hearings that would lead to his censure.[23] On May 31, 1955, a year after the *Brown* decision, the high court restated the "fundamental principle that discrimination in public education is unconstitutional."[24] It gave the South time for implementation—but African Americans kept the pressure on. In Greensboro, Bennett College professor Edward Edmonds led protests against inferior public schools and segregated swimming pools, while Dr. George Simkins began a successful drive to desegregate city-owned golf courses.[25, 26]

That summer, the murder of Emmett Till and the subsequent trial would bring black and white reporters to Mississippi and intensify the push for civil rights.[27] When Rosa Parks refused to give up her seat on a city bus to a white man, her challenge to the state and municipal laws inspired Montgomery's 48,000 Negro residents to launch a 381-day bus boycott—the first large-scale modern civil rights protest. *The New York Times* as well as television news programs began to see the race story not as a Southern story, but a national one. The aggressiveness of the Northern press and Northern sympathizers in the 1950s was feared by Southerners to be a repeat of the issues raised during slavery.[28]

A school dance, believed to be in the 1950s or '60s.

Integration was becoming visible. Chuck Berry began recording in 1955, helping to shape a new musical genre, rock and roll.[29] *The Register* was filled with ads in which African American faces appeared, as well as those of white movie and television stars. Current students might be amused by the responses to the "Inquiring Reporter" asking about the book rental system: "I think eight dollars per quarter is too much to pay for the rental of books," commented Shirley Garvin of Gastonia, North Carolina.[30]

The college continued to gain recognition, hosting both the National Technical Association annual convention and the North Carolina Science Fair and Workshop. The featured speaker was Dr. A. C. Stewart, a chemist at Oak Ridge National Laboratory.[31] Thirty-five different groups totaling 25,000 persons visited campus in 1955–56, and A&T welcomed thousands to Senior High School Day, an

Debating had been a major activity on campus for decades when this photo was taken of the Kappa Phi Kappa debating society in 1951.

open house for the community, and a Mother's Day reunion.[32]

During the 1950s and '60s, Drs. Gladys and George Royal conducted research funded by the Atomic Energy Commission, seeking "to lessen the deleterious effects on bone marrow of the high doses of radiation used in cancer therapy and worked to develop new treatments for animals and humans exposed to high levels of radiation from other sources."[33] Local corporations supported students with scholarships. Clarence E. Peoples, an electrical engineering student, became the first recipient of the Bur-Mills Scholarship,[34] while eight nursing students received three-year scholarships from the Richardson Foundation, Inc. It was the largest scholarship gift the college had received to that point.[35]

*The Register* paid tribute to 15 A&T graduates who had gone on to earn doctorates, beginning with M. F. Spaulding '25, who became the head of the Department of Agronomy at Tennessee State University.[36] A&T boasted the largest marching band in its history, with 135 pieces and a

Members of the A&T Marching Band and Concert Band gather for a photo in 1950–51 with bandleader Walter Carlson.

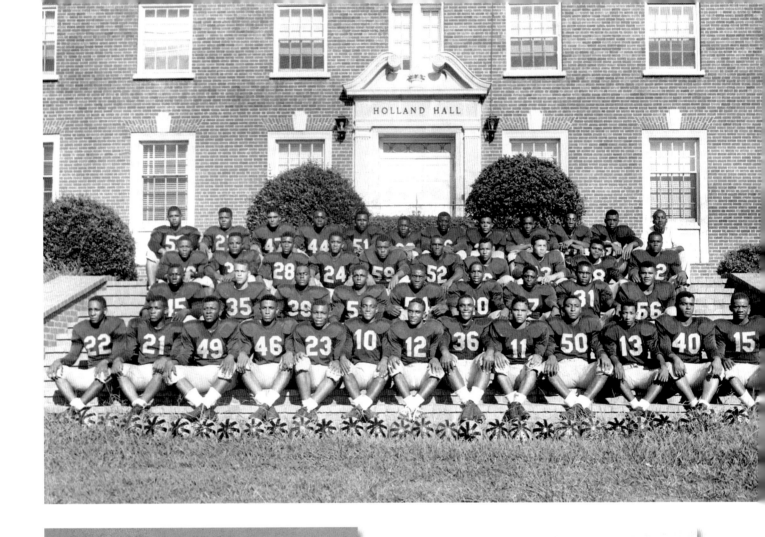

## A&T COLLEGE 1955
## FOOTBALL SCHEDULE

### HOME GAMES

Sept. 30 Virginia Union (Friday) 8 P.M.
Oct. 15 Maryland State      2 P.M.
         (HOMECOMING)
Oct. 22 Winston-Salem Teachers 2 P.M.
       (HIGH SCHOOL SENIOR DAY)
Nov. 5 Florida A&M Univ.     2 P.M.
        (FOUNDERS DAY)
Nov. 24 N. C. College       2 P.M.
       (CAROLINA CLASSIC)
       THANKSGIVING DAY
\* All Home Games to be played in
Greensboro Memorial Stadium

### AWAY

Sept. 24 West Virginia State    8 P.M.
        Dunbar, W. Va.
Oct. 29 Morgan State        2 P.M.
        Baltimore, Md.
Nov. 12 Virginia State       2 P.M.
        Petersburg, Va.
        —Over—

**Department of Athletics**

## AGRICULTURAL & TECHNICAL COLLEGE
### GREENSBORO, NORTH CAROLINA

L. A. WISE, *Chairman, Athletic Committee*
BILL BELL, *Director of Athletics and Head Coach*

**Save Time And Waiting In Line-Buy your tickets In advance at:**

Farley's Sweet Shop, 938 E. Market Street.
Coble Sporting Goods, 119 N. Greene Street.
Lee's Service Station, 712 E. Market Street.
Eccles Drug, 914 Gorrell Street.
Wynn Drug, 814 Gorrell Street.
A. & T. College registrar's office.

TOP: The 1956 Aggies football team.

BOTTOM: The 1955 A&T football schedule (left) and the reverse side (right). *Carolyn B. Gregory.*

12-member majorette corps.[37] Running back J. D. Smith Jr. was drafted by the Chicago Bears.[38]

On November 4, 1955, the college observed its 64th birthday with the dedication of Cherry Hall (engineering), Hodgin Hall, Bluford Library, Carver Hall, Moore Gymnasium, Ward Hall (dairy science), Benbow Hall (home economics), and Sebastian Infirmary. Gov. Luther Hodges' Founders Day address met an angry, and noisy, reception. "The interruption of Governor Hodges' discourse can not be truly called spontaneous. On the other hand, it did not come of formal planning. Most of the people present had heard or were aware of the context and presentation of Governor Hodges' speech this summer, on voluntary segregation. They didn't like it."[39] President Bluford was mortified by the discourtesy shown to the governor. He rebuked both students and faculty. By year's end, he was gone, dying on December 21, 1955.[40]

Warmoth T. Gibbs, dean of the School of Education, was elected college president in 1956, with Jerald Marteena taking the newly created post of dean of faculties.[41] Gibbs would come in on a rising tide of accomplishment: The Southern Association of Colleges and Secondary Schools had just approved A&T at the same level as other schools in the association—previously it had been rated on the level of Negro institutions. The visiting team

William King Jr. is shown outside the new Sebastian Infirmary in 1956. Student nurses were driven around the community to do public health work. The infirmary was named for Dr. Simon P. Sebastian, who taught at A&T and then returned as the college physician for many years. *ETHEL CROOKS.*

"praised the spirit of the students and were especially impressed with the building program."[42] In the fall of 1956, the college received a $500,000 appropriation for construction of a cafeteria, renovation of a biology lab, books, and engineering equipment.[43] The move toward accreditation led to "new money" from the legislature to support faculty raises, new faculty with doctorates, a library, and labs.[44] The fall of 1956 saw another record freshman class, at 775. A total of 569 veterans were enrolled.[45]

Leontyne Price visited in January 1956, singing classical and spiritual songs for a capacity crowd in Moore Gymnasium.[46] Surely in that audience were members of the college choir, preparing for a two-week concert tour that would take it to Washington, D.C., and New York City.[47]

Gibbs' inaugural address was carried in *The Register*. He said that the newly dedicated George Washington Carver Hall demonstrated "our desire to do research in North Carolina soils, minerals, fibers, animals, plants and problems relating to them." He took particular note of the growth in business, engineering, and nursing.[48]

But students were seeking more than a degree—they wanted change. In 1956, the student legislature of Woman's College passed a resolution favoring desegregation, 24-0 with 5 abstentions.[49] That fall, the first African American students enrolled there.[50] By the end of the year, students from the state universities and colleges had passed a resolution, introduced jointly by A&T and the University of North Carolina, to repeal the Pearsall Plan, a despised program to halt public school integration.[51]

The Montgomery Bus Boycott ended when the Supreme Court ruled in November 1956 that segregation

An Ag Extension group is shown with leader J. Jeffries (second from left). Jeffries, who graduated in 1939, was an assistant state extension agent in the 1940s through his retirement in 1962.

Women wait for a bus in downtown Greensboro. Integrating public transportation was a major element of the civil rights movement.

on public buses was unconstitutional under the 14th Amendment.[52] The Montgomery Improvement Association, founded to address bus segregation, was coordinated by the Rev. Dr. Martin Luther King Jr., who helped form the Southern Christian Leadership Committee (SCLC) in 1957.[53]

In the summer of 1957, Charlotte, Greensboro, and Winston-Salem approved desegregation. That fall, five African American children endured heckling as they walked through the doors of previously all-white Gillespie Park School in Greensboro. Josephine Boyd crossed the color line at Greensboro Senior High, later Grimsley High School.[54, 55] Also that year, the college gained a new name, becoming the Agricultural and Technical College of North Carolina, and its first white student, Rodney Jaye Miller. The first degrees in nursing were awarded in

June 1957.[56] The Greensboro Public Library opened its facilities to all citizens of the county.[57]

But as desegregation moved forward in North Carolina, another story was brewing in Arkansas, where black newspapers were renewing their advocacy. Daisy Bates and her husband L.C., editors and reporters for the *Arkansas State Press*, were staunch supporters of civil rights. Students known as the Little Rock Nine were recruited by Bates to integrate Central High School.[58] When Gov. Orval Faubus deployed the Arkansas National Guard to prevent black students from entering, King urged the president to take a stand, or "it will send the process of integration back fifty years."[59] Eisenhower, fearing international embarrassment, ordered soldiers to escort those African American students to school in 1957.[60] In 2001, Bates would have a state holiday declared in her honor.[61]

In the midst of the focus on civil rights, the Soviets launched the first man-made satellite and opened the "space race" with the U.S. The following year, a general self-evaluation study took place at A&T, part of a national review of education sparked by *Sputnik*.[62] Cold War tensions were felt on campus. Greensboro had been

Dr. F. A. Williams (second from right) is shown at a college event. He chaired the committee on civil defense.

named as a "target area" because of its telephone and petroleum hubs. "Dr. F. A. Williams, chairman of the College Committee on Civil Defense, stated that 'we must act immediately in acquiring the all-important know-how either for evacuating, or for taking cover from a 10-megaton Hydrogen Bomb should such become an apparent reality.'"[63]

The decade of the 1950s witnessed a return by women to domestic life. There was an air of tranquility, and the GI Bill allowed men to support large families. The number of televisions in the homes surpassed radios. Husbands made sure their homes were filled with the latest labor-saving appliances "as seen on television."[64] Not all women were buying quiet domesticity, however. A&T had a pair of identical twins, Yvonne and LaRose Griffin, who were studying architectural engineering.[65] Althea Gibson became the first African American tennis player to take a major title, winning the women's singles and doubles at

Wimbledon in 1957.[66] At A&T, male and female shared the growing interest in tennis.

This mixture of "business as usual" and dramatic change would continue, with African Americans making news in the arts, sports, and business even as they fought for basic rights to vote, shop, and live as they pleased. Early 1958 brought a visit by King to Greensboro, but he spoke at Bennett College at the invitation of President Willa Player, urging the overflow crowd, "We must learn to live together as brothers or we will certainly die together as fools."[67] Within sight of Bennett and A&T, the black community and its business district were being pulled apart by "slum clearance" projects.[68]

The year 1958 saw the creation of the Alvin Ailey Dance Theatre, and Eunice Johnson began the Ebony Fashion Fair in Chicago.[69] This popular show would come to Greensboro in the future. Perhaps in response, *The Register* featured a fashion photo spread that summer. "A must for any wardrobe is a SACK or CHEMISE," the newspaper advised. Bermuda shorts, argyle socks, and middy blouses were in evidence as well.[70]

In the fall of 1958, the Homecoming parade left the environs of the college to take a route through the downtown business area.[71] The campus chapter of the NAACP, formed during the final weeks of the past school year, had some 50 members in the fall of 1958,

A THRIVING BLACK BUSINESS DISTRICT CENTERED ON EAST MARKET STREET SERVED THE COLLEGE AND COMMUNITY, BUT MUCH OF IT WOULD BE LOST TO URBAN RENEWAL.

Mrs. Anderson is shown at Farley's Grill on East Market Street in the 1950s. This was a nice place to take your girl on Sundays, recalled Lewis Brandon III '64. *Ruth Anderson Smith.*

ABOVE: The Ethel Bakery Shoppe was among the establishments frequented by students. From left are Odell Harris Sr., Ethel Harris, and Odell Harris Jr. *Lewis A. Brandon III.*

RIGHT: "Mom" Parker, who operated a grocery store, is shown being crowned Queen of Maco Beauty College in the early 1950s. *Lucy Sligh.*

Majorettes for A&T College sometime in the late 1950s to early '60s strike a pose.

headed by Robert Herbin.[72] A&T remained loyal to its traditions while moving toward high-tech fields being showcased just down the road in the newly opened Research Triangle Park—an annex was nearing completion at Price Hall to house the masonry, painting, decorating, and drawing departments. Graduating engineers made their annual inspection tour, visiting Kerr

Dam, a cement manufacturing plant, Bethlehem Steel, and the naval yard at Philadelphia.[73] Fall enrollment for 1959 showed the School of Engineering in the lead with 850 students, followed by Educational and General Studies with 795, and Agriculture with 489 students. The college's gender balance was 1,459 men to 758 women, but just one woman was enrolled in electrical engineering. Those engineering majors were getting jobs—Boeing had just hired Charles Saunders, an electrical engineering grad, who joined half a dozen other recent graduates at the airplane manufacturing company.[74]

The National Science Foundation continued its ongoing support of student researchers, as well as a $58,300 grant for a summer institute for teachers of science.[75] On the humanities side, A&T became the first Negro college in the South to organize a program of African studies, under Fulbright Scholar Dr. S. M. Broderick of Sierre Leone.[76] In the 1950s and '60s, the college sent leaders and teachers to the newly postcolonial nations of Africa and Asia, and invited their scholars here. Yoshua Nkomo, president of the Southern Rhodesia African National Congress, visited the campus in the fall of 1959. "Freedom from shackles and colonialism must take place before colored peoples anywhere can assert themselves."[77] Dr. Frenise A. Logan, professor of history, brought acclaim to the college by winning the R.D.W. Connor Award for the best article published in the *NC Historical Review* that year.[78] *The Register* student newspaper, for the second year in a row, won a first place at the Columbia University Scholastic Press Association conference.[79]

Students struggled with finances, then as now. The costs for attending in 1959–60 were $312 for day students, or $629.50 (men) or $620.50 (women) for boarding and lodging. Out-of-state students were assessed an additional $269.50. "Among the specific fee increases will be athletics from $22.05 to $27, lecture from $3 to

A geography class prepares for a trip in 1960.

$4, [and] medical from $12 to $15."[80] Greek organizations were active, but not always financially possible for students. "I did not join a fraternity because it cost money. I did join a graduate chapter later," recalled Winser Alexander '64.[81]

An impromptu concert at Cooper Hall in 1959 featured "former Jazz Messengers Donald Byrd and Doug Watkins, Water 'Red' Davis from Dizzy's big band, and a youngster Jimmy Wormsworth."[82] This was the year that Lorraine Hansberry's A Raisin in the Sun became the first Broadway play produced by an African American woman. It would come to Harrison Auditorium in 1962, when Laverne Madison, a senior English major, directed a production.[83] Trumpeter Miles Davis recorded "Kind of Blue" with High Point native John Coltrane on saxophone. In Detroit, Berry Gordy started Motown Records.[84]

These were quite literally banner years for Aggie sports. The football team under Coach Bert Piggott won successive championships in 1958 and 1959.[85] The baseball team won the CIAA crown in 1959, and would

*Commencement ceremonies took place on the "quad" during the 1950s. LEWIS A. BRANDON III.*

renew the title in 1960 and 1961. The track team excelled at the Penn Relays that spring. "The beautiful plaque marked the first award ever received by an A&T-sponsored track team."[86] In basketball, "Cal Irvin and his basketball Aggies won successive CIAA championships in 1958 and 1959, the first since 1937 …. In 1959 his team was successful in reaching the NCAA small college competition where it placed third in the nation."[87] Joe Cotton was voted to the AP's Little-America squad—the first A&T player and first CIAA player to achieve this honor.[88]

The Air Force ROTC welcomed a Republic F-84-F Thunderstreak jet fighter used in the Korean War that was donated by the Air Force for display near Campbell Hall.[89]

The year closed out with a red-letter banner headline in *The*

*Register*: "A&T Made Member of Southern Ass'n." Full accreditation, a dream of Bluford, had come to fruition under his successor. Students went home for the holidays with that accomplishment in their minds, and the stirring sounds of Gloria Davey, the first Negro to sing "Aida" at the Metropolitan Opera, in their ears.[90]

The crowd cheers at a football game.

Star basketball player Al Attles (center) with teammates in 1958.

Zeta Phi Beta sorority is shown in this undated photograph.

But a year of accomplishment was also marked by setbacks. Students rallied in Moore Gym to protest a proposed $1 million budget cut. President Gibbs traveled to Raleigh to plead for partial restoration of the funds.[91] Advancements helped buoy their hearts, but Negroes still drank from colored-only water fountains, and ate and slept in Negro hotels or in the homes of other African Americans. Students knew that even with a college degree, employment opportunities would be slim except for teaching, preaching, and working in government jobs.[92] In Greensboro, American Federal Savings and Loan came into being after attorney J. Kenneth Lee, plaintiff in the suit that opened UNC-Chapel Hill to black students and a graduate of the UNC Law School, was turned down for a mortgage.[93]

But change was to come.

The 1960s began with a wave of protest that would continue with the growth of three new movements: the counterculture, Black Power, and women's rights. Millions would watch these movements unfold on their televisions, which also brought presidential debates into living rooms for the first time, with 70 million people watching candidates Kennedy and Nixon.[94]

Students celebrated Negro History Week with a visit by Sterling A. Brown, "poet, jazz enthusiast, critic and teacher," whose book *The Negro Caravan* is considered a seminal anthology of African American literature. He met with students, including winners in the writing contest on the topic of "The New Negro."[95]

Homecoming 1960 boasted a record-breaking crowd of 12,500 for the game, and a mile-long parade featuring almost 1,000 ROTC cadets.[96]

The college announced that evening classes would be offered for the first time, both regular courses and non-credit classes intended to

Riding in the Homecoming parade in 1960 are Liz Neal, Jeanne "Miss Junior" Bryant, and Shirley Canada. *Jeanne B. Holtzclaw.*

Segregated facilities remained across the South, as in this shot of the county courthouse in Halifax, North Carolina, taken sometime in the 1930s. *LIBRARY OF CONGRESS, LC-DIG-FSA-8A03228.*

Four A&T College students sit in seats designated for white people at the racially segregated Woolworth's lunch counter in Greensboro, North Carolina, on February 2, 1960. The students are (from left) Joseph McNeil, Franklin McCain, Billy Smith, and Clarence Henderson. This photo was taken on the second day of the now-famous Greensboro lunch counter sit-ins. *JACK MOEBES/NEWS & RECORD.*

EXTRA

# REGISTER

*"The Cream of College News"*

EXTRA

VOLUME XXXI No. 9          THE AGRICULTURAL AND TECHNICAL COLLEGE, GREENSBORO, N. C.          FRIDAY, FEBRUARY 5, 1960

<u>FOR SERVICE</u>          Reprinted by Special Permission — The REGISTER Staff, February 1, 1980

# Students Stage Sitdown Demand

### Get In Study Chores

Students from A&T College began Monday afternoon what they called a "passive sitdown demand" for service at the customer lunch counter at Woolworth's downtown five and dime store in Greensboro. Shown above are five students who-while they sit-are getting in a little study time. The counter has approximately forty stools, and at times during the third day (Wednesday, when this photo was made) there were only three or four seats left vacant by the students.

The special edition of *The Register* on February 5, 1960.

offer "advancement to adults." Two female "cadettes" joined the ROTC—Wilhelmina Perry and Ann Chavis would not be commissioned but could get academic credits.[97] The Greeks welcomed 40 new members. The college moved commencement—which had been held on the lawn for the previous 10 years—to the new City Auditorium.[98]

The event that put A&T in the national news came on February 1. For decades, A&T students have gained strength from the legacy of the A&T Four. But there is not a single eyewitness account of the historic hour when four freshman dressed in coats and ties walked to the downtown Woolworth's, sat at the counter, and were denied service.[99, 100, 101]

This pivotal story of Joseph McNeil, Franklin McCain, Ezell Blair Jr., and David Richmond occurred on the afternoon of February 1, 1960, but was not covered that night on television or the next day in any newspaper, although a Syrian American merchant who had counseled the students alerted the local papers.[102] Lee Kinard, a longtime news anchor in Greensboro, noted that at the time, WFMY-TV did not have a news department, a reporter, or even a vehicle. "News was not 24/7," he noted.[103]

The following morning, McNeil, McCain, Blair, and Richmond, known as the "Greensboro Four" and later the "A&T Four," returned with 23 other men and four women. This time, reporters from both television and newspapers were there. Only a few comments made the national media and there was a brief mention inside *The New York Times*.[104] Staff, students, and faculty on A&T's campus learned by word of mouth how the men had been refused service. The manager had let the students sit, then called the police, who had come by only to observe, and 15 minutes after the store closed, the four students had left and said they'd be back the next day.[105, 106] The United Press story was almost as vague.

In a special edition of *The Register*, Editor-in-Chief Albert L. Rozier Jr. reconstructed the initial conversation between Ezell Blair Jr. and a waitress:

Blair: "I'd like a cup of coffee, please."

Waitress: "I'm sorry. We don't serve colored here."

Blair: "I beg to disagree with you. You just finished serving me at a counter only two feet from here."

Waitress: "Negroes eat at the other end."

Blair: "What do you mean? This is a public place, isn't it? If it isn't, then why don't you sell membership cards? If you do that, then I'll understand that this is a private concern."

Waitress: "Well, you won't get any service here!"

Rozier also reported that a "Negro girl, a helper at the counter, confronted them, saying, 'You are stupid, ignorant! You're dumb! That's why we can't get anywhere today. You know you are supposed to eat at the other end.'"[107]

"They made a great giant step forward, even they had doubts as to whether sitting down would make a difference," said Henry E. Frye '53. "They were very respectable, dressed well, the kind of people good folks look at and say, 'You know it is just not right to let those people buy and not sit down and eat a hot dog when they were spending money in the store.'"[108]

This edition profiled the "Four Freshmen," Blair and Richmond, both from Greensboro, McCain of Washington, D.C., and McNeil of Wilmington, North Carolina. It was noted that students from white institutions had come forward to participate in the ongoing sit-in, also being refused service, and that there were plans for more demonstrations. Commentary and cartoons led the editorial page, including Rozier's editorial, stating, "There is no longer a place in America for second-class citizenship and first-class jeopardy."[109]

The sit-ins would draw wide support. The Bennett "Belles" were prominent, and students from white institutions participated in sit-ins that extended to other businesses such as the Kress store, where 45 students were arrested. Rozier and McNeil represented A&T at the National Student Conference on the Sit-in Movement in Washington, D.C., in April.[110] The sit-ins would continue until on July 25, 1960, when Woolworth's management relented.

During the sit-ins, city leaders asked President Gibbs to keep students on campus. Gibbs replied, "We teach our students how to think, not what to think."[111] In his annual report, Gibbs stated that "the students feel deeply and sincerely that they have important basic interests at stake in this situation … so strongly that threats of arrest or intimidation do not seem to deter them."[112]

Lucille Johnson Piggott '54 did not get to march. "When everybody else marched, I got up that night, got dinner and was ready to march and my husband said, 'Sugar, we got a little baby back in the crib, don't you think one of us needs to stay here?' 'Oh,' I said, 'I guess I was elected.'" She was working in Gibbs' office at the time, and "I heard him ask the question, how are the kids? We drove out there (the jail) one Sunday, and saw them when they were waving flags in the window."[113]

"I have always had interest in politics," recalled Lewis Brandon III '64. "I became a leader and brought more of my 'boys' down. We went and occupied the counter, people ignored us. Some days later, people would pour drinks on us. But we adopted the attitude that we would not fight. We stayed til the place closed and went back to A&T and walked the women to Bennett."[114]

Following the Woolworth's sit-in, protests spread in the South and ignited wider unrest. In Raleigh, North Carolina, in the spring of 1960, the Student Nonviolent Coordinating Committee (SNCC) was founded and became the nationwide liaison for protest. A&T students considered the tension between Booker T. Washington's "separate but equal" ideas and W.E.B. Du Bois': "One ever feels his two-ness,—an American, a Negro; two souls, two thoughts, two unreconciled strivings; two warring ideals in one dark body, whose dogged strength alone keeps it from being torn asunder."[115] During the summer and fall of 1960, Elijah Muhammad, leader of the Black Muslims, called for an all-black state. King was

A young couple on campus. HBCUs had offered black students an education while Jim Crow ruled the South, but marches and demonstrations would demand that educational opportunities be open to all.

arrested for sitting in at an Atlanta department store restaurant.[116]

Right-to-vote campaigns ran parallel with the civil rights demonstrations and boycotts occurring throughout the country. In May, President Eisenhower signed the Voting Rights Act of 1960. Federal courts could appoint voting referees to register blacks in areas where racial discrimination against voters had been proven.[117]

Desegregation of schools inched into the South both peacefully and violently in the early 1960s, most notably at the University of Alabama, University of Georgia, and University of Mississippi. Ole Miss was forced to admit James Meredith.[118] "Coming from a segregated background, we did not think of white schools because they would not accept us, but I knew of a city called Greensboro, I also knew about another city called A&T. If it was a band clinic, you went to A&T, if you went to a state organization, you were going to A&T. It fit my father's pocketbook," said Lewis Brandon III '64.[119]

Margaret Tynes opened the Lyceum Series in 1960. The daughter of a retired minister in Greensboro, the 1939–40 Miss A&T went on to Columbia University and Julliard. She was the first Negro to be featured on the NBC-TV *Opera Hour* and appeared with Ed Sullivan.[120]

Dr. Samuel DeWitt Proctor, a "liberal arts man," became the fifth president of the college, taking over from Gibbs on July 1, 1960.[121] He would

Willie Adams, drum major, in a shot from 1959–1960. He was an engineering major.

soon face the same budgetary challenges as previous leaders, requesting $4.2 million for the college, including $1 million for a student union.[122] By the fall of 1962, he was saying temporary goodbyes as he left to head the Peace Corps mission in the new nation of Nigeria.[123]

*The Register* noted the signing of professional football contracts in 1960 by A&T standouts Tommy Day, who joined the St. Louis Cardinals; Paul Swann and Johnny Wardlaw, who signed with Toronto of the Canadian League; and Harvey Stewart, who joined Montreal.[124] Later that year, Aggie basketball alumnus Alvin Attles signed a contract

with the Philadelphia Warriors.[125] Basketball and baseball player Hugh Evans chose to play baseball and then went on to be an NBA referee for 28 seasons before becoming a league official.[126] The Aggies claimed a special victory with the recovery of the Victory Bell which had been taken from campus in the fall of 1959.[127]

By 1961, Fidel Castro's rise in power was noted on A&T's campus, where professors Drs. Octavio and Maria Diaz were former Cuban residents.[128] Before President John F. Kennedy's inauguration, he was briefed on a plan by the Central Intelligence Agency to train Cuban exiles for an invasion. On April 17, 1961, 1,400 Cuban exiles launched the failed Bay of Pigs attack.[129] Meanwhile, students also were paying attention to the Congo Crisis as the newly independent country struggled through the early

Margaret Tynes, opera star and former Miss A&T, is shown performing in *Carmen*.

1960s. The International Relations Club hosted a panel on the issue.[130]

North Carolina welcomed a new governor, Terry Sanford, who had made friends at A&T when he "dropped in" with his campaign helicopter as ROTC cadets were drilling. He would invite those cadets and the band to march in his inaugural parade.[131] Sanford worked to improve the lives of North Carolinians with his "Go Forward" program on education as well as the North Carolina Fund, which became a model for anti-poverty programs across the nation.

The Freedom Rides of 1961 showed the world the length to which white Southerners would go to uphold segregation. On May 4, 1961, John Lewis was brutally beaten when he was one of seven black riders who tried to enter the white waiting room of the Greyhound bus terminal in Rock Hill, South Carolina. He would go on to become a notable congressman.[132] The interracial group continued its travels through the Deep South, despite being hampered by acts of violence. U.S. Attorney General Robert Kennedy recognized the dangers they faced, and asked the riders to delay until "an atmosphere of reason and normalcy has been restored."[133] On June 16, Robert Kennedy met with student leaders and urged them to concentrate on voter registration. By October, SNCC had joined forces with the NAACP, SCLC, and CORE in the voter education project.

Robert Wynn, a dairy specialist, working with students. He went to Nigeria in the early 1960s to assist with agricultural programs.

In 1961, the college's Agriculture Department was reorganized and Dr. William Reed said this would "prove advantageous to freshman students who are uncertain about their majors."[134] The newspaper commented on the need for more telephones on campus—there were just eight, in the dorms, the library, and the old canteen, an average of 265 students per telephone.[135] Twelve agricultural leaders from Ghana and Nigeria came to A&T in 1961 for a 14-week short course in farming.[136] Meanwhile, an agriculture student from A&T, Junius Byron Russell Jr., was in Egypt as one of four representatives of 4-H Clubs of America at the world agricultural fair.[137]

It was a spring of triumph and tragedy for the cadets. The Air Force ROTC unit won a first place at the Cherry Blossom Festival in Washington, D.C. The ROTC Ball opened the round of spring dances as "the biggest social event on the College calendar,"[138] but that same newspaper reported the death of Air Force Capt. William Woody Farmer, one of five who died when a B-52 bomber exploded in mid-air near Denton. He was a 1954 A&T graduate and president of the senior class and Pan Hellenic Society.[139]

Lawrence Winters, noted for his starring role in *Showboat*, presented a concert in November.[140] The busy life around campus was documented with newspaper ads for Triangle News Stand, Foushee's Cleaners, Elite

Student shutterbugs discuss photography.

Clothier, Sid's Curb Market, and the College Dairy Bar.

At the centennial of the Emancipation Proclamation, the Rev. Cleo M. McCoy of the A&T Chapel said, "The Negro, brought to these shores 100 years ago to help solve the white man's problems, is now considered the nation's problem."[141] Desegregation of the South took another step forward when Harvey Gantt, later a U.S. congressman, became the first Negro to register at Clemson College.[142]

In the summer of 1962, Fannie Lou Hamer was fired from her job on a Mississippi cotton plantation she had called home for more than 40 years

New Farmers of America members
show beef cattle at A&T College.

because she tried to vote. She became a major civil rights figure, registering blacks to vote through SNCC in Mississippi. "They kicked me off the plantation, they set me free," she said.[143]

Guilford College integrated its main campus by admitting two Kenyan Quakers for fall enrollment. That fall, the first African American student enrolled.[144] An Aggie made desegregation news when Catherine Hinson, a senior English major, became the first Negro saleslady at Brownhill's, a leading women's wear store in Greensboro.[145] Some 50 students from A&T and Bennett College were arrested in the fall of 1962 for staging sit-ins and stand-ins at the S&W and Mayfair cafeterias.[146]

When President Proctor accepted the call to the Peace Corps, Lewis C. Dowdy took over in his absence and guided the university through protests. His wife, Elizabeth Dowdy, reflected on campus life in the 1960s. "Dr. Dowdy and I thought these pains of freedom had to be endured. … Dr. Dowdy spent hours with the arrested students in makeshift jails in Greensboro. Pastors from the community met at our home, The Oaks, in order to discuss solutions."[147]

In the fall of 1962, the world was on the brink of nuclear war. An American U-2 spy plane photographed nuclear missile sites being built by the Soviet Union on Cuba. Soviet leader Nikita Khrushchev and President Kennedy found their way to a peaceful resolution, and the Limited Nuclear Test Ban Treaty was signed in June 1963: "For, in the final analysis, our most basic common link is that we all inhabit this small planet. We all breathe the same air. We all cherish our children's future. And we are all mortal."[148]

Malcolm X became national minister of the Nation of Islam, rejecting the nonviolent civil rights movement. A champion of African American separatism and black pride, he said that equal rights should be secured

Students compare notes at the 1962 freshman orientation.

"by any means necessary." Dr. Martin Luther King Jr. once said, "I feel Malcolm has done himself and our people a great disservice."[149] Once again the division among African American leaders resurfaced, echoing the conflict between Du Bois and Washington, and between the A&T Four and the sentiments of the Negro clerk at Woolworth's. An editorial appeared in *The Register*: "Walking past a local theatre the other night, I saw several of my fellow classmates coming out of a small door marked 'COLORED.' … It has been proven that we no longer have to go into the back or accept less than what we have coming to us …. One step in achieving this goal could very well be the staying out of doors marked colored …."[150]

King and the Rev. Ralph Abernathy were arrested on Good Friday of 1963. King had smuggled a pen into jail, and on scraps of paper, wrote his widely published "Letters from Birmingham Jail." The nation shuddered to watch television news accounts of police using attack dogs and fire hoses to break up demonstrations in Alabama—marches that included children.[151]

The college got good news in 1963 that the budget commission had approved $2.3 million for capital improvements, including purchase of the Lutheran College property.[152] Joe Taylor signed a contract to play for the NFL's Giants.[153] A swim team had debuted in 1962, and by 1963 was taking top honors at swim meets.[154]

A&T began offering instruction in computer programming for the first time.[155] Dr. Cecile H. Edwards, professor of nutrition and research, was named the nation's most outstanding Negro woman scientist.[156]

A&T's arts scene included an appearance by Carlos Montoya, the leading flamenco guitarist, and a theatre exchange with Pfeiffer College. Folk singer Odetta performed in the Lyceum Series, and was asked about her controversial "natural" hair.[157] William Mason, a junior at A&T, became the first black to play with the Greensboro Symphony Orchestra.[158] "Miss Murphy"—a stray dog that had become the campus mascot—was hit by a car and a campaign was started to cover her $56 vet bill.[159] Student Council elections in 1963 had Jesse Jackson, later a candidate for U.S. president, winning the presidency over Cary Bell, Jerome Murphy, and Winser Alexander, who would go on to become an interim provost and vice chancellor at his alma mater.[160]

In May 1963, demonstrations against business segregation reached a peak in Greensboro, with African Americans marching behind Jackson. The Greensboro Coliseum, which had opened four years before, became one of the detention centers. By the fall, "forty percent of restaurants and motels in Greensboro are desegregated, compared with nearly complete desegregation of facilities in Charlotte and Durham."[161]

The assassination of civil rights leader Medgar Evers sent shock waves throughout the country in June 1963, followed in two months by the death of Du Bois.[162] Ten days later, buses would be loaded in Greensboro to take participants to the then-largest single protest demonstration in U.S. history. King delivered his "I Have a Dream" speech at the Lincoln Memorial in Washington, D.C., where more than 250,000 blacks and whites assembled to push for equal rights.[163]

Following uplifting scenes from the march came devastating news: four African American girls died in the bombing of the 16th Street Baptist Church in Birmingham, Alabama.[164] A poem published in the student newspaper, "Visions of a Dying Church" by Jim Petteway, was written in response: "The tears of my people / I feel all around me. / And

those bodies, those / four innocent bodies / drift slowly, sadly."[165]

Little more than two months later, on November 22, 1963, the nation was shocked by the assassination of President John F. Kennedy. The effects on campus were immediate. The Blue-Gold basketball game and a showing of the movie *Ben Hur* were postponed. "Students are glued to radio and television sets receiving details of the incident while others are huddled in small groups about campus discussing the tragedy. Classes have been disrupted. Flags have been lowered to half mast."[166]

Following the assassination, Malcolm X spoke of the killing as an example of "chickens coming home to roost," meaning that Kennedy was a victim of the same kind of violence that tormented black people. Elijah Muhammad called

Malcolm X dangerous, suspending his duties. On March 12, 1964, he left the Nation of Islam.[167]

Dr. Proctor returned to the A&T presidency in September 1963 but resigned in April 1964, saying, "Despite my deep, personal loyalties to higher education in general, and the A. and T. College in particular, the urgency of the summons to serve the country—especially after the death of President John F. Kennedy—seemed overriding."[168]

The turmoil of 1963 led to the passage of the Civil Rights Act, prohibiting discrimination in public accommodations and employment, and President Lyndon Johnson signed the bill in the presence of civil rights leaders on July 2, 1964.[169] As legal barriers fell, African American artists were breaking new ground. Romare Bearden, born in Charlotte, produced his collage series, "Projections." Sidney Poitier won the Academy Award for best actor for his role in *Lilies of the Field*.[170]

Racial disturbances erupted in northern cities in the summer of 1964, with scores of injuries, property loss in the millions, and the National Guard called to control the unrest.[171] In the South, civil rights groups organized voter registration drives—A&T was the center for one conducted by the NAACP, the National Student YWCA, and the United Southern Christian Fellowship Foundation, as well as students from Northern and Midwestern states. "In Greensboro, the project involved more than 7,000 unregistered Negro voters" nearly 1,000 of whom became registered.[172] Three CORE workers disappeared and their bodies were found in shallow graves on a farm in Philadelphia, Mississippi. The FBI accused nearly two dozen white segregationists of complicity in their murders.[173]

The year ended with the U.S. Supreme Court upholding the Civil Rights Act and King being awarded the Nobel Peace Prize, the second African American to receive the recognition. Cassius Clay won the World

President Samuel DeWitt Proctor.

Women were demanding more rights as well, and would protest restrictive campus rules.

The Latin phrase *Mens et Manus*, meaning "Mind and Hand," is inscribed on the university's seal. It reflects A&T's early mission to assist people in their efforts for industrial and intellectual advancement.

Heavyweight Boxing Championship and announced he was Muhammad Ali, having joined the Nation of Islam as early as 1961.[174]

Lewis Carnegie Dowdy was inaugurated on April 10, 1964, as the college's sixth president.[175] He had been at the college for 14 years, serving as dean of the School of Education and General Studies and dean of instruction before becoming acting president.[176]

Changing times could be tracked in the headlines. *The Register* promised that "Computers, Pre-Registration Will Reduce Registration to Three Step Procedure."[177] By that fall, enrollment passed 3,200 with an estimated 1,200 freshmen. "All the dormitories are filled to capacity, and, in at least one, rooms

which in recent years housed two students now house three."[178]

Young women were a noticeably larger portion of the student body. Student leaders presented a list of recommendations rising out of a mass meeting of women students, asking for more freedom, including that "the excessive number of chaperones be curtailed" and that female students should gain the right to ride in cars.[179] An editorial asked if A&T was losing its distinction of being a man's world: "At the present rate, the time won't be long before a woman will again be president of the student council, editor of *The Register*, and editor of the *Ayantee*."[180] Science majors Daisy M. Hodge and Rita J. Southall attended a symposium at MIT on "American Women in Science and Engineering."[181]

The Aggies captured both the CIAA and NCAA Regional crowns in basketball.[182] Two mid-1960s athletes would go on to play professionally: Maurice McHartley with The American Basketball Association and Merl Code with the Canadian Football League.[183]

Engineering students William Edward Newell and Reginald Mitchiner were chosen for the Engineering Students Summer Training Program sponsored by GM.[184] A chapter of Phi Beta Lambda, a national society for students in business education, received its charter.[185] The *Ayantee* was dedicated to Dr. Darwin T. Turner, chair of the Department of English, noting that he had "entered college at the age of 13, was initiated into Phi Beta Kappa at age 15, and graduated in three calendar years at the age of 16."[186] Homecoming featured jazz vibraphonist Lionel Hampton and his orchestra playing for the dance, and he appeared in the parade.[187]

At A&T, the early 1960s saw a number of advances. In 1963, 91 of the state's 100 counties were represented in the student body, as well as 27 states and seven foreign countries.[188] East Indian, Chinese, Cuban, and Iranian faculty joined black and white Americans. The college had six

The basketball team is shown at the airport in March 1964, headed for the NCAA playoffs in Kentucky. Among the players shown are believed to be A. Sanders (fifth from left), Mulcaire (seventh from left), Wiley Briggs next to him, and then Jackson.

schools and offered master's degrees in agricultural education, chemistry, education, and industrial education. The quarter system was abandoned and semesters instituted in the 1965–66 academic year.[189]

A voter registration drive in Alabama led by King developed into a national protest movement in January 1965 as a shocked nation witnessed police bludgeon and tear-gas protesters in Selma. A federal judge ordered Alabama officials not to interfere and the 50-mile march was protected by federal troops. Some 50,000 people massed at the Alabama state capital to hear King criticize leaders such as Gov. George C. Wallace for interfering with voting rights.[190]

A&T opened a "War on Poverty" with $261,000 in grants to help families who were educationally

Lionel Hampton (with microphone) at Homecoming.

or culturally disadvantaged.[191] Dr. John Hope Franklin lectured on the civil rights revolution: "The area of Negro History is so exciting, so exotic that the Negro writer has been almost pushed out of the field."[192] An "Extra" edition of *The Register* celebrated the groundbreaking for the student union. "The structure, presently referred to as the A&T College Memorial Union Building, will honor all alumni who have lost their lives in combat."[193] Meanwhile, the latest war was having an impact on campus. *The Register* headlined, "Aggie Sentiment On Viet Nam/How Do You Feel—Or Do You Feel?"[194]

The student newspaper featured a photo of two co-eds with a prize turkey, noting that the college farm had produced more than 7,000 pounds of turkey for use in holiday dinners.[195]

An Aggie football standout, Cliff Matthews, signed as a catcher for the Baltimore Orioles,[196] while Aggie great Cornell Gordon was playing defense for the New York Jets.[197] Near the end of the year, halfback Melvin Phillips joined the San Francisco 49ers.[198]

Across the nation, tensions continued to grow. Malcolm X rejected the Nation of Islam's claim that all white people were evil and was assassinated in New York City in February 1965 by three African Americans tied to the Nation of Islam.[199] Younger activists also challenged the peaceful strategies of the old guard. Inner-city rebellions occurred in Watts, Newark, and Detroit. Prisoner rights movements were formed with Angela Davis, an assistant professor at UCLA and the first black woman on the FBI's Ten Most Wanted list.[200]

With the passage of the Voting Rights Act in 1965, the disenfranchisement of African American voters in the South was outlawed.[201] Edward Brooke of Massachusetts became the first African American to sit in the U.S. Senate since Reconstruction.[202] At the Howard University commencement, President Johnson pledged to bring blacks into mainstream America.[203]

TOP: Jackie Robinson (center), who had broken the color barrier in Major League Baseball, appears at A&T. President Lewis Dowdy looks on.

BOTTOM: Student nurses receive their military commissions in 1964. *ETHEL CROOKS.*

Commencement
in 1956.

**ENDNOTES**

1. November 17, 1956
2. Hornsby, A., 161-62
3. Hine et al., 500
4. King, D.S., 140
5. Hornsby, A., 162
6. Gibbs, *History*, 159
7. Spruill, 6
8. Jones et al., 27
9. Bedford, [10-12]
10. March 1950
11. Bluford, "Annual," 1953, 4
12. Bluford, "Annual," 1953, 8
13. Bluford, "Annual," 1952, 11
14. March 1950
15. Bluford, "Annual," 1952, 4
16. Bluford, "Annual," 1952, 14
17. Hornsby, A., 163
18. *Brown*, 1954
19. Hine et al., 500
20. Ifill
21. Roberts and Klibanoff, 66
22. Bluford, "Annual," 1954, 9-11
23. Sloan et al., [8]
24. *Brown*, 1955
25. "Historical"
26. Simkins
27. Roberts and Klibanoff, 86-87
28. Roberts and Klibanoff, 109, 111, 124
29. Hornsby, A., 165
30. September 27, 1955
31. November 24, 1955

32. Gibbs, "Annual," 1956, 6
33. Jones et al., 14
34. September 27, 1955
35. October 15, 1955
36. October 25, 1955
37. October 15, 1955
38. *Collection*, [15]
39. November 15, 1955
40. Kelley, 39-40
41. February 25, 1956
42. February 25, 1956
43. September 29, 1956
44. Gibbs, *History*, 68-70, 183-84
45. November 17, 1956
46. February 25, 1956
47. February 25, 1956
48. November 17, 1956
49. February 25, 1956
50. "Historical"
51. December 1, 1956
52. *Browder*
53. Hornsby, A., 169
54. "Bicentennial," July
55. Hawkins and McDowell
56. "A&T History"
57. "Bicentennial," July
58. Roberts and Klibanoff, 150-51
59. "Telegram"
60. PBS: "Timeline: Civil," 1
61. Stockley
62. Gibbs, *History*, 69
63. March 23, 1957
64. Sloan et al., 455
65. December 1, 1956

66. July 20, 1957
67. "Bicentennial," January
68. "Historical"
69. Hevesi
70. July 16, 1958
71. November 1, 1958
72. November 1, 1958
73. May 28, 1959
74. October 30, 1959
75. December 18, 1959
76. Gibbs, *History*, 52-53
77. November 13, 1959
78. December 18, 1959
79. April 1, 1959
80. May 28, 1959
81. Alexander
82. May 28, 1959
83. January 26, 1962
84. PBS: "Timeline: Civil," 1
85. Gibbs, *History*, 73
86. May 28, 1959
87. Gibbs, *History*, 73
88. April 1, 1959
89. December 4, 1959
90. December 4, 1959
91. April 1, 1959
92. Roberts and Klibanoff, 222
93. "American Federal"
94. Sloan et al., [9]
95. January 29, 1960
96. November 4, 1960
97. November 4, 1960
98. Gibbs, "Annual," 1960, 12-13
99. Branch, 271-274

100. Chafe, 98-99, 112-120
101. Wolff, 11-29
102. Roberts and Klibanoff, 222-23
103. Kinard
104. Roberts and Klibanoff, 223
105. Branch, 271
106. Wolff, 29
107. February 5, 1960
108. Frye, H.
109. February 5, 1960
110. April 29, 1960
111. "Joint Resolution," 2
112. Gibbs, "Annual," 1960, 1
113. Piggott
114. Brandon
115. DuBois, *Souls*, 3
116. Hornsby, A., 174-75
117. Hornsby, A., 175
118. Hornsby, A., 179
119. Brandon
120. September 30, 1960
121. July 22, 1960
122. September 30, 1960
123. January 12, 1962
124. July 22, 1960
125. September 16, 1960
126. *Collection*, [20]
127. September 30, 1960
128. October 31, 1962
129. "Bay of Pigs"
130. January 13, 1961
131. January 13, 1961
132. Lohr
133. "Riders"
134. February 10, 1961
135. February 24, 1961
136. April 14, 1961
137. May 12, 1961
138. April 14, 1961
139. April 14, 1961
140. November 17, 1961
141. January 16, 1963
142. Clemson
143. Johnson, T.A.
144. "Historical"
145. March 30, 1962
146. November 21, 1962
147. Dowdy, E.E.S.
148. "Cuban"
149. "Malcolm X"
150. March 30, 1962
151. Hine et al., 529-30
152. February 13, 1963
153. February 23, 1962
154. February 6, 1963
155. November 1, 1963
156. November 22, 1963
157. April 10, 1963
158. October 25, 1963
159. November 15, 1963
160. May 1, 1963
161. "Historical"
162. Hornsby, A., 180
163. Hine et al., 530
164. Hornsby, A., 182
165. September 20, 1963
166. November 22, 1963
167. "Malcolm X"
168. Kelley, 50
169. "Civil Rights Act"
170. PBS, "Timeline: Civil," 2
171. Hornsby, A., 185
172. April 10, 1964
173. Cobb
174. Hine et al., 556
175. April 10, 1964
176. March 20, 1964
177. February 28, 1964
178. September 18, 1964
179. February 7, 1964
180. February 7, 1964
181. October 23, 1964
182. March 6, 1964
183. *Collection*, [24, 28]
184. April 24, 1964
185. November 20, 1964
186. *50th Anniversary*
187. "Bicentennial," October
188. Gibbs, *History*, 127
189. October 1, 1965
190. Hornsby, A., 185-86
191. January 15, 1965
192. February 19, 1965
193. November 2, 1965
194. December 10, 1965
195. November 25, 1965
196. October 1, 1965
197. October 8, 1965
198. December 3, 1965
199. Hornsby, A., 186-88
200. Hine et al., 549
201. "Voting Rights Act"
202. Clemetson
203. Hornsby, A., 187

Muriel Traynham carrying textbooks on campus, a photo believed to be from the early 1950s. *Eula Whitley collection.*

CHAPTER FIVE

# Black Power
# and Activism

## 1966–1979

A&T cheerleaders raise a fist in a Black Power salute.

The civil rights movement had begun with waiting.

The A&T Four and their supporters waited to be served at the Woolworth's lunch counter, from February 1960 until that July. But what had been accomplished by patience seemed less adequate as the decade continued, and leaders both black and white were gunned down. Peaceful protests gave way to rage, and militancy increased year by year. Stokely Carmichael, whose "Black Power" slogan was well-known on college campuses, would give way to H. Rap Brown at the Student Nonviolent Coordinating Committee, and the Black Panther Party was created.[1, 2, 3]

While the campus was bubbling with ideas, from Pan-Africanism to Black Nationalism, from civil rights to women's rights, A&T was also going about the business of becoming a major research institution. "Between 1965–1982, the University received over $55 million from public funding agencies to support the research program; more than $18 million for special academic projects; and $53 million for developmental programs."[4] Reflecting the national debate, political and cultural discussions abounded on campus, and poetry, theatre, and music helped raise social consciousness. The *Negro Digest* published by John Johnson became *Black World*.[5]

"The summer of '66 claims several events, but the term 'Black Power' is a verbal giant which reigns

A cartoon from the October 4, 1966 issue of *The Register*.

Dr. Lewis Dowdy (center) and Dr. Jerald Marteena (right) accept a grant in 1966.

supreme as the most controversial phrase of the '66 heat wave," wrote Lee House Jr.[6] "The explosive phrase, 'we want black power,' has made headlines coast to coast, created a near break among civil rights organizations, and alarmed the general public." A&T would become known as a center for the Black Power movement.[7] Floyd McKissick of North Carolina succeeded James Farmer as the director of CORE and Carmichael took over at SNCC, transforming both into more militant organizations.[8, 9]

The growth of the black population in the late 1960s was reflected in the number of African Americans holding public office. Thurgood Marshall was appointed to the U.S. Supreme Court in 1967, the first black to serve in the nation's highest court.[10]

At A&T, a new club for "viewing political issues" was organized, in the same year that political science became a major. The Association of Social Science Teachers and the

National Convention of Sigma Rho Sigma Honorary Social Science Fraternity planned their annual convention at A&T, with the focus on "The Great Society."[11] Dr. Robert C.

John Johnson, publisher of *Ebony* magazine, during a commencement visit.

Students take the lead in academics as the keynote speakers at the 1966 fall English Emphasis program. They are (from left) Margaret Shivers, Sandra Carlton, Cynthia Moore, Yvette Roberts, Phillistine Goode, and Augusta Allen, with program chair Carrye Kelley.

Dr. Lewis C. Dowdy is shown riding with Walter H. Riddick (right), a prominent mortician whose horses won numerous show prizes, building the university's reputation during Alumni Week in Norfolk, Virginia, in 1966.

Weaver, a former instructor of economics, was nominated to head the newly created Department of Housing and Urban Development.[12] President Dowdy became a director of the Greensboro Chamber of Commerce, another first.[13] Radio station WANT debuted as a class project by students majoring in electrical technology. WNAA's current general manager, Tony Welborne, was one of those students.[14] Sometimes, however, growth didn't keep pace with needs.

Since the early years of the university, complaints about the food service had been perennial. In 1966, protests over the food were made visible with picket lines, rallies, and

newsletters and sparked a new organization: Student Organization for Unified Leadership (SOUL).[15] A&T students were taking action in the community as well, joining students from other colleges for the Greensboro United Tutorial Services at low-income housing sites.[16] They could see new opportunities opening up with government agencies and defense contractors, and banks sought Aggies for college checking accounts.[17, 18] The coronation of Nannie Kearney as Miss A&T marked the start of something new: the Coronation Ball, attended by the college's then-oldest living alumnus, the Rev. Arthur Rankin, part of the Class of 1901.[19] Student Jerome

Morehead was presented with the highest lifesaving award given by the American Red Cross. He rescued five children on a tragic day in June 1965 that claimed four other lives at a 4-H camp near Swansboro.[20]

Robert Beamon, a freshman track star, was selected in 1966 for a worldwide track event in Puerto Rico. Elvin Bethea and Roy "Spaceman" Thompson, later a coach at A&T, were the only Aggie track athletes to compete in the Atlantic Coast Regionals Meet (NCAA).[21]

The culture was changing, as fashion features advised students on how to wear "granny glasses" and the proper length of skirts—short and shorter. The Vietnam War was heating up. The Army ROTC posthumously awarded the Purple Heart and Bronze Star to the parents of 2nd Lt. William E. Davis Jr., an Aggie killed in action in December 1965.[22]

The demolition of one of the original campus buildings was a fitting visual for a year in which the old began giving way to the new; Crosby Hall, completed in 1896 as the mechanical building, had housed a number of departments.[23] Later that spring, three new buildings were dedicated: the Memorial Student Union, biology building, and a women's dorm.[24]

Julian Bond, a founder of SNCC and representative in the Georgia General Assembly, spoke for the Men's Council meeting.[25] Men's Week was followed closely by Religious Emphasis Week, and by Women's Week.[26]

Mrs. Lewis (Elizabeth) Dowdy is honored with a corsage as the Women's Weekend banquet speaker.

An official gathering honors Aggie administrators (from left) M. F. Holt, Clyde DeHugeley, S. B. Simmons, Dr. W. T. Gibbs, H. Clinton Taylor, L. A. Wise, Dean J. M. Marteena, C. E. Dean, T. A. Clark, C. Cunningham, Alma Morrow, and W. J. Fisher.

The A&T basketball team won the 1967 CIAA title. A 105-82 win over the Winston-Salem Rams was considered the biggest of the season, as "the Aggie defense took some of the glitter off Earl Monroe as he was held to a season's low of 20 points, 24 points below his average."[27] The Philadelphia 76ers drafted Aggie standouts Teddy Campbell and George "Red" Mack.[28] One week after the celebration for the basketball championship, the A&T Rifle Team took the CIAA crown.[29]

The college helped preserve a local institution, L. Richardson Hospital, as Dr. F. A. Williams led the A&T faculty and staff in a fund-raising drive.[30] A&T also continued to work with UNCG on Upward

Bound, a program to overcome the economic, cultural, and educational deprivations of teenagers, through a $175,054 grant from the U.S. Office of Economic Opportunity.[31]

A new name appeared, North Carolina Agricultural and Technical State University, as it became a regional university. It was the only predominantly black institution in a group that included East Carolina, Western Carolina, and Appalachian State.[32]

Protests against the Vietnam War held particular importance for young black people. Howard Fuller of the North Carolina Fund was hosted by Delta Sigma Theta Sorority at its vesper service. Fuller warned that "only two places are black people

Training the next generation of teachers remained a priority for A&T. This is a 1967 summer institute for high school teachers supported by the National Science Foundation. *Lewis A. Brandon III.*

well represented—in Vietnam and in poverty."[33] English professor Richard Vission participated in the March on the Pentagon.[34]

The move to militancy, as demonstrated in the reports of the Watts riot, prompted President Johnson to establish the National Advisory Commission on Civil Disorders, headed by Illinois Gov. Otto Kerner. Its 1968 report warned that America was "moving towards two societies, one white, one black—separate and unequal."[35]

The years 1968 and 1969 would mark the loudest protests and the greatest grief, as the campus came under fire from the National Guard and a student was killed.

Some 200 A&T students carrying signs and coffins marched to downtown Greensboro in February to protest the shooting of three students by police at South Carolina State College.[36] Protest was joined with action—a voter registration drive was planned at a meeting including representatives from Bennett College and UNCG.[37] For the most part, however, the campus was quiet in the early part of 1968. The university's postman of 38 years, Allison Gordon, retired. He had come to the college in 1922 when it was just "three buildings and a barn."[38]

Elvin Bethea was drafted by the Houston Oilers. The six-foot-five 255-pound lineman was captain of the football team and a member of All-NAIA, CIAA All-Star, and Daily News All-State teams.[39] As a gymnastics

team was being formed, the swim team was disbanded.[40]

Radio station WANT featured the *Soulfinger Show*, *Wonderful World of Jazz*, and *Light Classical Showcase*. A&T alum 1st Lt. Cato Reaves, who had received the Distinguished Flying Cross, returned to participate in the New Career Opportunities Conference.[41]

Dr. Martin Luther King Jr. understood a new direction was needed for the struggle he defined and began to attack the war. On March 31, 1968, President Lyndon B. Johnson told the country he would stop the North Vietnam bombings.[42] Days later, King was assassinated in Memphis where he went to support striking sanitation workers. A day earlier, King had given his last and perhaps most prophetic speech: "I just want to do God's will. And He's allowed me to go up to the mountaintop, and I've looked over. And I've seen the promised land.'"[43]

Hundreds of thousands attended King's funeral. President Johnson declared a day of mourning. Riots broke out in as many as 125 cities. President Johnson told Joseph Califano Jr., his domestic policy adviser, "Everything we've gained in the last few days we're going to lose tonight."[44]

"It took less than a couple of minutes for two or three hundred students to gather at the administration building after the news of Dr. Martin Luther King, Jr.'s death had swept across the campus," wrote managing editor Prince Legree in *The Register*. "The building was vacant so

The Memorial Student Union
was a center of campus life.

the marchers moved to Murphy Hall cafeteria, where Dr. Dowdy was being honored at a dinner …. Dowdy spoke to the group. 'Are you disillusioned? You are doing exactly what our common enemy wants you to do.'" A memorial service was set for the next day, and the marchers moved out to the downtown.[45]

Throughout the spring, students organized, protested, and debated the direction of A&T. The university abolished compulsory ROTC. Dowdy also formed a Blue Ribbon Committee to consider student grievances and announced plans for an African-Afro-American culture center.[46]

A country already reeling was staggered with the June assassination of Sen. Robert Kennedy as he campaigned for the Democratic nomination for president and riots in Chicago at the Democratic National Convention. Still, the national mood in the fall of 1968 could be described as one of hope. Arthur Ashe won the U.S. Open, the first black to do so. Shirley Chisholm became the first black woman to serve in Congress. Eighty blacks were elected into office in the South.[47]

The university was reorganized and when students returned to this reshaped university, *The Register* had a

While compulsory ROTC was abolished in the late 1960s, it remained a strong force on campus. Here, Air Force ROTC cadets in 1972 are shown near the fighter jet that marked the Campbell Hall headquarters.

new motto: "Complete Awareness in Times for Complete Commitment."[48]

Observers called the period from 1968 to 1975 the "second phase" of the black student movement, as students were determined to see educational reform that would embrace the culture, issues, and spiritual awareness of black people. One "student power" demonstration, in November 1968, saw students from A&T make up the majority of protestors at a teach-in by Greensboro colleges.[49]

"The Achievement of Black Americans" was the theme for a Homecoming that broke records with more than 18,000 in attendance. Winning floats in the mile-long parade included Omega Psi Phi, the Physical Education Department, and the Architectural Engineering Department.[50] Football coach Hornsby Howell was named Coach of the Year for District 26 of the NAIA and the CIAA.[51]

Louis E. Lomax, a controversial journalist and author of *The Negro Revolt* and *To Kill a Black Man*, spoke on Black Power. "The question is not if blacks will become violent but what will we be forced to do?" he asked.[52] Two weeks later, a student boycott of classes ended after being marred by vandalism in the dining hall.[53] Stokely Carmichael spoke to students: "When we feel psychologically equal to him (the white man) we must plan a strategic program to prepare for revolution … a revolution that we can win."[54]

President Johnson, who during his time in office saw the country experience the most violence and disorder since the early 1890s, was followed by Richard Nixon,[55] who created the Environmental Protection Agency and endorsed an Equal Rights Amendment to prohibit gender discrimination, but also destabilized Roosevelt's New Deal alliance.[56] As Nixon escalated the war in Vietnam with invasions in Laos and Cambodia, opposition grew.

The Student Government Association started the New Year with a sit-in at the Dudley Building, but left after reaching an agreement with the Faculty Senate.[57] Student leaders would follow up with a new constitution and a comprehensive list of grievances.[58] Dick Gregory praised A&T for its leadership, saying, "10 years ago they raided Panties—Today we raid Administrations and they say today's youth have lesser morals. Never before have we had more responsible youth than today."[59] He could have pointed to major accomplishments by Aggies: Lawrence McSwain was the first black student to become president of the North Carolina Student Legislature.[60] Sandra A. Carlton received a Danforth Fellowship for graduate studies,[61] and Luther Brown Jr. became A&T's first Woodrow Wilson Fellow.[62]

Jeffrey C. Feggins recalled Summer Music Institutes at A&T in 1968–69 under the direction of Dr. Howard T. Pearsall, choir director. "As

Ellis Corbett, serving as grand basileus of Omega Psi Phi Fraternity, presents a $500 check to Charles Evers in September 1969, to help the town of Fayette, Mississippi. When Evers took over as mayor and an all-black city council was installed, it was discovered that the town treasury had been depleted. Evers was the brother of slain civil rights leader Medgar Evers.

a freshman, I joined the University Choir and was a loyal member from September 1970 to May 1974," he wrote. "We traveled by bus to all major cities singing and performing on stage. We were greeted by former Aggies, and alumni from our university who sponsored us." Feggins, who graduated in 1974, said, "I was surrounded by great teachers, musicians, vocalists, and friends."[63]

Late winter brought a 12-inch snowfall. A collection of African art and artifacts went on display in the Taylor Art Gallery in the basement of the Bluford Library.[64] Willie Pearson was drafted by the Miami Dolphins.

Food service was again at the heart of a spreading series of protests in March 1969—but not over the meals. A three-day labor dispute was settled after striking food service workers, with the support of the student body, refused to serve meals until their demands were met, including a minimum wage of $1.80 per hour. The settlement didn't come without controversy, however. Students marched to the president's home; when police arrived to escort them away, "the students then marched to East Market Street where cars were stoned, traffic was held up, and windows were broken." Police used tear gas, but rock-throwing continued and police reported small arms fire. Two A&T students suffered minor gunshot wounds, according to police, who arrested three students in connection with the disturbance.[65] Similar strikes took place at UNC-Chapel Hill and at UNCG.[66]

The university was chosen for a conference to organize black students: the Student Organization for Black Unity, or SOBU. The Wesley

Foundation hosted the Rev. Archie L. Rich, who discussed black theology.[67] Afro House opened in a former day school nursery as an Afro-American cultural center.

In other highlights, the Aggies defeated Delaware State to take the baseball CIAA crown.[68]

The events from May 21 to 25, 1969, vividly depicted the tensions between students who followed the legacy of King and those who sought a different path. The disturbance began at segregated Dudley High School. Student Council write-in presidential candidate Claude Barnes was denied his landslide victory—allegedly, because school officials believed him to be a Black Power activist. Hostilities spread to the campus after three days, and gunfire broke out between the National Guard and A&T students. Willie Grimes, an A&T student not involved in the protests, was shot and killed while returning to his dormitory.[69] To this day, it's unknown how Grimes was killed, or by whom.[70] The National Guard incursion on the campus was described as "the most massive armed assault ever made against an American University."[71] The National Guard withdrew after searching the A&T dormitories; hundreds of students were taken into protective custody.[72]

"I can remember hearing the gunshots in the night as bullets penetrated the walls of Scott Hall," related Elizabeth Dowdy. "I can recall the tanks blocking Bluford Street near the entrance of our driveway at The Oaks residence. … But through it all to my amazement, there was calm, tolerant understanding patience that my husband Dr. Dowdy exhibited during all this upheaval with deep concern for the students as he walked around campus to see that all was well."[73]

The State Advisory Committee to the U.S. Commission on Civil Rights held open hearings into the May disorders. President Dowdy said that city authorities had not notified him of an

Members of Willie Grimes' fraternity move his casket from the school, where funeral services were held. He was killed in 1969, as violence rocked the campus. *The Daily Reflector/ Joyner Library Collection.*

intended "sweep" at Cooper and Scott halls, and male students were "subjected to tear gas and were marched from their living quarters in towels thrown around the waist and pajamas." Dowdy also said that he had not requested the National Guard. "When asked again for the amount of damages, Dowdy answered, '$56,000 … yet the damage done to the 1,300 students there will be harder to repair … in terms of human dignity.'" This group would issue a report in March 1970 that said, "There must be continuous attention focused on the unequal treatment afforded blacks in Greensboro to prevent crises from arising."[74, 75]

The National Guard was sent into the campus in May 1969. *NEWS & RECORD.*

When the National Vietnam Moratorium was held at A&T on October 15, sponsored by the university's Veterans Program, the bloodshed of March was remembered. "When the National Guardsmen and police forces unnecessarily wrecked our campus, I then realized that I had fought the wrong war," said Jack Douglas, a senior from Greensboro.[76] Despite debates over the war, the ROTC continued on campus, and excelled, with the Army ROTC winning the number-one rating during competition in the summer of 1969.[77]

While students sought more rights, the university was focused on academic progress. The School of

Three women model A&T hats in 1969.

Engineering was accredited by the Engineers Council for Professional Development, joining NC State and Duke as the only schools in North Carolina with that designation. The campus had two new buildings: a men's dormitory, and the communications building scheduled to open in the spring.[78] Seven A&T student teachers spent five weeks in Camden, New Jersey, teaching in inner-city schools.[79] A&T had its first black chairman of the Board of Trustees with the election of John S. Stewart, president of Mutual Savings and Loan Association.

As the tumultuous year came to a close, Stevie Wonder performed, the A&T Band received its first new uniforms since 1959,[80] and Merl Code was named to the AP Little All-American football team.[81]

The 1970s would bring changes in the image of black Americans. The business magazine *Black Enterprise* began to attract the growing black middle class. Fifteen members of Congress formed the Congressional Black Caucus. Hank Aaron became

Richard E. Moore was prominent in the life of the campus community in English and journalism and the A&T Public Information Office for more than 28 years.

Students work in the School
of Business and Economics
Computer Center.

The Aggie dog presided over some major athletic triumphs in the 1970s.

the home run king, and Reggie Jackson set records in several World Series. *The Jeffersons*, one of the first sitcoms about an African American family, became one of television's longest-running and most-watched programs.[82, 83]

The arrival of a new decade brought a new school to A&T, as the School of Business and Economics was formed. The Computer Science Center was dedicated and the $1.5 million Crosby Communications Center with its little theatre and journalism facilities "represented a major step in strengthening the University's offerings in the humanities."[84] A three-day workshop studied the possibilities of merging A&T and UNCG—an issue that would simmer throughout the decades.[85]

On May 4, Ohio National Guardsmen shot and killed four white students at Kent State. Ten days later, on the campus of historically black Jackson State University, two black students were shot and killed. Both events were covered by the media; the Jackson State shootings attracted less attention.[86]

The Rev. Jesse L. Jackson, director of Operation Breadbasket, was named one of the Ten Outstanding Young Men of 1969 by the U.S. Jaycees.[87] He would return to his alma mater to deliver the commencement address,[88] then in the fall, called A&T "a sanctuary in which revolutionary thoughts and ideas must be developed."[89]

The A&T basketball team, nationally ranked, beat Lincoln University

The Rev. Jesse Jackson was often on campus. Here, he rides with his sons in a Homecoming parade.

JESSE JACKSON & SONS

Students watch a demonstration in a chemistry lab in the 1970s.

117-58 in its first appearance at Madison Square Garden in a benefit for the United Negro College Fund.[90]

Major grants continued to roll in. Dr. Gerald Edwards, director of the Division of Natural Sciences and Mathematics, and his wife Dr. Cecile Edwards, chair of the Department of Home Economics, received $102,000 to study malnutrition.[91] A&T received a $96,000 grant from the Department of Housing, Education and Welfare to prepare teachers to "teach the black experience and Black students."[92] NASA awarded $39,000 to the School of Engineering, among the first NASA support given to a predominantly black college. Union Carbide was also making grants to researchers in engineering.[93]

The A&T theatre group won first prize at the National Association of Dramatic and Speech Arts, and Hollis Pippins was judged the best actor.[94] Dr. John Kilimanjaro was overseeing the design and construction of the Paul Robeson Theatre.[95]

Science and technology continued to be a major emphasis. Moon rocks were exhibited on campus.[96] A&T launched a program to increase the number of black certified public accountants. The university boasted a new Control Data 3300 computer, supported by grants from the

National Science Foundation, Control Data, and other foundations and corporations.[97]

A parade of black luminaries visited A&T, including James Brown, the Alvin Ailey Dance Theatre, and The Impressions.[98] As with Brown's "Say It Loud, I'm Black and I'm Proud," the words of another visitor would be important in the new black identity. Nina Simone, who had released "To Be Young, Gifted and Black," performed in Moore Gymnasium.[99]

One of A&T's signature organizations, the Gospel Choir, came into being from discussions between Athletic Director Albert Smith and Vernon Hatley, a senior who would become president of the 87-member group.[100] In sports news, Mel Holmes was named to the AP Little All-America football team.[101]

Julian Bond closed out the year at a "Save the Black Schools Banquet" sponsored by SOBU.[102] Two years later, the National Save Black Schools Conference was held at A&T.[103]

Minister Louis Farrakhan discussed Black Muslim beliefs early in 1971. "In the time for your rise, we as Black people must be very careful for our enemies are laying traps everywhere. One of these traps is selling drugs to the young Blacks."[104] His message was timely, as a local newspaper had written a controversial story about drug use on A&T's campus, with a dramatic front-page photo and articles noting the increased use of marijuana, LSD, and hard drugs.[105]

A&T's budget request included $3.5 million for a health and physical education building, and $7.1 million for two science buildings.[106] The university was also growing through gifts from alumni: support for scholarships had increased from $7,000 annually in the 1960s to $100,000 each year for the past two years. Dowdy called the increased alumni support "one of the most encouraging aspects of the University's overall development."[107] More than 300 school administrators, teachers, students, and parents attended the Teachers, Administrators and School Integration (TASI) Conference at A&T.[108] For the first time, the university awarded faculty prizes for teaching (Carrie Walden of Nursing) and service (Ernestine Compton of Physical Education). The Department of Sociology and Social Work was named the most outstanding department.[109]

The yearbook staff sponsored a new contest for Miss Black Awareness, with Angela Collins winning.[110] Ray's Kingburger on Bessemer Avenue offered Kingburgers at half price on Tuesdays.[111] The campus was torn up with installation of an underground electrical distribution system.[112]

A&T's long association with the CIAA came to an end, as it became one of the founding schools in the Mid-Eastern Athletic Conference (MEAC) beginning in the fall of 1971.[113] In May 1971, the Aggies took the CIAA Southern Division baseball crown,[114] winning overall by default

Students and faculty working under a USDA grant in the early 1970s are pictured. Front row (from left): students gathered around Dr. Samuel Dunn, chairman of the Plant Science Department. Back row: Musa Kamara, Kurt Hafer, Harvey Hermanson, E. S. Carr, G. B. Reddy, Lee Yates, Dr. Isiah Ruffin, Dr. Eugene Marrow, Lewis A. Brandon III, Dr. Charles A. Fountain, and Mr. Grandee. NICHOLAS BRIGHT, COURTESY LEWIS A. BRANDON III.

when the Northern Division playoff did not take place.[115]

Title IX, which would lead to an explosion in women's sports, was still a year away when the first extramural women's basketball game on A&T's campus was played, with the Aggiettes losing to the Bennett Belles.[116]

James Farmer, former Department of Health, Education and Welfare director and former CORE national director, was the speaker for Founders Day 1971, urging "new affirmative action." Future astronaut Ronald McNair, then a senior professional physics major, received a Ford Doctoral Fellowship to study at MIT, which would later dedicate a building in his honor.[117] A&T maintained scholarly links with Africa, as a Harvard history professor, Dr. Kenneth Onwuka Dike, lectured[118] and singer Miriam Makeba performed.[119]

Attention turned to school desegregation and the Vietnam War. In the fall of 1971, the Greensboro school system was integrated with the institution of cross-town busing.[120, 121] Black Monday protests drew 4,000 students to Raleigh "in opposition to the Reorganization of Higher Education in NC bill";[122] nevertheless, A&T became a constituent institution of The University of North Carolina, one of 16 public senior institutions, in 1972. President Dowdy's title also changed to Chancellor Dowdy.[123, 124]

Rep. Shirley Chisholm told students she was running for president because people are "tired of tokenism, and tired of see-how-far-you-have-come-ism."[125] One of the signal arts organizations of the era came to campus, as the Dance Theatre of Harlem performed.[126] The university had its first woman physician at Sebastian Infirmary, Dr. Barbara Jean Graveley.[127]

Although the original Smith-Lever Act was far-reaching, it was amended to be more inclusive of schools beyond the original 1862 Land Grant Institutions. In 1971, the funding formula was amended, with an appropriation of $12.6 million directly to the 1890 Land-Grant Universities. A&T was flush with new money: the university received two federal grants totaling $1,112,000 from the Department of Agriculture through the Hatch Act and Smith-Lever Act.[128] Among researchers active on campus was Dr. N. M. Chopra, who worked with both NC State and the Council for Tobacco Research USA on tracking how pesticides broke down in tobacco smoke. He had to equip a laboratory for this research and "designed a cigarette smoking machine which would comply with the smoking standards … a professor of A&T's Technology Department made that machine for me."[129]

As the United States continued to grapple with reform, rebellion, and war, President Nixon's most dramatic foreign policy achievement was the opening to China.[130] Back home, Congress approved the Equal Employment Opportunity Act,[131, 132, 133] laying a foundation for affirmative action.[134] By 1980, more than one million black people had enrolled in colleges, and thousands attended the best universities and professional schools in the country.[135]

Black women were gaining a higher profile: Sandra Hughes became a reporter at WFMY-TV in Greensboro in 1972 and later came to A&T to teach journalism. Dr. Alfreda Webb, a professor of animal science, became the first African American woman to serve in the NC General Assembly.[136] Alma Adams, later to be a state legislator then U.S. Representative, graduated with the first MS in Arts Education.[137]

The university received approval to offer a master's degree in engineering. A&T had its first poet-in-residence, Keorapetse Kgositsile, from South Africa, supported by a grant from the National Foundation for the Humanities.[138] Later in the year, poet Sonia Sanchez visited.[139] Work began to renovate old Vanstory Hall, the last of the original buildings.[140] Closed-circuit television arrived, offering plays, demonstrations, lectures, and more.[141]

The Aggie basketball team won the first MEAC regular season title, then took the championship.[142] Three Aggie football players were drafted: Ralph Coleman and Lonnie Leonard by Dallas, and Willie Wright by Oakland.[143] The Elizabeth S. Dowdy Women's Invitational Basketball Tournament was launched by Tyrone Bolden, coach of the Aggiettes.[144] A&T fielded a golf team for the first time. Later that year, Cal Irvin stepped down as basketball coach to devote all his time to his position as athletic director.[145]

Tony Brown also visited A&T for the Department of Sociology and Social Work's Urban Affairs Institute in 1973. From left: Dr. James C. Johnson, Social Work Department; Dr. John Marshall Stevenson (later changed to Kilimanjaro), editor and publisher of *Carolina Peacemaker*; speaker Tony Brown (standing), at that time editor and writer of *Tony Brown's Journal*; Dr. Lewis C. Dowdy, chancellor; and Dr. Gloria Scott. DAVID JOHNSON.

Tony Brown and Ossie Davis spoke to the National Association of Dramatic and Speech Arts Convention; some 300 people attended the three-day event.[146] A&T's Karate Dojo hosted the A&T Southeastern Open Karate championships.[147] Co-ed visitation was approved for the Senior Dorm, and student identification cards were now required.[148]

Gen. Daniel "Chappie" James, the only black general in the U.S. Air Force and a Tuskegee Airman, appeared at the annual ROTC celebration and cadets ball. He spoke of the opportunities in the service, and said, "When you're busy hollering 'freedom now,' you have to have a place to be in which to be free."[149] Among the cadets at that event was likely Jacqueline M. Pattishall, who would be the first black female in the nation to complete a regular Air Force ROTC program.[150]

"Old Smokey" was retired as the A&T power plant shifted from coal to oil. Dr. Quiester Craig arrived as the new dean of the renamed School of Business and Economics.[151]

The Agriculture Department prepared to send a delegation to the national convention of the Future Farmers of America, once closed to blacks. At the national convention two years later, Cedric Jones won the FFA Legion of Merit citation for his work in establishing the A&T Alumni Chapter.[152] The first-place float in the Homecoming parade was the School of Agriculture entry featuring a revolving globe above a pyramid.[153]

Chancellor Dowdy was elected president of the National Association of State University and Land-Grant Colleges, becoming the first black to head a major higher education association.[154]

The year 1973 dawned with the signing of the Paris Peace Accords, but fighting continued until April 1975, when Saigon fell. Nixon campaigned very little but gained a second term, only to preside over his administration's self-destruction over the Watergate break-ins.[155]

A new Centrex telephone system went into operation at A&T and the switchboard disappeared in favor of direct dialing. A new parking system also was ready to go into effect. Some of Mattye Reed's collection of African art went on exhibit in the Clinton Taylor Art Gallery.[156]

Joyce Bass is identified in this shot of campus life from the 1970s.

Poet Maya Angelou signs a book at the Uhuru Bookstore on East Market Street in 1974 for Dorothy M. Eller, English professor at A&T. *Lewis A. Brandon III.*

Greensboro National Bank, the only national bank in the state controlled by blacks, opened with great fanfare. Henry E. Frye '53 and J. Kenneth Lee

Mattye Reed is shown with some of the African art in the gallery that would bear her name.

'45 were principals. The ceremonies included a recently released POW, Air Force Maj. Norman A. McDaniel, an Aggie alumnus.[157] McDaniel spoke to ROTC cadets later that month and credited trust in God for helping him endure torture and imprisonment.[158]

Another veteran, Willie Edward Jenkins, who had returned to A&T to earn his bachelor's degree in 1949, went on to become an architect and found his own firm in Greensboro in 1962. From the mid-1960s to the mid-'80s, he designed six buildings on the campus, including Communications (1973), Williams Cafeteria (1974), Aggie Stadium (1980), and Engineering (1984).[159]

The second half of the 1970s was dominated by national crises and by a fight for A&T's very survival.

Nixon's second term included the Middle East crisis and resulting oil embargo, as well as the escalating Watergate scandal. On August 9, 1974, he resigned in the face of almost certain impeachment.[160] Gerald Ford became the only president to come into office under the 25th Amendment to the Constitution.[161] Public interest in the Watergate scandal was high and *Washington Post* reporters Carl Bernstein and Bob Woodward emerged as models for aspiring journalists.[162] Journalism programs around the country grew: the Department of English, which housed the journalism program, saw a steady increase in the number of majors.

Meanwhile, battles over the desegregation of the UNC system led to serious discussion of merging colleges. A&T was asked to increase the number of white students from 254 to 300.[163] Two weeks later, the Department of Health, Education and Welfare (HEW) rejected the UNC desegregation plan again.[164] Later that year, A&T fought a tough battle to gain the new veterinary medical school, only to see the nod go to NC State.[165] A&T students rallied in 1975 against a large tuition increase and perceived efforts to phase out black colleges.[166] The debate came back to a boil in 1978 when HEW threatened to cut off federal funding to the UNC system because of its refusal to meet desegregation demands.[167] In 1979, the federal government again rejected North Carolina's desegregation plan for its state universities.[168]

As this drama unfolded, campus life went forward. The School of Business and Economics received a substantial grant from the W.K. Kellogg Foundation to support program development.[169, 170] The Alfred P. Sloan Foundation approved a $100,000 grant as part of a nationwide effort to increase minority participation in engineering.[171] The social work program received full accreditation from the Council on Social Work Education, one of the first in the nation to do so,[172] and A&T partnered with West Virginia University in a $1.7 million project to assist agricultural development in East Africa.[173]

A&T students, like everyone else, struggled with the gasoline shortage that year.[174] If they were confined to campus, they had one reason to rejoice: the new dining hall opened.[175] The activism of the 1960s was not forgotten, however: 200 students from area universities gathered in the Holland Bowl and marched to the municipal building to protest capital punishment.[176]

Aggies were in the news for their accomplishments. Professor Zoe Barbee became the first African American woman elected to the Guilford County Board of Commissioners,[177] but was killed in a car accident soon after.[178] Lt. Thomas Brown, a 1974 graduate, was the first Army "flyer" to be commissioned out of the Army ROTC.[179] It was only fitting that a new jet was installed that year in front of Campbell Hall.[180]

In sports news, a soccer team was organized at A&T.[181] Three brothers from Roanoke, Virginia—Al, Winston, and Ricky Holland—were all playing for the football team.[182] The baseball team won a MEAC crown, as did the wrestlers, and wrestling coach Mel Pinckney was named the MEAC Coach of the Year.[183] The basketball team won the MEAC tournament and Warren Reynolds was named the top basketball coach in the MEAC. The Athletic Department announced the beginning of a fund drive for a new 20,000-seat football stadium.[184]

Later that year, the football squad added its laurels: Hornsby Howell

Former Aggie athletes often returned to campus, like Al Attles in this photo believed to be from the 1970s.

was named Football Coach of the Year in the MEAC, and tight end Walter Bennett was named to the AP College Division All-America team.[185]

The Society of Physics Students won the 1975 Marsh W. White Award presented by the American Institute of Physics, selected from over 450 colleges and universities.[186] A new sorority was chartered: Nu Gamma Mchumba. The final word is not Greek, but means "African Sweetheart."[187] Dr. Albert Spruill, dean of the Graduate School, was elected president of the Southern Conference of Graduate Schools.[188] Dr. Gloria Scott, professor of education and director of institutional research, became the first black elected president of the Girl Scouts of the USA.[189]

Speakers visiting campus included Julius Chambers, president of the Legal Defense Fund of the NAACP and member of the NC Board of Governors,[190] and Vernon Jordan, executive director of the National Urban League.[191] The A&T Marching Band gained a new name in 1975, the Blue and Gold Marching Machine.[192]

The bicentennial year would bring soldiers home from war, and hopes for peace in the Middle East.[193] At A&T, engineering continued to grow, students continued to protest, and women's rights became a new cause.

Vietnam veterans faced different challenges than the World War II generation. The effects of Agent Orange were just starting to be discussed. At A&T, a tutorial service

was started to help veterans succeed.[194] The university, meanwhile,
was removing architectural barriers
and installing ramps to open the campus to students with disabilities.[195]

The Board of Governors approved
an M.S. in Adult Education and
B.S. in Transportation, Industrial
Engineering, and Landscape
Architecture, making A&T the first
predominantly black university to
offer these bachelor's degrees.[196] The
Department of English was authorized to offer the M.A. in English and
African American Literature, a degree
unique in the nation.[197] A new program in Food Science was sponsored
by the departments of Animal Science
and Home Economics, and coopera-
tively between A&T and NC State.[198]

A&T was selected to coordinate
a $550,000 program to interest more
minority students in engineering.[199]

For the second consecutive year, a student from the School of Engineering
won a scholarship from Bell
Laboratories.[200] Aggie alumna Ruby
Murchison, a seventh-grade instructor in Fayetteville, North Carolina,
was honored at the White House as
National Teacher of the Year.[201]

Things were looking up for the
tennis team with the opening of new
courts.[202] The basketball team won
the MEAC championship and James
"The Bird" Sparrow was named *Jet*
magazine All-American.[203] Aggie
wrestlers won both the MEAC and
the Visitation championships, making it to the semi-finals of the NCAA
regionals.[204] The women's bowling
team won first in its division at the
Inter-collegiate Bowling Conference
Tournament.[205] Tampa Bay drafted
George Ragsdale, who had set an A&T
rushing record.[206]

Aggie cheerleaders
in 1976.

James Sparrow

Forward Elmer Austin fires for two points over
Winston-Salem defenders in a 1971 game.

ABOVE: Sinclair Colbert (#52) and Ron Johnson (#30) in action.

LEFT: Basketball standout James Sparrow is pictured with coach and athletics director Cal Irvin.

The Aggies became a dominant force in the MEAC, taking several basketball titles.

Home Economics students in Child Development at Christmastime, 1970s. *Vashti Niles.*

The importance of family is demonstrated by the Webbs. Haywood Webb '09 (seated at left) is shown in 1977 when he was the oldest living alumnus. He is pictured with his sons, all A&T graduates: Harold '48 (seated, at right), Reginald '50 (back row, at left), Burleigh '43, and Haywood Jr. *Harold H. Webb.*

Poets/activists Ron Ayers and Gil Scott-Heron appeared at Moore Gymnasium.[207] Holland Hall residents marched on the chancellor's home to protest conditions at the dorm.[208] A week later, students gathered on the steps of the Dudley Building for a protest about the cafeteria.[209] The 180-piece A&T Band presented a special concert on the steps of the U.S. Capitol on October 23,[210] but a month later went on strike to protest conditions in the Music Department.[211]

Women's liberation was in the news—and on campus. Cathy Sedwick, a member of the Young Socialist Alliance, spoke on "Black Women's Liberation."[212] A&T's Detachment 605, Air Force ROTC, inducted its first female commander, Cadet Lt. Col. Wilma Slade.[213]

The novel *Roots* won a special Pulitzer Prize for author Alex Haley in 1976. When the novel became a mini-series in early 1977, it became one of the most-watched shows in the history of television. Many alums remember vividly where and with whom they watched this series. Haley spoke at the Greensboro Memorial Auditorium that spring, saying, "If one truly wants to say he knows American history, it is a fact that one does not know history if he does not know the role Black people played in its development." The Board of Trustees approved renaming Senior Dorm as Haley Hall.[214]

Controversy over affirmative action continued after passage of the Equal

Employment Act, but the federal mandate led to new employment opportunities, and the growth of the black middle class was significant. In 1977, the Supreme Court ruled against universities using racial quotas in determining admission, in the Bakke case.[215]

National dignitaries were on campus for dedication of a solid state engineering research laboratory in Cherry Hall, one of three in the nation, and construction was set to begin for a $2.8 million physics building.[216]

When the Department of Mathematics moved to Marteena Hall, Merrick Hall was dedicated to the School of Business and Economics. The school also announced the creation of the United Parcel Service Endowed Chair, to enhance faculty development, research, and student development in transportation.[217] Nearly $500,000 in grants from the W.K. Kellogg Foundation helped support the School of Business and Economics and the mass communications curriculum.[218]

Other good things were happening across campus. Teacher education programs and the undergraduate programs in industrial technology were accredited.[219] The trustees approved construction of a new women's dorm.[220] A report on the Minority Biomedical Sciences program noted that, since 1972, more than 111 students had participated. The Association of Childhood Education formed a chapter at A&T.[221]

The university lost two head coaches on the same day, as basketball coach Warren Reynolds and football coach Hornsby Howell both stepped down.[222] A&T's standout Dwaine "Pee Wee" Board was named to the Mutual Black Network All-America football team and voted the nation's Defensive Player of the Year.[223]

The first Black Arts Festival and Symposium was held at A&T in May,[224] and noted musical visitors to campus included Ray Charles[225] and jazz legend Earl "Fatha" Hines.[226]

Student protestors met with Chancellor Dowdy to discuss dorm living conditions.[227] Police officers and students were hospitalized after a smoky fire broke out in Curtis Hall.[228] Later that year, Housing and Urban Development lent A&T $1.4 million to make improvements at the dormitories.[229]

Angela Watson, an A&T senior, won the Miss Black North Carolina title.[230] WNAA-FM became the new call sign for the former WANT.[231] Joseph M. and Kathleen Bryan gave $45,000 to assist University Relations—the largest single gift ever received from an individual.[232]

Jimmy Carter became America's 39th president, focusing on economic and energy crises, but was baffled by the inability of Americans to solve these problems. In a 10-day meeting at Camp David with 130 leaders from all walks of life, Carter concluded that the nation was facing "a crisis of spirit." Carter went on to negotiate the historic Camp David Accords.[233]

As 1978 opened, Ronald McNair was named one of the first black

An aerial view of the stadium, long before electronic scoreboards.

astronauts.[234] Shortly thereafter, A&T was selected by NASA to test the feasibility of curriculum and research sharing by satellite.[235]

The A&T Wilmington 10 defense committee held a support rally for an April 1 statewide demonstration seeking pardons for the group.[236] Eight young black men, a minister, and a female anti-poverty worker had been convicted in 1971 on charges related to the firebombing of a white-owned grocery. By October, only the Rev. Ben Chavis was still behind bars as the others were released on parole.[237] The convictions would be overturned by a federal appeals court in 1980.

A mobile teaching laboratory, "Newspaper Technology … On the Move," visited A&T[238] and the university's first Mass Media Careers Conference was held in April 1978.[239]

A fundraising drive for a new Aggie Stadium led by the Greensboro

Jaycees raised nearly $500,000, and the university committed $1.8 million through a bond issue.[240] The Aggies routed NC Central 96-74 to take the MEAC title in basketball,[241] then went on to win the MEAC tournament—the fifth championship in seven years.[242] Aggie alumnus Kenny Free was named the first full-time commissioner for the MEAC.[243]

The Air Force ROTC began accepting applications for pilot flight training for women.[244] Lt. Col. Joseph Monroe, a graduate of the Air Force ROTC at A&T, became the first black officer nominated as a permanent professor at the U.S. Air Force Academy.[245] The ROTC sponsored its first Turkey Trot, a five-mile run through Greensboro.[246]

Imam Wallace D. Muhammad, leader of the world community of Al-Islam in the West and recipient of the "Four Freedoms Award," spoke on campus, saying that Jim Crowism still existed.[247] A husband-wife team, Dr. Wyatt D. Kirk, chairman of the Education Department, and Dr. Sarah Virgo Kirk, associate professor of social work, began a three-year project to measure the impact of racism on personality development of blacks.[248]

Early in 1979, students protested visitors from the Department of Health, Education and Welfare, asking that HEW improve living conditions on campus, increase funding, and cease trying to phase out black schools.[249] Dr. Dowdy took to the pages of *The Greensboro Record* to ask if black colleges could survive. "Greensboro's Bennett College and A&T State University offer case studies in the financial, social and political pressures that threaten either to close them or sharply alter their existence."[250]

Max Robinson, ABC anchorman, served as the keynote speaker at the Mass Media Conference[251] and returned to speak at commencement.[252] Ossie Davis and Ruby Dee presented a program of legends, stories, and drama from African folk tales to contemporary literature.[253]

Tenor Seth McCoy made his debut at the Metropolitan Opera, the third black male in Met history to sing in a starring role. A graduate of Dudley High School and A&T, he was just past 50 years old.[254]

Joe Brawner was named MEAC Player of the Year.[255] The Aggies defeated Howard to again capture the MEAC basketball championship.[256] The new gymnasium was completed and named for the late Ellis F. Corbett,

organizer of the Aggie Club and Boosterettes, while the new social sciences building was named for former president Warmoth T. Gibbs Sr.[257]

The undergraduate business program was accredited by the American Assembly of Collegiate Schools of Business, the first HBCU in the state to receive this recognition.[258]

In the news for 1979 were the defeat of the Equal Rights Amendment in the state[259] and the meltdown at Three Mile Island.[260] The Senate ratified treaties turning the Panama Canal over to Panama.[261]

As the year came to a close, violent events would shatter confidence locally and globally.

On November 3, 1979, members of a Communist organization that had sought to strengthen local unions gathered for a "Death to the Klan" parade in Greensboro when armed men converged on the area, opening fire and killing four activists and wounding 10 more. A fifth member of the protest group died the next day.[262] Although the Klan-Nazi shootings made national headlines, the event was quickly overcome by another story.

President Carter allowed the Shah of Iran to seek treatment for terminal cancer in the U.S., causing outrage in Teheran. On November 4, 1979, Iranian militants overran the U.S embassy and took 53 American hostages. That crisis would dominate U.S. foreign policy for more than a year, with a failed rescue attempt in April 1980. That fall, Ronald Reagan was elected president.[263]

## ENDNOTES

1. Hornsby, A., 191-92
2. Hine et al., 544-46
3. PBS, "Timeline: Civil," 3
4. Jones et al., 16-17
5. Hine et al., 559
6. House
7. Biondi, 158
8. Hine et al., 546
9. Carmichael
10. Hornsby, A., 192-93
11. February 25, 1966
12. January 21, 1966
13. November 18, 1966
14. February 25, 1966
15. March 4, 1966
16. November 18, 1966
17. October 7, 1966
18. October 14, 1966
19. November 5, 1966
20. October 14, 1966
21. May 27, 1966
22. March 18, 1966
23. February 17, 1967
24. April 23, 1967
25. February 17, 1967
26. February 24, 1967
27. March 10, 1967
28. May 12, 1967
29. March 17, 1967
30. March 17, 1967
31. April 7, 1967
32. September 22, 1967
33. December 14, 1967
34. November 2, 1967
35. Kerner, 1
36. February 22, 1968
37. February 29, 1968
38. January 18, 1968
39. February 22, 1968
40. February 8, 1968
41. March 8, 1968
42. "LBJ"
43. King, Dr.
44. Risen
45. April 18, 1968
46. April 25, 1968
47. Hornsby, A., 194-96
48. September 20, 1968
49. November 9, 1968
50. November 15, 1968
51. December 19, 1968
52. November 22, 1968
53. December 13, 1968
54. December 19, 1968
55. Moss, 417
56. Hine et al., 563
57. February 14, 1969
58. February 7, 1969
59. February 21, 1969
60. March 14, 1969
61. March 20, 1969
62. March 28, 1969
63. Feggins
64. March 7, 1969
65. March 20, 1969
66. "Historical"
67. May 2, 1969
68. May 17, 1969
69. "Historical"
70. Hawkins
71. Biondi, 159
72. North Carolina Advisory, 16
73. Dowdy, E.E.S.
74. North Carolina Advisory, 19-21
75. March 20, 1970
76. October 24, 1969
77. Dowdy, "Annual," 1970, 6
78. September 19, 1969
79. Dowdy, "Annual," 1970, 12
80. November 24, 1969
81. December 12, 1969
82. PBS, "Timeline: Civil," 4
83. PBS, "Timeline: Modern," 1
84. Dowdy, "Annual," 1970, 22
85. February 20, 1970
86. Hornsby, A., 205
87. January 16, 1970
88. May 8, 1970
89. September 25, 1970
90. January 16 1970
91. February 27, 1970
92. March 6, 1970
93. April 24, 1970
94. April 20, 1970
95. College of Arts & Sciences, [1]
96. October 2, 1970
97. October 9, 1970
98. October 9, 1970
99. October 10, 1969
100. October 23, 1970
101. November 6, 1970
102. December 16, 1970
103. *National Save Black Schools*

Students stand on the stairs at Cooper Hall.

104. January 15, 1971
105. February 12, 1971
106. January 15, 1971
107. February 19, 1971
108. January 15, 1971
109. Dowdy, "Annual," 1971, 9
110. February 19, 1971
111. February 25, 1971
112. May 7, 1971
113. December 16, 1970
114. May 7, 1971
115. May 28, 1971
116. March 5, 1971
117. March 26, 1971
118. May 14, 1971
119. November 12, 1971
120. "Historical"
121. Hawkins and McDowell
122. October 29, 1971
123. September 22, 1972
124. Dowdy, "Epoch," 3
125. October 8, 1971
126. October 8, 1971
127. September 3, 1971
128. October 22, 1971
129. Chopra, 13
130. Moss, 468
131. "Equal," eeoc.gov
132. "Equal," gpo.gov
133. Nixon, "Statement"
134. Fullinwider
135. Moss, 521
136. January 21, 1972
137. College of Arts & Sciences, [2]
138. January 14, 1972
139. March 17, 1972
140. January 28, 1972
141. February 10, 1972
142. March 10, 1972
143. February 10, 1972
144. March 3, 1972
145. August 25, 1972
146. April 21, 1972
147. April 14, 1972
148. August 25, 1972
149. April 28, 1972
150. Moore, "First"
151. September 1, 1972
152. October 22, 1974
153. November 3, 1972
154. November 17, 1972
155. Moss, 483
156. January 26, 1973
157. March 2, 1973
158. March 30, 1973
159. Hodges
160. Moss, 489
161. Moss, 495
162. Harry Ransom Center
163. April 19, 1974
164. April 30, 1974
165. December 3, 1974
166. April 25, 1975
167. March 24, 1978
168. March 27, 1979
169. February 22, 1974

170. School of Business, 2
171. February 8, 1974
172. College of Arts & Sciences, [2]
173. December 6, 1974
174. March 1, 1974
175. August 23, 1974
176. April 23, 1974
177. November 8, 1974
178. February 18, 1975
179. November 26, 1974
180. January 11, 1974
181. April 9, 1974
182. September 6, 1974
183. April 11, 1975
184. February 28, 1975
185. December 5, 1975
186. January 21, 1975
187. March 18, 1975
188. March 4, 1975
189. October 31, 1975
190. March 21, 1975
191. April 18, 1975
192. May 2, 1975
193. Moss, 506
194. October 12, 1976
195. October 22, 1976
196. September 28, 1976
197. College of Arts & Sciences, [3]
198. April 13, 1976
199. October 5, 1976
200. April 23, 1976
201. March 26, 1976
202. February 6, 1976
203. April 6, 1976
204. March 2, 1976
205. April 13, 1976
206. April 16, 1976
207. March 30, 1976
208. September 17, 1976
209. September 21, 1976
210. October 15, 1976
211. November 16, 1976
212. October 19, 1976
213. November 19, 1976
214. April 26, 1977
215. *Regents*
216. January 21, 1977
217. School of Business, 2
218. September 16, 1977
219. January 10, 1978
220. January 28, 1977
221. September 9, 1977
222. March 4, 1977
223. December 5, 1978
224. "Black Arts"
225. September 13, 1977
226. September 29, 1978
227. April 8, 1977
228. September 23, 1977
229. October 28, 1977
230. August 26, 1977
231. October 28, 1977
232. November 11, 1977
233. Moss, 507
234. January 17, 1978
235. January 20, 1978

236. March 31, 1978
237. October 31, 1978
238. March 31, 1978
239. April 28, 1978
240. September 8, 1978
241. February 17, 1978
242. February 28, 1978
243. May 5, 1978
244. February 10, 1978
245. December 5, 1978
246. January 12, 1979
247. February 21, 1978
248. September 12, 1978
249. February 27, 1979
250. Dowdy, "[Can]"
251. March 30, 1979
252. April 20, 1979
253. October 11, 1979
254. February 23, 1979
255. February 23, 1979
256. February 27, 1979
257. November 2, 1979
258. School of Business, 2
259. March 27, 1979
260. April 3, 1979
261. Moss, 507-08
262. "Bicentennial," October
263. Moss, 510

Judge Elreta Alexander-Ralston was the first African American woman to graduate from Columbia University Law School (1945), was part of the first integrated law firm in the South, and in 1968 became the first African American woman in the nation elected to the bench as a district court judge.

CHAPTER SIX

*The Technological Age*

1980-2000

**Mission Specialist Ron McNair trains in weightlessness in this shot from the Lyndon B. Johnson Space Center.** *NASA.*

In the last decades of the 20th century, the university continued to play a leading role in political activism and African American affairs, even as it became a more global institution. A&T reached the stars, but also mourned the death of the astronaut who carried the Aggie colors into space.

Chancellor Lewis C. Dowdy stepped down, marking the end of an era. Inaugurated as president in 1964, he had guided the university through times of great challenge as well as great growth. Dr. Edward B. Fort, a historian by training, became chancellor in 1981 and led the university to national prominence in engineering and technology education. More than 30 academic programs debuted during his administration, and A&T awarded its first doctorates.[1]

This was the era of the computer. In 1972, approximately 6,000 computers were in use in America; by 1980, there were tens of thousands. Steven Wozniak and Steve Jobs created Apple,[2] while Microsoft, founded in 1975, became dominant in the mid-1980s with the arrival of MS-DOS.[3] Silicon Valley became the home of dozens of small computer companies.[4]

Innovations in space travel were highlighted by the short but illustrious career of Ronald E. McNair. A 1971 physics graduate, he returned to speak for convocation at the dawn of the decade,[5] and would offer steady encouragement of space sciences at

Aggies are hoping to become the next business mogul or technology star. The annual Career Fair helps them make that first connection. Here, a General Motors representative talks with students.

A&T, including the shuttle experiment program. "In September 1967 I arrived at A&T, a predominantly black institution, to pursue a degree in physics, though I could barely say the word," he commented. "I went on to graduate in physics, with honors, on schedule and armed with the tools that would launch my career on a trajectory through graduate school, into the industrial laboratories and, ultimately around the earth aboard the space shuttle."[6] In 1983, A&T signed contracts with NASA for research valued at $1.7 million, the largest research grant ever for the School of Engineering.[7] Aggies boarded buses

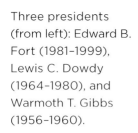

Three presidents (from left): Edward B. Fort (1981–1999), Lewis C. Dowdy (1964–1980), and Warmoth T. Gibbs (1956–1960).

Dr. Ronald McNair '71 (right) is shown with Dr. Thomas Sandin of physics. *Thomas Sandin*.

for the Kennedy Space Center to view his first shuttle flight on January 29, 1984.[8] Two years later, McNair died in the *Challenger* explosion,[9] but the university's student-built laboratory would fly aboard the space shuttle *Endeavour* in his honor in 1994.[10]

The 1980s were sometimes called the "me decade," but political awareness was not forgotten at A&T. The decade opened with tributes, 20 years after the sit-ins, as the Woolworth's store hosted the Greensboro Four and a historical marker was placed. Andrew Young, civil rights leader and former U.S. ambassador to the UN, charged that blacks in North Carolina were becoming complacent.[11] A&T and visiting college students staged a rally and heard from the Rev. Ben Chavis of the Wilmington 10.[12] Later in the year, some 300 Aggies were among 12,000 students who gathered in Washington for a Black College Day rally.[13] Rosa Parks urged students to "become concerned, aware and dedicated to the quest for freedom, equality and peace for all mankind."[14]

The university farm in the 1980s. International exchange programs often involved agriculture.

The university's increased global involvement showed in the 400 international students on campus, as well as exchange and training programs with African and Caribbean nations.[15] Fifteen Nigerians graduated from a two-year industrial technology program,[16] and a Chinese ag-ed team visited.[17] Basketball Coach Gene Littles recruited a Senegalese player.[18] By 1981, the campus had 500 international students representing 50 nations, and students were having difficulty in finding housing.[19]

The university was growing, with $18 million in construction projects, including a new $2.2 million social sciences building and a new radio station.[20] Construction was under way for the new administration building and veterinary sciences building.[21] The football stadium would open in September of the following year.[22] Gov. Jim Hunt cut the ribbon on a demonstration solar-heated home and Garrett House became a solar demonstration facility.[23, 24]

Constance Hill Marteena left a bequest of $120,371 to fund the Marteena Scholars program in mechanical engineering. Her husband, Jerald M. Marteena, former dean of engineering, was memorialized in the naming of the new $2.7 million physical sciences building.[25] The computer science program was approved as part of a redesigned Department of Mathematics and Computer Science.[26]

For the first time at A&T, the Department of Military Science's cadet battalion was commanded by a woman, Beverly Godfrey.[27] The University Choir got a standing ovation for recreating *Wings Over Jordan* at the annual meeting of the Association for the Study of African-American Life and History. A&T's choir had appeared in that show, the first autonomous black radio program, in the 1930s–1940s.[28]

When Chancellor Dowdy stepped down for health reasons in October,[29] Dr. Cleon Thompson Jr. was named interim chancellor.[30]

The year 1980 brought a new athletic director to campus, Bert

Tailgating becomes a popular part of football season.

Piggott,[31] and that fall, A&T hosted its first cross-country meet.[32] Football coach Jim McKinley was named Coach of the Year.[33]

In January 1981, President Ronald Reagan launched his "supply side" economic program. Social spending was slashed by $41 billion, and the repercussions of Reaganomics would be felt on the A&T campus for many years.[34]

The Delta Sigma Theta Sorority presented its Jabberwock Pageant to raise scholarship funds, as it had since 1964.[35] The landscape architecture program prepared to graduate its first class, also a first among HBCUs.[36]

Dr. Edward Fort, named chancellor in late August, said, "I envision an expanded world-class university, one that sustains its destiny as a major economic development force in this state and nation."[37] A&T's engineering school was among six HBCUs participating in a $1.8 million package for faculty development from Exxon Education Foundation.[38] Businesses and industry were investing on campus, and A&T cooperated with the Greensboro Chamber of Commerce, Winston-Salem State, and Bennett in sponsoring an international trade show.[39] A&T also joined Appalachian State and UNC Wilmington to form the Appropriate Technology Consortium, focused on renewable or recyclable resources.[40]

The year 1982 was a big year for Aggie sports. Dwaine "Pee Wee" Board became the second Aggie to claim a Super Bowl ring, as a San

Francisco 49er. The first was Cornell Gordon with the New York Jets.[41] A&T's basketball squad defeated Howard to take the MEAC title[42] and Donald Corbett repeated as Coach of the Year.[43] Maurice "Mo" Forte was named the football coach in April,[44] and Orby Z. Moss Jr. was hired as athletic director in the fall.[45]

Dr. Rosalyn S. Yalow, 1977 Nobel Prize winner, lectured on radioactivity in the Natural Science Honors Colloquium sponsored by Minority Access to Research Careers.[46] Maya Angelou spoke to a packed house, focusing on black American poetry and reading from her own work.[47] Radio station WNAA was building a tower and planned to go to 10,000 watts by December.[48] In the next year, it would go to a 24-hour format and be named the Black College Radio

Station of the Year.[49] Chancellor Fort visited the White House to mark the anniversary of an executive order to strengthen the nation's HBCUs.[50] A&T received a $650,000 Title III grant to strengthen academic and administrative programs.[51]

The years from 1982 to 1985 saw major accomplishments for black Americans. Alice Walker's novel *The Color Purple* won the 1983 Pulitzer Prize and the National Book Award. Michael Jackson's *Thriller* soared, Vanessa Williams was crowned Miss America in 1983, and Harold Washington became the first African American mayor of Chicago.[52] Two former Aggies made history: former state senator Henry E. Frye became the state's first black Supreme Court justice,[53] and Edolphus Towns became the first Aggie elected to Congress.[54]

Engineering students were recognized at the NACME Forum in 1982 in Dallas, Texas. Among the honorees is Carlton Coles of A&T (back row, third from left).

The fountain in front of the student
union is a popular gathering place.

Noteworthy accomplishments at A&T included the School of Agriculture receiving its largest single grant ever, $4 million from the USDA, to renovate research facilities and purchase land and equipment.[55] The Richard B. Harrison Players won the Kennedy Center/ American College Theatre Festival's Best College Production. In addition, a BFA in Professional Dramatics was approved.[56] The School of Nursing gained full accreditation by the National League of Nursing.[57]

It wasn't all bookwork, however. Aggies enjoyed A&T's first outdoor all-day concert as part of the 1983 Aggiefest, featuring Grand Master Flash.[58] Students were styling at Blumenthal's with Levi jeans at $16.97 and Izod shirts at $18.97. A Wachovia ad touted a new automated teller machine system, including one on Bessemer Avenue.[59]

Maxine Laverne Jones was selected as one of the 10 Outstanding Young Women in America for 1982.[60] Rep. Towns addressed commencement exercises,[61] which included the graduation of twins Lorrance and Torrance Lawson, the last of seven children from a Roxboro farm family to matriculate from A&T.[62] Legislative leaders gave the go-ahead for an $8.4

Aggie Lawrence McSwain '70 continued his career by moving from the district attorney's office to become a district court judge. Here, he is congratulated by family, friends, and colleagues.

million engineering building,[63] and a new undergraduate degree in communications was approved.[64]

Aggie sports rolled again in 1983 as James "The Bird" Sparrow claimed the A&T scoring record in basketball[65] and A&T took the MEAC basketball championship.[66] The Aggie cross-country team won the MEAC championship,[67] as did women's volleyball.[68] Tailback Mike Jones represented A&T at the Freedom Bowl.[69]

Two special visitors highlighted the year. Home run king Hank Aaron came to campus for the Sickle Cell Banquet.[70] Shomari "Peedie" Snipes, a child with the rare aging disease progeria, visited campus and became an honorary Aggie, and was featured on the cover of *Jet* magazine.[71]

The Rev. Jesse Jackson, frequently on campus as a member of the Board of Trustees as well as a speaker, visited as part of a voter registration crusade throughout the South.[72] Months of anticipation culminated in the announcement of his candidacy for president.[73] During his vigorous campaign, Jackson garnered 18 percent of the vote. In 1988, Jackson tried again, but lost the nomination to Michael Dukakis:[74, 75] "Dr. Martin Luther King Jr. lies only a few miles from us tonight. Tonight he must feel good

as he looked down on us. We sit here together, a rainbow, a coalition—the sons and daughters of slavemasters and the sons and daughters of slaves, sitting together around a common table to decide the direction of our party and our country."[76]

The late King's contributions were recognized when, in 1984, A&T's Board of Trustees authorized his birthday as a university holiday.[77] President Reagan had signed the national holiday into law in November 1983.[78]

The city was buffeted by emotional currents that spring. In March, classes were cancelled as A&T and the city of Greensboro turned out to honor astronaut Ron McNair with a convocation, a march downtown, and McNair's address to the Annual Army/Air Force Banquet and Ball.[79] Less than a month later, *The Register* headlined, "All White Jury finds klansmen and Nazis not guilty." Five demonstrators had been killed and six wounded in the 1979 incident at a Greensboro housing project.[80]

Robert Maynard, the first black publisher and editor of a major metropolitan daily newspaper, spoke to the Mass Media Careers Conference.[81] Other visitors that year included Lerone Bennett, historian and *Ebony* editor;[82] Dick Gregory;[83] and Roberta Flack, a native of Black Mountain, North Carolina, who performed a benefit show for the James B. Hunt senatorial campaign at the Corbett Sports Center.[84]

A Jesse Jackson campaign bumper sticker. The former SGA president ran for president of the United States in 1984 and 1988.

4President.org

Architectural engineering students prepare their float for the Homecoming parade. *VICKI COLEMAN.*

A&T participated in a $19 million grant to improve livestock management in Niger,[85] and the Center for Energy Research and Technology was founded in 1984 as "a multidisciplinary research, teaching and outreach facility."[86] The Minority Biomedical Research Support program and Health Careers Opportunity Program worked to promote access by minorities to health research and the health professions.[87]

Charles D. Bussey, a 1955 English graduate and the first A&T grad to attain the rank of general in the U.S. Army, was named chief of public affairs for the Department of the Army and promoted to major general.[88] "At A&T, I had teachers and professors who cared, and unique opportunities to get involved," he said.[89]

Reagan returned to the White House in a landslide, and Chancellor Fort warned that higher education budget cuts would affect A&T.[90]

Reagan opposed civil rights laws and supported a constitutional amendment outlawing busing to achieve school integration.[91] Jail populations increased, until by the end of the 1980s, over a million Americans were incarcerated. Another pressing problem was the Reagan Administration's refusal to acknowledge AIDS (Acquired Immune Deficiency Syndrome). Traffic in marijuana, cocaine, and heroin thrived, with America in the mid-1980s the world's major consumer of illegal drugs.[92] However, there were pockets of success. Reginald Lewis acquired Beatrice International Food Co. with sales over $1 billion, inspiring generations of African American business moguls and Wall Street executives.[93, 94]

The year 1985 marked the 25th anniversary of the sit-ins, with speeches by the A&T Four and the unveiling of a bas-relief in the student union.[95] The campus had a

The seven members of the Space Shuttle 51-L flight, which was lost on takeoff. Front row (from left): Mike Smith, Commander Dick Scobee, and Ron McNair. Back row: El Onizuka, "Teacher in Space" Christa McAuliffe, Greg Jarvis, and Judy Resnik. *NASA.*

spate of prank bomb threats, and six people eventually were charged.[96, 97] Such events had the campus on edge, but traditional pranks continued—students who participated in a "panty raid" faced a $40 fine.[98]

Natalie Cole and Frankie Beverly spoke out against apartheid during a discussion sponsored by Students United for a Free South Africa.[99]

J. W. R. Grandy, superintendent of grounds, retired after 42 years.[100] At graduation, marketing major Robert Nicholas Carter, a 29-year-old father who commuted 72 miles to attend classes, was the top-ranking honor graduate.[101] The naming of 15 buildings and streets was a highlight of Founders Day.[102] Theatre Arts won the National Lorraine

Hansberry Playwriting Contest and the American Revolution Playwriting Contest for *The Peace Maker.*[103]

Members of the university's Student Space Shuttle Program led by Dr. Stuart Ahrens, physics professor, were anticipating McNair's shuttle flight in early 1986. Their student-designed spaceflight experiments, inspired by McNair, eventually flew on *Endeavour* in 1994.[104] But on February 11, 1986, after the loss of the *Challenger*, the front page of *The Register* was a single photo of McNair with the motto, "With his dreams, he reached beyond the stars, thus giving us courage to dream and achieve." An estimated 3,500 people crowded into Moore Gymnasium for a memorial.[105]

The Aggies retained the MEAC basketball title for a fifth year.[106] In football, the Aggies beat Delaware State for a share of the 1986 MEAC title.[107]

Six students enrolled in the new engineering Ph.D. program, a cooperative effort with NC State and UNC Charlotte.[108] The chancellor set a new library as his number-one priority and requested $15.5 million to build it.[109] Dr. Sidney Evans, director of agricultural research, received the George Washington Carver Award and was inducted into the Public Service Hall of Fame.[110]

Apartheid was an ongoing topic of conversation for A&T students. During Southern African Awareness Week, an exiled South African spoke[111] and the Rev. Jesse Jackson told students that registering and voting were part of their "moral obligation to fight Apartheid."[112] The Board of Trustees chairman pledged to provide information concerning the university's investments to a student anti-apartheid group.[113]

A new theatrical tradition began in 1986 with the debut of *Black Nativity*, which would become a holiday staple for the Triad.[114]

The Division of Industrial Education and Technology, which traced its beginnings to early "trade programs," became the School of Technology in 1986, as its programs proved to be a good avenue to job placement. In 1987, the new school offered 10 undergraduate degrees. Master's degrees followed and a Ph.D. in Technology Management. Price Hall, the school's original home, was renovated in 1988, and a new $7.9 million Samuel and Angeline Smith Hall was dedicated in the fall of 1998.[115]

In the final years of the Reagan presidency, the Iran Contra scandal erupted, the stock market crashed, and Reagan softened his approach to the Soviets with his speech in

A scene from *Black Nativity*.

Here, a group of students walk near Crosby Hall in 1995.

Brig. Gen. Clara Adams-Ender directed the nursing corps at Walter Reed Hospital, part of an Aggie legacy of military leadership.

West Berlin on June 12, 1987: "Mr. Gorbachev, tear down this wall!"[116]

The end of the Cold War was accompanied by better times for the economy, and expanding opportunities for women. Sandra Day O'Connor, the first woman to be appointed to the U.S. Supreme Court, represented many who entered the professional and corporate worlds as well as politics. Laws were enacted to help women obtain credit, start businesses, and buy homes.[117, 118] Oprah Winfrey appeared on Chicago television in 1984 as the first African American woman to host a popular talk show "where she kicked off her heels and pulled up her chair into homes across the heartland."[119] By 2014, she became *Forbes*' only African American billionaire.[120]

Issues of black identity and participation in American life continued to be debated on campus. More than 50 A&T students joined 20,000 protesting racial policies in an all-white Georgia County.[121] Former Cleveland mayor Carl Stokes spoke as part of Black History Month.[122] In Greensboro, Aggie Sylvester Daughtry became the first black police chief.[123]

Other national and international issues remained in the news. Students answered "man on the street" surveys about AIDs, and Gov. Jim Martin declared AIDS Awareness Week.[124] The Warmoth T. Gibbs Lecture Series was inaugurated.[125] Students listened to Isaac Hayes talk about the recording industry during a stop at WNAA,[126] and heard S.O.S. and Salt and Pepa perform during a week-long anti-apartheid festival which had replaced Aggie Fest.[127]

In other student news, the Kappa Alpha Psi Fraternity chapter was honored as the national Chapter of the Year.[128] A&T's Gospel Choir won first place in the National Collegiate Gospel Competition in New York City.[129] Senior Anita Hudson was one of 30 HBCU students honored with the Student Award for Excellence in Science and Technology by President Reagan.[130]

Nursing alumna Clara Adams-Ender '61 received her star and promotion to brigadier general in Washington, D.C., where she was chief of the Department of Nursing at Walter Reed Army Hospital. She was the only black female general on active duty with the U.S. Army and the second Aggie to achieve that rank, joining Maj. Gen. Charles D. Bussey.[131] Both generals served as commencement speakers.

Jesse Britt, an Aggies receiver, became an NFL player in the fall of 1986 with the Pittsburgh Steelers.[132] The Aggie basketball team won the MEAC tournament.[133]

In 1988, two years to the day after his death, Ronald McNair was memorialized with the rededication of the engineering building in his honor.[134] Later in the year, A&T was selected for an $8.4 million NASA program with NC State to help send manned vehicles to Mars and beyond.[135] A&T was also

selected to operate a $3.6 million Space Technology Development and Utilization program.[136]

Susan Taylor, editor of *Essence* magazine, told students to take charge of their lives. "Do you know who you are? You are that group that W.E.B. Du Bois challenged. You are the talented tenth."[137]

The theatre program's Bachelor of Fine Arts gained accreditation in 1988, a first for an HBCU and for the UNC system, and only the second in the nation.[138]

Bill Hayes was lured away from Winston-Salem State to become A&T's new head football coach.[139] Alan Hooker, who held most of A&T's passing records, was signed by the Dallas Cowboys.[140] A&T

An architect's rendering of McNair Hall. *E. Jenkins.*

senior Ruth Morris competed in the Summer Olympics as a member of the track and field team for her native Virgin Islands.[141]

Virginia McKee, administrative assistant to the chancellor, was honored with a luncheon as she began her 40th year of service. She had worked with six presidents/chancellors.[142] Members of the Legislative Black Caucus helped break ground for the new library.[143] The university partnered with the Southeastern Forest Experiment Station to encourage more blacks to enter forestry and natural resources fields.[144] A new master's degree was initiated in Plant and Soil Science.[145]

The final year of the decade opened with Yolanda King, daughter of Martin Luther King Jr., addressing black apathy at the convocation honoring her father.[146] Jazz trumpeter Wynton Marsalis spoke to a capacity crowd,[147] and poet Nikki Giovanni encouraged students to be proud of their heritage. "If we haven't taught the world anything else we've taught the world how to forgive," she said.[148] Public Enemy appeared in a predawn Homecoming dance, having recently topped the charts with "Fight the Power."[149]

Dr. Benjamin Carson, director of pediatric neurosurgery at Johns Hopkins Children's Center, spoke at Honors Convocation, telling students that he struggled academically in his early years and that faith played a major role in his success.[150]

As the AIDS epidemic continued, awareness was increasing at A&T. Jackie Greenlee, health educator at the Sebastian Health Center, warned students that they must change their habits: "AIDS does not discriminate."[151] Student government backed the idea of condom machines in the dorms and students voted 827 to 292 in favor.[152]

The C.H. Moore Agricultural Research Facility was dedicated, keeping the name of the former Charles Moore Elementary School that once occupied the building.[153] A&T retained third place for research funding in the 16-school public system.[154] Dr. Alex Williamson received the research achievement award from the National Association for Equal Opportunity in Higher Education,[155] and AT&T donated $1 million for equipment and scholarships.[156] The National Science Foundation awarded $2.5 million for telecommunications research.[157]

Dr. Ben Carson (left) with Chancellor Edward Fort and Dr. Edward Hayes, vice chancellor of academic affairs.

The 1990s saw notable achieve-
ments, including an increase in
the number of black public offi-
cials in major cities. In Virginia,
Douglas Wilder became the first
African American governor since
Reconstruction.[158] Black women
excelled. In 1993 alone, three black
women became the first in their fields:
Dr. Jocelyn Elders as surgeon general,
Toni Morrison winning the Nobel
Prize in Literature, and Rita Dove as
poet laureate of the United States.[159]
August Wilson won his second Pulitzer
Prize,[160] and his plays were performed
by the A&T Theatre Department.

The recession of the early 1990s
saw about nine million workers without jobs. Housing starts, car sales,
and businesses suffered as the weak-
ness of the U.S. economy saw an ero-
sion of middle-class family finances,
including African Americans who
had experienced gains in the 1980s.[161]

As the 1990s dawned at A&T,
African American heritage was
celebrated in poetry, music, and art.
"Afrocentric consciousness is on the
rise," headlined a story about the
movement that began in the 1960s.
"Blacks have not been given credit
for their contributions to the world,"
said history instructor Sandrea
Williamson.[162] The 30th anniversary
of the sit-ins included renaming
the adjoining street as February
One Place. A monument was also
unveiled outside the Memorial
Student Union.[163] The Hon. Minister
Louis Farrakhan addressed an estimated 10,000 people in the Corbett
Sports Center, discussing the wave
of black-on-black crime.[164] Dizzy
Gillespie appeared as part of the
Black American Arts Festival.[165]
Vandorn Hinnant, a 1981 art graduate, was the first to be exhibited
in the Artist Gallery at Greenboro's

Actors Ruby Dee
and Ossie Davis
(left) meet with
students during one
of their visits.

A detail shot of the North Carolina Agricultural and Technical Centennial Story quilt, "Common Roots," which took almost three years to make. Fifty-nine blocks depict events and people that figured prominently in the life of this great institution. More than 100 people lent their talents to design the blocks or do the stitchery. The quilt remains on display in the Bluford Library.

new Green Hill Center for North Carolina Art.[166]

A&T reached out to help Bennett students who were displaced after a fire in a dorm.[167] The Pershing Rifles, a military fraternal organization, honored former member Ernest "Willie" Grimes, who had been shot and killed in 1969 following a day of unrest at Dudley High School.[168] A group of quilters, including faculty, staff, students, alumni, and community friends, was at work on a project to celebrate the university's centennial in 1991.[169]

Dr. Willie James Burden became the new athletic director.[170] Miss A&T Sharron K. Jenkins won the title of Miss Hall of Fame during that inaugural year for A&T in the National Black College Alumni Hall of Fame Queens Competition in Atlanta.[171]

Aggies returned in 1991 to the sounds of war. "Aggies called to serve in 'Operation Desert Storm,'" read the headline in *The Register*:[172] "Several students withdrew from the university to serve in the battlefields of the Middle East." The Gulf War was waged by a coalition led by the United States in response to Iraq's invasion and annexation of Kuwait. President George H. W. Bush ordered an Allied air assault, and 700,000 troops attacked Iraqi positions, leading to a swift victory. Cable News Network played a major role as American audiences watched around the clock.[173] On campus, support groups sprang up, with a "Say a Prayer Program" and a Wall of Heroes.[174]

President Bush had a more divisive issue later in the year, when he nominated Clarence Thomas to replace retired justice Thurgood Marshall on the Supreme Court. Thomas was confirmed, but only after sensational televised hearings in which a former employee, Anita Hill, accused Thomas of sexual harassment.[175]

January 1991 also marked the launch of the centennial celebration, "Celebration and Challenge: A Second Century." Author Alex Haley and John Jacob, president of the National Urban League, spoke in the Centennial Lecture Series. The new F. D. Bluford Library was dedicated.[176]

Tensions exploded in May 1992 when a California jury acquitted four white police officers charged with brutally beating Rodney King, an African American suspect, as a bystander videotaped the incident. America heard his voice, "Can't we all get along?"[177] but the Los Angeles riots resulted in over 50 deaths and $1 billion in damage. Students debated the King event and other social issues, with the plight of African Americans living in inner cities revealed in John Singleton's *Boyz in the Hood*[178] and Spike Lee's 1989 *Do the Right Thing*. The decade also brought the deaths of rapper/actor Tupac Shakur and rapper Notorious B.I.G. (Biggie Smalls), killed allegedly in East-West Coast rivalry.

Violent crime rates continued to mount during the Bush presidency, and police budgets, prison

Chancellor Fort speaks at the 100th anniversary celebration.

Astronaut Mae
Jemison greets fans.

sentences, and prison construction all increased.[179] Attorney General Richard Thornburgh commented on "the first civil right, the right to be free of fear, in their homes, on their street, and in their communities."[180]

Even as earthly troubles continued, the Hubble Space Telescope gathered astounding images of deep space, and A&T continued its leadership in the space sciences, as one of 12 institutions selected for the Ronald McNair Post-Baccalaureate Achievement Program to prepare low-income and first-generation students for summer research programs.[181] Dr. Mae Jemison, the first female black astronaut, gave the address at the McNair tribute, saying, "Students force the university to keep up, grow, expand and to face the changing world."[182]

The 120-piece Marching Machine was declared Best All-Around Group in the Battle of the Bands at the

The horn section of the A&T Marching Band in practice.

Children play and learn at the Child Development playground.

institution by the Historically Black Research University Foundation for Science and Technology, enhancing funding for science, engineering, technology, and business programs.[186]

The Board of Governors approved A&T's doctoral programs in electrical and mechanical engineering[187] and the former library building became the Interdisciplinary Research Center.[188] A&T received a $1.2 million Title III grant from the U.S. Department of Education.[189]

On a more controversial note, the Faculty Forum voted against instituting a mandatory six hours of black studies classes, instead choosing to strongly encourage such classes as core options in curricula. This would spark a protest in the fall semester and a call for a re-vote.[190] In early 1994, A&T made six hours of black studies mandatory.[191]

invitational Bronze Classic, held in Atlanta.[183] At the beginning of the year, quarterback Connell Maynor was named Offensive Player of the Year for the MEAC.[184]

Funding for research continued to grow. A&T was one of four HBCUs selected in the Dow Chemical Co.'s Take Initiative Program, and received a $1.4 million grant from the U.S. Department of Education for academic and support programs.[185] The university was designated as a research

Aggies remember special Homecoming events, from the Gospel Show to the Comedy Connection. This ticket is from 1993. *STEPHANIE LUSTER-TEASLEY.*

GENERAL ADMISSION
TKT. NO. 189
★★★★★★★★★★★★
NO REFUND-NO EXCHANGE

N.C.
A & T
S.G.A.
PRESENTS
AGGIE NATION
COMEDY
CONNECTION
HOMECOMING 93
* * * * * * *
CORBETT
SPORTS CENTER

ADM. $2.00

TUE 8:00 P.M.
ADMIT ONE - THIS DATE
OCT. 19, 1993
★★★★★★★★★★★★
TKT. NO. 189
GENERAL
ADMISSION

Senior theatre majors Roz Fox and Theron McConneyhead won at the Region IV American College Theatre Festival and went on to the national festival.[192] Charter members were inducted into the university's new chapter of the Golden Key National Honor Society.[193] In alumni news, a 1969 A&T chemistry graduate, James Mitchell, was named the 1993 Black Engineer of the Year.[194]

Three Aggie football players were taken in the NFL draft: Craig Thompson by the Bengals, and Kevin Little and Reggie White by the Chargers.[195]

William Jefferson Clinton's arrival at the White House was met with enthusiasm and the question, what improvements would African Americans see? Shortly after taking office, he signed the Family and Medical Leave Act of 1993,[196] proposed the first balanced budget in decades, and achieved a budget surplus.[197] His first term saw terrorism challenge America, with the 1993 truck bomb explosion in the garage under the World Trade Center in New York City and the 1995 Oklahoma City bombing.[198]

The death of Thurgood Marshall brought an end to an era on the nation's high court.[199] A month later, another hero would die, as tennis great Arthur Ashe was lost to AIDS.[200] Two months later, the campus would be mourning as former president Gibbs died at the age of 101.[201]

In 1993, the Division of Research, formerly the Office of Research Administration, became the official unit to administer all sponsored program activities. Dr. Ernestine Psalmonds became the first vice chancellor for research.[202] A&T received a $3 million grant from the W.K. Kellogg Foundation to support doctoral programs in electrical and mechanical engineering,[203] followed closely by a $5 million grant over five years from the U.S. Department of Transportation.[204]

The Aggies baseball team rolled to win the MEAC championship, the first since 1974, under new coach Keith Henry.[205]

A&T officials were elated after North Carolina voters passed a $310 million University Improvement Bond Referendum. A&T stood to gain more than $13 million, including money for a new technology building.[206] A major announcement topped

The baseball team celebrates after a win. *University Relations/Charles E. Watkins.*

Faculty march in regalia at Founders Day 1994.

the news in early 1994, as plans were unveiled to turn the closed Woolworth's store into a museum honoring the A&T Four and civil rights efforts.[207]

A&T students were reaching new heights in academics. Ten Air Force cadets took off from PTI as the first participants in the joint Civil Air Patrol/ROTC Test Program.[208] A&T won the National Association of Industrial Technology Outstanding Student Chapter Award.[209] Gloria Dyson Peay and Lonnie Cathey Jr., longtime university employees and students in the School of Business and Economics, returned from an all-expenses-paid trip to Germany through the Hoechst Celanese Marketing Challenge.[210] The laboratory built by physics professor Dr. Stuart Ahrens and A&T's Student Space Shuttle Program was approved to launch on the shuttle *Endeavour* in August.[211] The university hosted its first Honda Campus All-Star Challenge[212] and the

1994 Black Student Summit.[213] The Interdisciplinary Waste Management Institute was approved by the General Administration.[214] This unit offers a certificate program, coordinates instruction and research in waste management, and serves as a clearinghouse for the university's environmental efforts.

Speaking on campus during this time were Gov. James Hunt and Lori Hayes, alumna and actress.[215] Rep. Eva Clayton of the First Congressional District, the first black woman to be elected to that post in North Carolina, was the 1994 commencement speaker,[216] while Randall Robinson, executive director of TransAfrica, spoke in 1995.[217]

The Aggies made the NCAA tournament, defeating longtime nemesis South Carolina State for the bid to face Arkansas.[218] At the end of the semester, basketball coach Jeff Capel announced he was leaving for Old Dominion University.[219]

Computers were becoming a part of daily campus life. Here, Chancellor Fort looks at a screen in the Computer Center (second from left), while chancellor-to-be Harold Martin watches from the far right.

# ROBOTICS LABORATORY

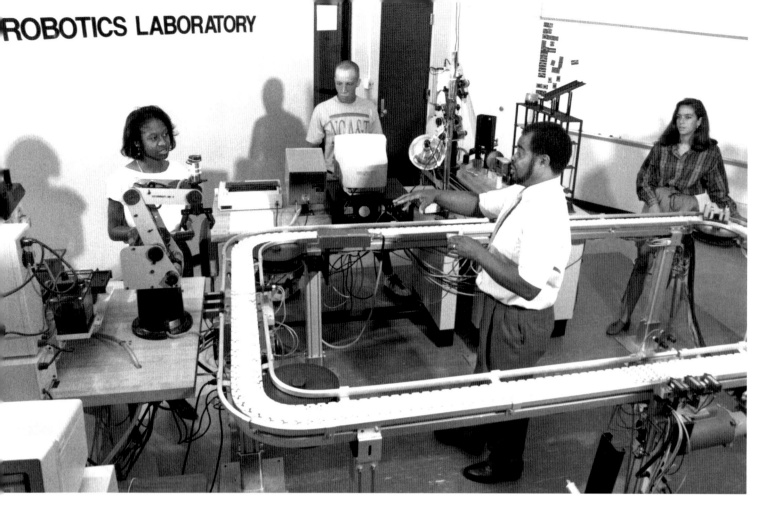

TOP: The School of Technology was operating a robotics laboratory in 1993.

BOTTOM LEFT: Dr. Willie Willis instructs a student at the animal science laboratory.

BOTTOM RIGHT: Gathered in the engineering lab are (from left) Dr. Reza Salami, Dr. Robert Sadler, Dr. Kunigal Shivakumar, Dr. Vishu Avva, Lonnie Sharpe (dean), Hobson Skeen, Dr. Earnestine Psalmonds, and Dr. Derome Dunn '78.

LEFT: CSPAN comes to campus, bringing real-world experience to journalism students.

BELOW: M. R. Reddy of Natural Resources and Environmental Design is shown working with a gas chromatograph.

Students work at Macs in computer room 271.

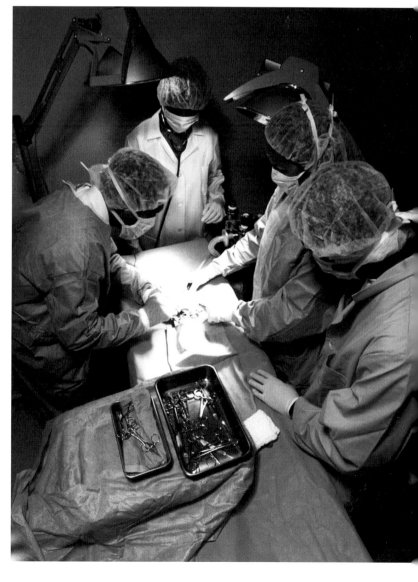

Surgery in the animal science laboratory.

At the midpoint of the decade, the founders of Google met as Sergey Brin gave Larry Page a tour of Stanford. Two years later, Google.com was registered as a domain.[220] Electronic companies based in the United States led the world in desktop computers, software applications, and telecommunications. High school and college graduates entered one of the strongest job markets for young people in decades.[221] At A&T, classrooms were redesigned to accommodate computers, and the School of Technology received a $2.3 million grant for the Center for Electronics Manufacturing.[222]

As vans, pickup trucks, and SUVs became popular, they found a lot of fans on the A&T campus.

A&T won its first-ever women's MEAC track title. First-year head coach Ruth Morris was named top women's coach, while Roy Thompson received the same honor after leading the Aggies to their second straight men's track championship.[223]

From 1995 to 1998, the economy grew at an annual rate of 3.4 percent, recovering from recession. America led the world in efficiency, and U.S. automakers controlled the market for popular minivans, light trucks, and sports utility vehicles.[224] All could be found in the parking lots of A&T—where student violators found themselves facing

Engineering students have their bags packed for a trip with professor Ron Bailey.

"boots on wheels" and heavy fines in A&T's Parking Division.[225]

Domestic violence and sexual abuse were discussed more openly. America was consumed by media coverage of O.J. Simpson, who fled police on the California freeway and then faced trial for murder.[226] His acquittal sparked controversy—"the basic reaction at A&T was overwhelming relief over the jury's decision, as evident by the cheers and applause in Crosby Hall and Student Union when the verdict was read."[227]

Buses filled with men from A&T and surrounding communities traveled to Washington to participate in the Million Man March.[228] Debates erupted as groups who felt marginalized from mainstream America demanded cultural and political equality. The term "multiculturalism" appeared, and conservatives tried to eliminate federal funding for the arts, humanities, and public television.[229, 230]

A&T became the first black university to design and produce integrated circuit chips, with funding by the National Science Foundation and the Microelectronics Center of North Carolina.[231] A&T hosted the first national student conference of the National Alliance of NASA University Research Centers,[232] and the Ronald McNair Fellowship Program to support students in space program research was established in the College of Engineering.[233]

The Joint Master of Social Work formation working group brought together faculty from A&T and UNCG, meeting in 1983 at UNCG's Piney Lake Retreat Center. Standing (from left): Robert Wineburg, Abdulla Hagey, Sarah Kirk, Jerry Finn, Tom Scullion, Larry Shornack, and David Johnson. Seated: Christine Boone, Patti Spakes, Ruthena Smith (Marley), Virginia Stephens, Yolanda Burwell, and George Allen. *DAVID JOHNSON.*

A&T meets an illustrious rival, Wake Forest, during the Tim Duncan (#21) era.

The Fugees, Tribe Called Quest, Busta Rhymes, and Outkast were slated for Homecoming, but SGA's decision to hold the concert at the Greensboro Coliseum for the first time in four years created rumors that a merger with UNCG was imminent.[234] In an interesting juxtaposition, UNCG and A&T did unite to offer a Joint Master of Social Work program.[235] A&T was ranked first among HBCUs for allocations from the U.S. Department of Agriculture.[236]

No one was more able to unite America than Michael Jordan, who led the Chicago Bulls to their fifth NBA championship in 1997. The slogan was "I Want to Be Like Mike," and

A&T was, as the Aggies became one of three Division I men's basketball teams to feature Jordan's clothing line.[237] The campus was also elated when Tiger Woods in 1997 became the first African American and the youngest golfer ever to win the Masters.[238] A&T's football standout Toran James was signed by the San Diego Chargers.[239]

The Aggie Shuttle service began on February 10, 1997, operating 10 hours a day. AggieONEcard debuted in three phases, starting with admission to the cafeteria and athletic events, and library privileges.[240] The organization formerly known as Mo'del Unique became Couture.[241] The A&T theatre program marked its 99th year[242] and one of its graduates, Licia Shearer, made her big-screen debut in the hip-hop comedy, *How to Be a Player*.[243]

The AIDS Memorial Quilt was displayed at Moore Gym from November 30 to December 2.[244] Among other changes on campus, Barbee and Cooper halls added Internet service, and registration for the spring semester of 1998 was done by telephone, with plans to move to the Web.[245] Dr. Chi Anyansi-Archibong became president of the North American Case Research Association.[246]

The Lady Aggies swim team debuted in the fall of 1997; a bowling team had been added in the spring

An A&T emblem was placed on the *Ferry Cape Point*, one of 16 North Carolina ferries bearing the colors and emblem of the UNC system schools.

Dr. Japhet Nkonge and Dr. Chi Anyansi-Archibong, faculty in the expanding School of Business and Economics.

semester.[247] Chris McNeil was Division I-AA first team All-American defense, and Division I-AA Defensive Player of the Year. He joined James Clyburn at the postseason Hula Bowl.[248]

Although fewer than half of all Americans of voting age went to the polls, those who did gave Clinton 49 percent of their votes, Bob Dole 41 percent, and Ross Perot 9 percent.[249] Personal demons, however, would haunt Clinton's presidency. As a result of issues surrounding personal

indiscretions with intern Monica Lewinsky, Clinton became the second U.S. president to be impeached. He was found not guilty by the Senate.[250] On the world stage, Clinton sent peacekeeping forces to Bosnia and bombed Iraq when Saddam Hussein stopped UN weapons inspections.

The year 1998 marked a special year for A&T, as the first doctorates were awarded in May. Alfred Burress, an electrical engineer, was the first candidate to defend his dissertation.[251] The Physics of Materials Laboratory was established with a $2 million grant from the National Science Foundation and $500,000 from the state.[252] A&T was ranked the number-one producer of minority

Dr. Gilbert Casterlow conducts a summer calculus workshop. A&T has a long history of leadership in STEM disciplines.

graduates in STEM disciplines.[253] A&T's women's bowling team had an undefeated season and second consecutive MEAC title.[254]

In the fall of 1999, at the request of then-vice chancellor for academic affairs Dr. Harold L. Martin Sr. and under the leadership of Dr. Peter Meyers, the University Honors Program began with 50 students and a few specially designated general education classes.[255] The program has since grown to over 600 students representing nearly every academic department on campus. "We aim to develop the students academically and socially as they prepare to enter into the next phase of their lives." Graduates have gone on to Harvard, Vanderbilt, and a host of other major graduate programs.[256]

Clinton's final years in office included the grim task of addressing the nation about the Columbine High School massacre. He proposed an expanded NATO, proposed a significant increase for civil rights enforcement,[257] and was praised for promoting the well-being of women, minorities, and the poor.[258]

The decade closed with the announcement that student fees were going up to pay for a parking deck, cafeteria renovations, expanded Aggie Shuttle, and 24-hour computer labs.[259] The new H. Clinton Taylor Art Gallery opened in the renovated Dudley Building, and the Richard B. Harrison Players were again national winners in the American College Theatre Festival, for *David Richmond*.[260]

Awards were instituted honoring researchers, with Dr. Celestine Ntuen selected as Outstanding Senior Researcher, and Dr. Yong Song as Outstanding Young Investigator.[261] The Minority Institution Technology Support Services Program was set up to support defense-oriented information technology and communication efforts at a group of colleges.[262]

The barbershop in the Memorial Student Union was a place to get a quick trim.

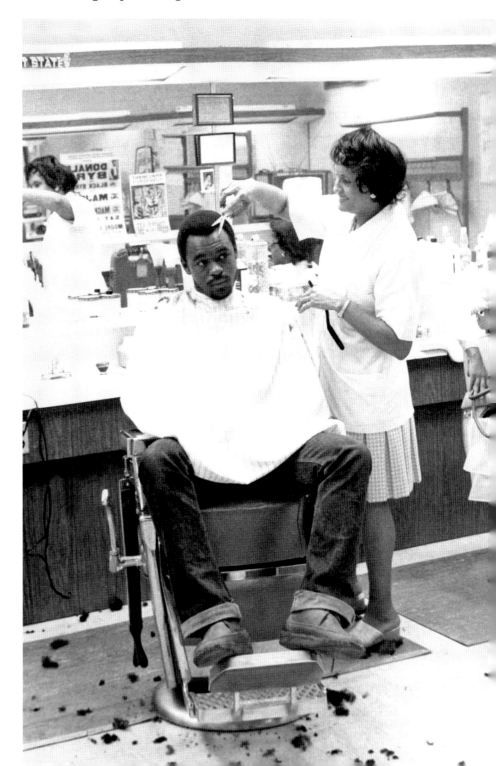

Maurice Hicks
in action.

North Carolina was struck by another disastrous storm. Hurricane Floyd's floodwaters devastated small towns and agricultural areas in the eastern part of the state.[263]

The A&T Fellowship Gospel Choir won top honors in competition in New York.[264] John Hope Franklin returned to the campus where he had taught 62 years before, speaking to the History Department Honors Program,[265] and high school students filled Crosby Hall for the second High School Media Workshop.[266] Justice Henry E. Frye marked another first as he became chief justice.[267]

Roy Thomas stepped down as basketball coach, and assistant Curtis Hunter took over.[268] The football team beat number-one-ranked Tennessee State to move to the second round of the Division I-AA playoffs. Coach Bill Hayes was named Conference Coach of the Year.[269]

Aggies celebrated the past and looked forward to a bright future at the 1999 Homecoming, where Tom Joyner headlined events as part of "The Greatest Homecoming on Earth."[270] A&T received a $3 million grant from Ford Motor Co., the largest corporate gift received to that point,[271] and celebrated its first winter commencement.[272]

The final year of the millennium was marked by some notable moments. Chancellor James Renick was installed.[273] Chemistry professor Dr. Vallie Guthrie, who had started the Greensboro Area

Mathematics and Science Education Center (GAMSEC) in the 1980s to improve math and science skills among secondary school students, was honored with the Presidential Award for Excellence in Science, Mathematics, and Engineering Mentoring.[274] The School of Agriculture became the School of Agriculture and Environmental and Allied Sciences.[275] Troy Pelshak, former Aggies defensive end, earned a Super Bowl ring as a rookie with the St. Louis Rams.[276]

A&T students worked hard to get out the vote for a referendum on the Michael K. Hooker Higher Education Facilities Financial Act, which had been signed by Gov. James B. Hunt Jr. in May 2000. This would mean $153.8 million for improvements at A&T. The $13.1 billion statewide referendum passed on November 7, and planning began to reshape the campus for the next century.[277]

Chancellor James C. Renick is shown with Vernon Stallings '65 and his wife Patricia '64. The Stallings Ballrooms in the expanded Memorial Student Union was named in his honor.

## ENDNOTES

1. "A&T History"
2. Moss, 518
3. McCracken
4. Reimer
5. March 28, 1980
6. Moore, "Hails"
7. November 8, 1983
8. November 29, 1983
9. February 11, 1986
10. September 30, 1994
11. February 5, 1980
12. February 5, 1980
13. September 30, 1980
14. February 22, 1980
15. September 5, 1980
16. January 18, 1980
17. September 5, 1980
18. January 11, 1980
19. January 23, 1981
20. March 18, 1980
21. April 25, 1980
22. August 28, 1981
23. March 14, 1980
24. February 15, 1980
25. August 26, 1980
26. College of Arts & Sciences, [3]
27. September 16, 1980
28. October 24, 1980
29. October 3, 1980
30. October 17, 1980
31. January 11, 1980
32. October 17, 1980
33. December 9, 1980
34. Moss, 536-38
35. March 27, 1981
36. April 10, 1981
37. "Program Upgrades"
38. November 13, 1981
39. February 16, 1982
40. February 23, 1982
41. February 23, 1982
42. March 15, 1982
43. March 19, 1982
44. April 6, 1982
45. September 3, 1982
46. March 19, 1982
47. December 7, 1982
48. September 10, 1982
49. April 8, 1983
50. September 28, 1982
51. October 22, 1982
52. PBS, "Timeline: Modern," 1
53. January 14, 1983
54. November 5, 1982
55. January 21, 1983
56. College of Arts & Sciences, [3]
57. December 9, 1983
58. April 8, 1983
59. September 16, 1983
60. February 25, 1983
61. May 6, 1983
62. May 6, 1983
63. July 1, 1983
64. September 16, 1983
65. January 14, 1983
66. March 15, 1983
67. November 8, 1983
68. November 11, 1983
69. December 9, 1983
70. September 30, 1983
71. December 9, 1983
72. October 21, 1983
73. November 4, 1983
74. PBS, "Timeline: Modern," 1
75. PBS, "Decision"
76. Jackson
77. January 13, 1984
78. Reagan, "King, Jr."
79. March 30, 1984
80. April 17, 1984
81. March 30, 1984
82. March 16, 1984
83. March 23, 1984
84. September 7, 1984
85. February 24, 1984
86. Jones et al., 36
87. Jones et al., 37
88. December 7, 1984
89. Moore, "Hails"
90. February 22, 1985
91. Moss, 559
92. Moss, 555
93. Edmond, "Reginald"
94. Edmond, "Off"
95. February 12, 1985
96. April 19, 1985
97. May 3, 1985
98. February 1, 1985
99. November 25, 1985
100. April 25, 1985
101. May 3, 1985
102. September 24, 1985
103. College of Arts & Sciences, [4]
104. April 11, 1994
105. February 11, 1986
106. March 18, 1986
107. November 14, 1986
108. November 14, 1986
109. September 26, 1986
110. December 5, 1986
111. September 19, 1986
112. September 19, 1986
113. September 26, 1986

## NORTH CAROLINA A&T STATE UNIVERSITY TEACHING EXCELLENCE AWARDEES

UNC Board of Governors Award for Excellence in Teaching

**2015** Dr. Jerono Rotich, Human Performance and Leisure Studies

**2014** Angela K. Miles, School of Business and Economics

**2013** Stephanie Luster-Teasley, College of Engineering

**2012** Teresa Jo Styles, College of Arts and Sciences

**2011** Robert L. Howard, School of Business and Economics

**2010** Antoine J. Alston, School of Agriculture and Environmental Sciences

**2009** Doretha Foushee, College of Arts and Sciences

**2008** Jothi V. Kumar, College of Arts and Sciences

**2007** Mary Smith, College of Arts and Sciences

**2006** Jacqueline A. Williams, School of Business and Economics

**2004** Patricia Shelton, School of Nursing

**2003** Sandra C. Alexander, College of Arts and Sciences

**2002** Susan Wilson, School of Nursing

**2001** Musibau A. Shofoluwe, School of Technology

**2000** Genevieve L. Williams, School of Education

**1999** Arjun D. Kapur, School of Technology

**1998** Marihelen Kamp-Glass, School of Agriculture and Environmental Sciences

**1997** Nancy L. Glenz, School of Technology

**1996** Gilbert Casterlow Jr., College of Arts and Sciences

**1995** Kofi Obeng, School of Business and Economics

114. College of Arts & Sciences, [4]
115. School of Technology
116. Reagan, "East-West Relations"
117. Moss, 540
118. Patterson, J.T., 210-11
119. Jacobs
120. Eum
121. January 30, 1987
122. February 6, 1987
123. January 16, 1987
124. November 6, 1987
125. College of Arts & Sciences, [4]
126. February 27, 1987
127. May 1, 1987
128. February 6, 1987
129. April 10, 1987
130. October 2, 1987
131. September 11, 1987
132. February 13, 1987
133. March 23, 1987
134. January 29, 1988
135. September 9, 1988
136. January 20, 1989
137. September 23, 1988
138. October 28, 1988
139. April 29, 1988
140. April 29, 1988
141. October 7, 1988
142. September 2, 1988
143. November 18, 1988
144. November 4, 1988
145. NCA&TSU Timeline, [8]
146. January 20, 1989
147. February 3, 1989
148. February 17, 1989
149. October 11, 1989
150. March 24, 1989
151. March 13, 1989
152. October 27, 1989
153. April 21, 1989
154. September 15, 1989
155. April 21, 1989
156. October 27, 1989
157. NCA&TSU Timeline, [8]
158. PBS, "Timeline: Modern," 2
159. PBS, "Timeline: Modern," 3
160. PBS, "Timeline: Modern," 2
161. Moss, 575-76
162. January 19, 1990
163. February 2, 1990
164. November 16, 1990
165. February 16, 1990
166. November 2, 1990
167. January 19, 1990
168. February 23, 1990
169. March 23, 1990
170. October 5, 1990
171. Rashid
172. January 18, 1991
173. Moss, 595-96
174. January 25, 1991
175. Patterson, J.T., 251
176. "A&T History"
177. Moss, 577
178. PBS, "Timeline: Modern," 3
179. O'Neill, 45

180. Johnston, A20
181. January 25, 1991
182. February 4, 1991
183. November 11, 1991
184. January 18, 1991
185. November 11, 1991
186. November 23, 1991
187. March 27, 1992
188. March 27, 1992
189. March 2, 1992
190. April 13, 1992
191. February 21, 1994
192. February 14, 1992
193. May 8, 1992
194. March 26, 1993
195. May 8, 1992
196. "Family Medical Leave Act"
197. "William J. Clinton," 42
198. Clinton, "PDD 39"
199. January 29, 1993
200. February 12, 1993
201. April 23, 1993
202. Jones et al., 40
203. February 12, 1993
204. April 23, 1993
205. April 23, 1993
206. November 8, 1993
207. February 7, 1994
208. February 7, 1994
209. January 31, 1994
210. February 21, 1994
211. April 11, 1994
212. March 21, 1994
213. March 28, 1994
214. Jones et al., 41
215. "A&T History"
216. May 2, 1994
217. May 5, 1995
218. March 21, 1994
219. May 2, 1994
220. Page and Brin
221. Moss, 576
222. NCA&TSU Timeline, [9]
223. May 5, 1995
224. Moss, 576
225. October 30, 1997
226. Moss, 578-79
227. November 7, 1995
228. November 7, 1995
229. Moss, 583
230. Patterson, J.T., 291
231. Jones et al., 41
232. NCA&TSU Timeline, [9]
233. Jones et al., 41
234. October 16, 1996
235. December 12, 1996
236. NCA&TSU Timeline, [9]
237. October 2, 1997
238. PBS, "Timeline: Modern," 4
239. College of Arts & Sciecnes, [5]
240. September 26, 1997
241. October 9, 1997
242. October 2, 1997
243. October 9, 1997
244. October 30, 1997
245. November 20, 1997

246. November 20, 1997
247. October 2, 1997
248. December 4, 1997
249. O'Neill, 211
250. Moss, 613
251. January 31, 1998
252. Jones et al., 43
253. NCA&TSU Timeline, [10]
254. March 12, 1998
255. December 3, 1999
256. "Honors Program"
257. Clinton, "Timeline"
258. O'Neill, 382
259. February 12, 1999
260. College of Arts & Sciences, [5]
261. Jones et al., 43
262. Jones et al., 44
263. "Hurricane Floyd"
264. April 16, 1999
265. November 11, 1999
266. November 11, 1999
267. November 11, 1999
268. March 22, 1999
269. December 3, 1999
270. November 5, 1999
271. December 3, 1999
272. NCA&TSU Timeline, [10]
273. February 4, 2000
274. February 5, 2001
275. NCA&TSU Timeline, [10]
276. February 18, 2000
277. October 23, 2000

Veda Stroud (front and center) is shown with a group of Golden Aggies. Alumni celebrating their fiftieth anniversary are traditionally honored at Commencement. Born in 1916, Stroud graduated from A&T and went on to Columbia University. She returned and taught at A&T from the 1940s to 1970s, where her husband Virgil headed the Political Science Department.

CHAPTER SEVEN

*The New Millennium*

2001–2014

The band won the Honda Battle of the Bands in 2014. This artful shot is from the 2013 event. *CHARLES WATKINS/UNIVERSITY RELATIONS.*

The 21st century began with high hopes and controversy on January 1, 2001. With many still focused on Florida recounts, George W. Bush was inaugurated on January 20, the second time a president's son entered the White House, the first being John Quincy Adams, son of the second president.[1]

At A&T, the decade opened with the first awarding of the Human Rights Medal. Lewis A. Brandon III, a 1960 alumnus and social activist, received the medal at the breakfast marking the sit-in movement.[2] The university signed an agreement to accelerate work on the International Civil Rights Center & Museum at the site of the sit-ins.[3]

In what would become a recurrent refrain, the state's budget shortfall led to a "freeze" on the UNC system budget. The School of Business gained approval for new master's degrees. In student life, many dreaded the fallout from a court decision that stopped Napster from sharing copyrighted music,[4] and fashion shows highlighted student designs and new trends. The Office of International Programs and the Office of Disability Support Services were more visible and offered new options. The Memorial Student Union expansion was celebrated,[5] while plans were being made for proceeds of the state bond issue—40 projects including demolition of Haley Hall and opening of Aggie Suites.[6]

An aerial view of the campus in 2014, showing the many buildings that changed the face of A&T in the 21st century.

The women's bowling team headed to the national championships, a first for an HBCU.[7] A&T's Jazz Ensemble took part in the first Piedmont Jazz Festival, with events across Greensboro and High Point.[8] Yaxi Shen became the first woman to receive a doctorate at A&T, in electrical engineering.[9]

James Brown performed in Greensboro for the 13th and last time, at the Coliseum complex.[10] Brown had added two A&T students to his band in the 1960s, Maceo and Melvin Parker, after hearing them play at an East Market Street club. Brown can be heard on recordings saying, "Maceo, blow your horn," and Aggies knew he was "one of their own."[11] Graduates shared "Aggie Pride" every time an alumnus contributed to the global society.

As the fall semester began, Chancellor James Renick spent two nights in a dorm getting to know students. Chris Wallace, a reporter for *The*

*Register,* wrote, "Imagine waking up one day at 5:30 a.m. to the sound of news reporters and camera crews outside your dorm room. What about going to the restroom to brush your teeth, and the chancellor of your university is next to you brushing his?"[12, 13]

On September 11, 2001, feelings of security disappeared when airborne terrorists hijacked jets, attacking the World Trade Center and Pentagon and crashing one in Pennsylvania,

TOP: Fashion takes the stage at the CoutureVerge Fashion Show. *University Relations.*

BOTTOM: Chancellor James Renick moved into the residence halls to learn what student life was like.

killing nearly 3,000 people.[14] A candlelight vigil filled the new Stallings Ballrooms, as students shared prayers, songs, and testimonies. "It's shocking. It really makes you think and realize that anything is possible at any time," said student Karl Walker.[15] Imam W. Deen Mohammed, son of the Nation of Islam founder, told an Interfaith Unity Week event that the suicide bombers would not find their actions acceptable to God. Soon came a new threat, bioterrorism, with anthrax mailings killing people from Florida to New Jersey.[16]

Still, campus life went on. P. Diddy and Patti LaBelle were named to headline Homecoming.[17] Vanstory Hall became A&T's first 24-hour co-ed dormitory. The Metro Aggie Club and the NY/NJ Connection worked together to support 9/11 families with proceeds from a penny drive and gym jam.[18]

During the early years of the decade, A&T students took part in state and national Model United Nations conferences. Student and faculty participation in international conferences continued to rise. The

The February One Monument, located in front of the Dudley Memorial Building, celebrates the A&T Four/ Greensboro Four. Pictured at the February 1, 2002, unveiling of the sculpture are (from left) David Richmond Jr. (son of the late David Richmond) and the three surviving members.

Board of Governors authorized the Center for Energy Research and Technology in 2002, directed by Dr. Harmohindar Singh, who facilitated the national funding consortium.[19] The first Ronald E. McNair Symposium on Science Frontiers was held.[20]

Faculty member and sculptor James Barnhill worked to capture the essence of the A&T Four in bronze. The atmosphere was euphoric at the 2002 unveiling of the 15-foot monument in front of the Dudley Building.[21] The Foundation launched a $100 million campaign, "From Generation to Generation."[22]

Maurice Hicks was named MEAC Offensive Player of the Year, Black College Offensive Player of the Year, and Division I-AA All-American, though his season was cut short with a knee injury. Also named All-Americans were Marcus Bryson and Qasim Mitchell.[23] Mitchell would later sign with the Cleveland Browns.[24] The A&T cheerleaders won an MEAC championship[25] and volleyball player Amanda Padilla was MEAC Rookie of

U.S. Congresswoman Eva M. Clayton (seen with Jibreel Khazan and Joseph McNeil) received the 2014 North Carolina A&T State University Human Rights Medal. *Charles Watkins/University Relations.*

A critique session in the studio during the National Association of Black Journalists Short Course.

the Year.[26] Charles Davis, a former Wake Forest basketball star, became athletic director.[27]

A&T's Department of Communication hosted the 10th annual National Association of Black Journalists Short Course.[28] Later in the year, pioneering female journalists were honored as Women in Journalism stamps were unveiled at the Stallings Ballroom.[29]

Williams Cafeteria reopened as a much larger and updated facility and the police department moved to Ward Hall.[30] "Online classes take off for A&T," the headline read, as Blackboard became a major element

in students' education.[31] A&T enrolled a record 10,000 students in 2003–04, a year in which a chapter of the Phi Kappa Phi University Honor Society was chartered.[32] Jannette Suggs retired after more than 30 years as administrative secretary to the dean of the School of Business and Economics, and the Students in Free Enterprise team won its 10th consecutive regional championship.[33]

Two years after 9/11, the campus grappled with the reality that School of Engineering alumnus Khalid Shaykh Muhammad was one of 16 high-value detainees sent to Guantanamo Bay. A December 8, 2006, memorandum for the U.S. Southern Command stated that Muhammad was the alleged mastermind of the 2001 attack.[34] According to David Klett, a mechanical engineering professor, "It came as a real surprise to learn that one of our graduates was among the 10 most wanted terrorists on the FBI's list and had a $25 million reward on his head."[35]

George Small, a former Aggie player, was named football coach in January,[36] and that November, the Aggies became the 2003 MEAC football champions, beating the Hampton Pirates.[37] Elvin Bethea became the first Aggie to join the National Football League Hall of Fame. Bethea, an executive with Anheuser-Busch, said, "I've always felt that it doesn't matter whether you attended a small school or a large school as long as you work hard and give 100 percent toward

your goals that hard work, good work ethics and focus are going to help you achieve your goals."[38]

Nobel Prize winner Dr. Carl E. Wieman visited campus for the colloquium and Nobel lecture,[39] and A&T hosted NASA Awareness and Job Explorations Days in October.[40] A newspaper article focused on A&T students' interest in video games,[41] while campus computer users were plagued by network viruses that caused fall registration to be extended.[42]

Dr. Johnny B. Hodge retired as band director after 23 years.[43] The A&T Marching Machine won first place in the Defeat the Beat/Battle of the Bands competition in Charlotte under new director Kenneth Ruff.[44] They would begin marching under a new banner, as A&T's new logo was unveiled featuring an updated bulldog with a spiked collar.[45]

NFL Hall of Famer Elvin Bethea is shown at Homecoming 2003 speaking with students. *Charles Watkins/University Relations.*

The university's new logo and other marks are unveiled in 2003 at Aggie Stadium. *Charles Watkins/ University Relations.*

The E. Gwynn
Dancers are shown
in a performance
in 2000.

The Visual and
Performing Arts
Department also
conducts educational
outreach, as shown in
this 2003 photo.

Chancellor Stanley F.
Battle, a classically
trained singer,
performs in concert.

The Blue and Gold Marching Machine wowed the crowds at the 2012 Macy's Thanksgiving Day Parade.

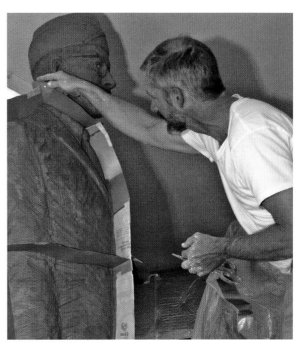

Sculptor Jim Barnhill is shown at work on the February One Monument of the A&T Four. *Charles Watkins/University Relations.*

A chorus sings during a performance of *Black Nativity.*

The Rev. Dr. Wayman Bernard McLaughlin Sr. died in 2003, shortly after retiring after nearly 35 years as the only philosopher teaching at A&T. A Danville native, he was the second African American to receive a doctorate from the Philosophy Department at Boston University, a classmate and friend of Martin Luther King Jr.[46]

*Black Nativity* moved off-campus to Triad Stage in downtown Greensboro, allowing renovations at Paul Robeson Theatre.[47] Legendary CBS newsman Andy Rooney visited.[48] The Gillette Co. launched a partnership with A&T, committing to $1 million in scholarships and paid internships over three years.[49]

In the early 2000s, Professor Jagannathan Sankar began discussions for the Center for Nanoscience and Nanomaterials. The university received

its largest single-year grant—$2.8 million from the Office of Naval Research—for that same center.[50] In January 2004, the Division of Research was reorganized as the Division of Research and Economic Development, directed by Dr. Narayanaswamy Radhakrishnan.[51]

In the fall of 2004, A&T learned that it had met the criteria for the Doctoral/Research Intensive Category established by the Carnegie Foundation for the Advancement of Teaching.[52] Also that year, the university partnered with the U.S. Department of Agriculture's Natural Resources Conservation Service, with one of three technology centers and a remote sensing lab relocated to Greensboro.[53] A&T also received significant grants in the area of health research. Alzheimer's disease researcher Dr. Goldie Byrd received $4.6 million over five years from the National Institutes of

Newsman Andy Rooney of *60 Minutes* speaks to a journalism student, Brett Harrington, during his visit to campus.

The new Science Building. *Jessie Gladdek/University Relations.*

Health for Building Genetics Research.[54] The School of Nursing, in partnership with John Hopkins University, received a $2.3 million, five-year grant to create the Center for Health Disparities Research.[55]

During the 2004 elections, A&T provided a platform for both parties. Vice presidential contender Sen. John Edwards and his family held a rally near the Dudley Memorial Building.[56] Others visiting campus included John Kerry's campaign staff, and local and state politicians such as Erskine Bowles,[57] Alma Adams, Mel Watt, and Brad Miller.[58] The year 2004 would mark the passing of former president Ronald Reagan,[59] and the re-election of George W. Bush.[60]

Jerry Eaves was named basketball coach early in the academic year.[61] Aggie cheerleaders regained the MEAC championship,[62] and A&T football made history, facing off against Division I-A Wake Forest.[63] Former Aggie Curtis Deloatch made the New York Giants team.[64] The union added PlayStation 2 gaming consoles.[65] A&T alumna Sharon Warren appeared as Ray Charles' mother in the film *Ray*,[66] while faculty and students from theatre, dance, and journalism took part in a cultural exchange program in South Africa. Football Hall of Famer Jim Brown returned to speak at a sports honors banquet.[67]

The business and economics building was named for longtime dean Dr. Quiester Craig,[68] and a dedication ceremony was held for the adjoining General Classroom Building housing the College of Arts and Sciences.[69] Two years later, the college would dedicate its new Science Building.

A new student organization appeared on campus: People Recognizing Individual Diversity and Equality, or PRIDE. Its goal was to educate the campus on gay, lesbian, bisexual, and transgender (LGBT) issues.[70]

Janice Bryant Howroyd, CEO of Act I Group, donated $10 million to her alma mater in the form of a life insurance policy of which A&T is the beneficiary. This marked the second-largest gift ever given to an HBCU.[71] With the growth in enrollment, alumni, students, faculty, and staff were more than ever supportive of athletics and activities such as Homecoming, which in 2004 brought an estimated $12 million in revenue to the city. Students began to take an interest in NASCAR when the Drive for Diversity visited the campus as a first step in diversification in the NASCAR racing industry.[72]

Students embraced the age of "new media" on Facebook and Twitter, and in blogs and podcasts.

RIGHT: The Aggie Dog.

BELOW: Latiera Streeter greets the audience at her coronation as 2004's Miss A&T. *Greenlee/University Relations.*

The new scoreboard shines at Founders Day 2005 as SGA president Justin D. Ramey speaks. *CHARLES WATKINS/ UNIVERSITY RELATIONS.*

Facebook, founded in 2004 by Mark Zuckerberg, surpassed 100 million users in 2008 and 1.23 billion in December 2013.[73] Students said it was a good way to keep in touch, but warned of its addictive qualities.[74] In 2006, 140-character text messages became news as Jack Dorsey tweeted, "just setting up my first twttr."[75] The Information Technology and Communications Division anticipated the explosion of technology and positioned the university to accommodate the changes.[76] A new high-tech Aggie Stadium scoreboard was an instant hit with students and fans.[77]

A&T played a significant role in bringing an understanding of new and social media not only to students, but to the region. In 2005, the South's first tech conference was

Converge South brought discussions of state-of-the-art social media and digital communications to A&T and the region. This session is in the renovated Crosby Hall.

organized by Sue Polinsky; Ed Cone, John Robinson, and Allen Johnson of the *News & Record*; and Journalism and Mass Communication chair Dr. Teresa Styles.[78] Converge South[79] brought noted bloggers to campus such as Jim Buie, Jay Rosen, and Jeff Jarvis, and national figures such as the late Elizabeth Edwards.[80]

Fall seemed to be the time for tragic events. Hurricane Katrina battered the Gulf Coast, the most costly and destructive natural disaster in U.S. history.[81] Surreal scenes followed, as people walked across the Danziger Bridge, leaving New Orleans and seeking refuge in Gentilly, while others were rescued from rooftops or took shelter in the Superdome.[82] A&T established a Hurricane Katrina Relief Fund called Aggies Care.[83] The Foundation accepted contributions to help

affected A&T students and a "Strip Takeover" by SGA gathered clothes, food, water, and other donations.[84]

The Department of Journalism and Mass Communication received initial accreditation by the Accrediting Council on Education in Journalism and Mass Communication, the second program in the state to have that distinction.[85] The Institute for Advanced Journalism Studies hosted a series on media and black life[86] and a symposium "Can What We Don't Know About Africa Hurt Us?"[87]

A&T and UNCG combined forces for a Millennium Campus, with the North Campus at the site of the former NC School for the Deaf and the South Campus on part of the A&T farm.[88] The Alumni-Foundation Event Center opened.[89, 90]

The cheerleaders repeated as MEAC champions[91] and the baseball

The Alumni-Foundation Event Center has a ceremonial opening on December 16, 2005.

This mural, "Graduation," was created by Joseph Holston in 2005 to depict the pageantry and promise of commencement. Its prominent placement welcomes visitors to the Alumni-Foundation Event Center. © *Joseph Holston, courtesy the artist.*

team became MEAC regular-season champs, the team's first title since leaving the CIAA.[92] DeLores "Dee" Todd became the university's first female athletics director.[93] Outfielder Jeremy Jones was named Black College Player of the Year and MEAC Player of the Year.[94]

The Department of Political Science won five awards at the Model United Nations.[95] Students and faculty traveled to Washington to take part in the Millions More Movement.[96] A&T students, faculty, and staff joined Phi Beta Sigma Fraternity and SGA to pay tribute to Rosa Parks, who died October 24, 2005.[97]

A&T unveiled a new fight song to replace "Old Aggie Spirit." Bicycles became popular on campus as gas prices rose. A&T's Kappa Alpha Psi chapter won the HBCU step show.[98] Forty thousand people were expected for Homecoming, and the Essence College Tour and Gospel Fest had A&T as its first stop.[99]

Parking complaints were addressed in 2006 as construction began on a $6.3 million parking deck.[100] Meanwhile, those tasked with maintaining order gained a major accolade, as the University Police Department (UPD) became the first HBCU department to meet the over 400 standards for accreditation by the Commission on Accreditation of Law Enforcement Agencies.[101] The UPD was re-accredited in 2012, and now has a staff of over 100, including sworn full-time police officers as well as security officers who patrol the campus, enforce regulations, and assist visitors. More than 400 cameras are monitored, as well as various alarm and access systems. The Community Action Team has a K-9 patrol and two bike officers.[102]

Freshmen were barred from bringing cars on campus, but could regain that privilege for the spring by

Terrence Jenkins, a graduate of the Journalism and Mass Communication program, went on to become "Terrence J." and appeared in major films and television series. *CHARLES WATKINS/ UNIVERSITY RELATIONS.*

achieving a 3.2 or better GPA. Walter Stith played in the Hula Bowl.[103]

Speakers brought new ideas before students. Michael Eric Dyson packed the student union for a discussion on MLK's life and legacy.[104] Cornel West spoke to the HBCU Think Tank 2006,[105] while Alphonso Jackson, secretary of Housing and Urban Development, was the commencement speaker.[106] Thomas Friedman spoke after students read his book, *The World Is Flat*, as the Text-in-Community selection.[107]

For the first time, A&T hosted the National Black Unity Festival.[108] Controversial topics resonated on campus: HIV/AIDS, same-sex relationships, and the use of the "N" word. A chapter of the Student Global AIDS Campaign was formed.[109] New data on the rise of HIV infection among college students in North Carolina served as a catalyst to increase outreach in the fight against the disease.[110]

The first African American International Grandmaster of chess, Maurice Ashley, visited.[111] Students from various schools participated in the 20th Annual Ronald E. McNair Commemorative Celebration. In 2006, there were 179 programs nationwide honoring Ronald E. McNair's legacy.[112] Chancellor Renick announced his resignation[113] and Interim Chancellor Lloyd V. Hackley began his tenure in May 2006.[114] The Grammy award-winning gospel group Sweet Honey in the Rock reopened the renovated Harrison Auditorium.[115]

More corporations hired graduates for positions in the United States and abroad and "Aggie Pride is now Worldwide" became a new slogan.[116] Career fairs, long a tradition at A&T, showed students how to dress and interview while connecting them with prospective employers.[117] The Study Abroad Fair by the Office of International Affairs helped students realize their dreams of travel and education.[118]

A robotics demonstration at the McNair Symposium, part of a range of educational programs that bear Ronald McNair's name at his alma mater and across the nation.

In remembrance of slain Florida teen Trayvon Martin, almost 200 Aggies lay down on the lawn in front of Gibbs Hall, March 25, 2012.

Tristan Bailey carries on a legacy of service at 2013 Martin Luther King Jr. Day through volunteerism with Greensboro Urban Ministry. *Charles Watkins/ University Relations.*

The Oaks, the former president's home on campus, is rededicated as a one-stop help center for veterans of all eras.

ABOVE: On Martin Luther King Jr. Day in 2007, Phi Beta Sigma Fraternity brings awareness to the homeless by staging a sleep-out. *Charles Watkins/ University Relations.*

LEFT: Teams of Aggies traveled to the Gulf Coast to help victims of Hurricane Katrina.

Chancellor James C. Renick (left) is shown with Irwin Belk and First Lady Peggy Renick at the dedication of the new track that bears Belk's name.

A&T became the first HBCU to host an NCAA regional track event, at its new Irwin Belk Track and Field.[119, 120] Three years later, the U.S. Junior Olympics came to campus, bringing more than 7,000 athletes from across the country.[121, 122]

"It is not my intent to alter the tremendous history of this institution. In fact, it was the history of great men such as the A&T Four that brought me here," said Dr. Stanley F. Battle as he became the new chancellor.[123] The Dowdy Scholars Program,

named after the sixth president of A&T, gave financial support to promising students.[124] Yvonne Johnson, an A&T alumna, became the first black mayor of Greensboro.[125]

In January 2007, President George W. Bush sent 30,000 additional troops to Iraq; A&T saw student-soldiers once again deployed.[126] Hodding Carter III, journalist and spokesman for the Department of State during the Iran hostage crisis, provided perspective on the Iraq war.[127]

In 2007, the National Oceanic and Atmospheric Administration created the Interdisciplinary Scientific Environmental Technology Center based at A&T to monitor the oceans, climate, and weather in cooperation with NOAA's Earth Science Research Laboratory in Boulder, Colorado.[128]

Phi Beta Sigma held its annual Sleep Out for the Homeless, as members spent the night in cardboard boxes and collected canned goods, clothing, and money to help the homeless. This service project started by A&T's Eta chapter in 1988 brought national recognition in 2000, and became mandated nationwide.[129] The "Make Hip-Hop Not War" campaign came to A&T.[130]

Rachel Wilson, a senior sociology major, was named Miss Black North Carolina USA.[131] Student Monique Johnson, who has a rare form of dwarfism, won CBS's *Assignment America* challenge.[132]

The tragedy at Virginia Tech topped the news during the spring semester,[133] but in the fall, A&T students were watching Jena, Louisiana. White students were accused of placing a "Whites Only" sign and hanging nooses on a tree in the school courtyard, leading to a summer of violence and intimidation. A busload of A&T students headed to the town to protest the sentences imposed on the "Jena Six"—black students accused of attacking a white classmate.[134]

The Muslim Student Association was newly active on campus.[135] Under Chancellor Battle's leadership, the university announced the "Cosby Kids" partnership with Guilford County Schools and Guilford Technical Community College to help local children succeed. Bill Cosby pledged his name, time, and wealth to the effort.[136]

Technology transfer efforts became important, as A&T labs launched spinoff companies such as Provagen, Premiere Analytics, Filtata, Inc., and Advaero, LLC. In the fall of 2008, A&T joined an elite group when the National Science Foundation awarded an $18 million grant for an Engineering Research Center.[137]

In 2008, *The Register* asked, "Are we ready for a black president?" The campaign for the White House was on.[138] Few people knew much about the senator from Illinois, but as his memoir indicates, Obama had "the audacity of hope." One excerpt focused on a topic relevant to A&T: "Since Lincoln signed the Morrill Act and created the system of land grant Colleges, institutions of higher

A member of Golden Delight performs. *JESSIE GLADDEK/UNIVERSITY RELATIONS.*

Scott Hall is demolished to make way for Aggie Village, a community complex of four residence halls, each bearing the names of the A&T Four—Franklin McCain Hall (built in 2003), Joseph McNeil Hall (2003), Ezell Blair Jr. Hall (2005), and David Richmond Hall (2005). Bullet holes from the building, a result of gunfire in the unrest of the 1960s, were preserved and remembered in an evening of poetry, theatre, and music. *Charles Watkins/ University Relations*.

learning have served as the nation's primary research and development laboratories. It's through these institutions that we've trained the innovators of the future, with the federal government providing critical support for the infrastructure—everything from chemistry labs to particle accelerators—and the dollars for research that may not have an immediate commercial application but can ultimately lead to major scientific breakthroughs."[139]

Obama's campaign galvanized voter registration, and students were active in campaigning and getting out the vote. However, such political, cultural, and scientific engagement was nothing new at A&T, as evidenced by the caliber of its visitors: Dr. David Satcher, former U.S. surgeon general; poet Rita Dove; former CEO Carly Fiorina of Hewlett Packard; actor James Earl Jones; and House Majority Whip Jim Clyburn.[140] Cornel West and Tavis Smiley addressed the 40th anniversary of the Kerner Report on the state of black America. The event was sponsored by the Institute for Advanced Journalism Studies and director DeWayne Wickham. The performance *Bullet Holes in the Wall: A Reflection of Courage in the Struggle for Liberation* paid tribute to A&T's activist legacy.[141]

It was a big year for Aggie athletics. The women's swim team won the HBCU championship.[142] Alexandria

Spruiel and Loreal Smith qualified for the NCAA Indoor Track and Field championships, the first Aggies to do so.[143] The Lady Aggies basketball team had its first postseason appearance in 14 years in the Women's National Invitation Tournament.[144] Sprinter Calesio Newman qualified for the NCAA East Regional,[145] and former footballer Will Billingsley signed with the Miami Dolphins.[146]

Greensboro would get a close look at "change" as Barack Obama appeared at War Memorial Auditorium in April.[147] Michelle Obama took the stage at the Carolina Theatre to lead a "Women for Obama" rally.[148] CNN's "Black in America" tour came to A&T in 2008,[149] Obama and Biden later campaigned in downtown Greensboro, and the Rev. Al Sharpton and *The Great Debaters* star Jurnee Smollet visited to promote voting.[150]

Jasmine McInnis became the first Mr. Black North Carolina.[151] The Leadership Studies Program graduated its first doctoral class in the spring of 2008.[152] Aggie Alert debuted in

Barack Obama and Joe Biden campaigned in Greensboro in 2008.

A shirt celebrating King's legacy provides a visual link with the past on the night of Obama's election as the nation's first black president. *Charles Watkins/University Relations.*

Emotions range from tearful to triumphant on that historic night. *Charles Watkins/ University Relations.*

response to the nation's experiences with shootings, bomb threats, and weather disasters.[153] The School of Business and Economics opened its new "trading room" even as the financial bailout was in the news.[154]

A&T had an ongoing commitment to Katrina victims that began

the next spring after the hurricane, when 29 Aggies took part in a spring break mission to clean up and rebuild areas of New Orleans devastated by Hurricane Katrina.[155] In 2008, 36 students and seven faculty members traveled to the Gulf Coast early in the year,[156] while others spent their fall break volunteering in the Lower Ninth Ward of New Orleans.[157]

Obama was elected and Aggies rejoiced at an election night watch party and by gathering around the reflecting pool in Aggie Village.[158] "Who among us in our wildest dreams, would have dared to think that ... our nation would have elected Barack Obama as president. Let us be mindful as we continue to pursue our dreams for A&T," said Elizabeth Dowdy.[159]

President Obama's inauguration brought hundreds of thousands to the Mall in Washington, D.C., including students from A&T. Others participated in a watch party at the Memorial Student Union. Marcus Bass, SGA president, said, "I think that for a lot of us the election was the big breaking point. But in his (Inaugural) speech, he really spoke to all Americans. Something that we forget as African-Americans is that we aren't the only people who know struggle. Struggle is the American story."[160]

Three Lady Aggies basketball players reached 1,000 points: Amber Bland, Ta'Wauna Cook, and Brittanie Taylor-James.[161] Taylor-James was later named MEAC Player of the Year. Patricia Cage-Bibbs became MEAC Coach of the Year for leading the

team to the regular season and tournament championships.[162] The cheerleaders won their third consecutive MEAC championship.[163]

Legendary pop singer Michael Jackson died in the summer of 2009, sparking the most widespread public mourning since the death of Elvis Presley. Other national events included the drama off the coast of Somalia in which SEAL snipers killed three pirates and liberated a captive. Obama received the Nobel Peace Prize.[164]

Landline phones largely disappeared from the dorms.[165] Dr. Sullivan Welborne, vice chancellor for student affairs, announced his retirement after 38 years of service at A&T.[166] The

Dr. Sullivan Welborne (right) closed out nearly four decades of service at A&T. He is shown here with Chancellor Battle (left) and the Rev. Al Sharpton.

Amber Bland is shown in action. She was one of three Lady Aggies on the same team to reach 1,000 points in the same season.

The Joint School of Nanoscience and Nanoengineering (JSNN) came about as a result of having two universities in the same city, but tens of thousands of lost jobs in textiles and tobacco and furniture also drove the need to create the jobs of the 21st century. *Jessie Gladdek/University Relations.*

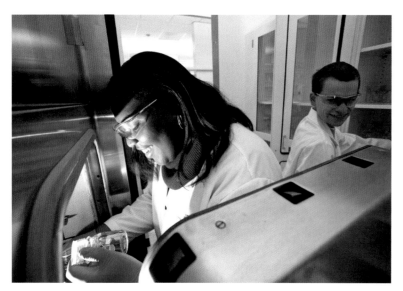

The JSNN has a diverse student population that is approximately 30 percent female. *Jessie Gladdek/ University Relations.*

A&T Marching Machine became the first band to perform at a NASCAR event, performing at Lowe's Motor Speedway.[167]

Research took a giant leap forward as ground was broken for

the Joint School of Nanoscience and Nanoengineering (JSNN), a 100,000-square-foot research facility at the South Campus, Gateway University Research Park.[168] Students would conduct basic applied research, with the ability to gain master's degrees or doctorates.[169] Dr. James G. Ryan was named the founding dean.[170]

Also in 2009, food researcher Dr. Mohamed Ahmedna was named director of the Center of Excellence for Post-Harvest Technologies at the North Carolina Research Campus in Kannapolis. "One of Ahmedna's most notable inventions is a pat-ent-protected post-harvest process that inactivates allergens in whole peanuts."[171] A&T received a five-year, $2.5 million grant from the National Science Foundation participate in a national consortium studying "Evolution in Action." A&T also was selected to lead a National Science Experiment on water quality and climate change.[172]

In 2010, Chancellor Harold Martin was installed as the twelfth leader of North Carolina A&T. Under Martin's leadership, the university would see growth and change in academic units as well as athletics. Among his early initiatives was to reinstate the Board of Visitors, an advisory committee for the chancellor, chaired by Royall M. Mack Sr. '69.[173]

Haiti was struck with a massive earthquake, and tens of thousands died. The National Association of Black Journalists chapter started Project Haiti, which was picked up by SGA.[174]

The International Civil Rights Center & Museum opened in the former Woolworth's building, a half-century after the A&T Four sat down at the segregated lunch counter. Present for the event were Joseph McNeil, Jibreel Khazan (formerly Ezell Blair Jr.), and Franklin McCain, as well as the Rev. Jesse Jackson and Gov. Bev Perdue.[175]

Kappa Alpha Psi returned with 41 new members. The fraternity had been suspended for three years on a hazing investigation, as the nation turned a more critical eye to initiation rituals.[176] The Aggies flag football squad won its fourth consecutive state championship.[177]

Dr. Jagannathan Sankar, Distinguished University Professor of Mechanical and Chemical Engineering and White House Millennium Researcher, received the UNC system's highest faculty honor in April 2010. Sankar works in areas affecting medical implants and surgical procedures, adaptive engineering,

Chancellor Harold Martin is installed.

construction safety, and homeland security.[178] In the fall of 2012, the STEM Early College at N.C. A&T[179] welcomed its first class. Those students joined the all-male Middle College at A&T, established in 2003.[180]

The chancellor's commitment to improving technology on campus was coming to fruition with upgrades to Blackboard and Google Mail for students. The university also increased its online presence.[181] Two other new initiatives marked 2011: the Quality Enhancement Project began a five-year effort to improve students' critical thinking skills,[182] and a new interdisciplinary master's program in nanoengineering was established.[183] The Dennis Hayle Stop the Violence Walk returned for a second year, sponsored by Omega Psi Phi. Hayle, a member of the fraternity, had been shot in 2009 and his murder remained unsolved.[184]

The Lady Aggies basketball team rolled up a 30-game home win streak before falling to Hampton University on a game broadcast on ESPNU.[185] The football team broke a seven-year Homecoming "curse" by defeating Delaware State 42-24.[186, 187]

The Aggie football team celebrated "redemption" on the field after a 2011 Homecoming victory over Delaware State. It was the team's first Homecoming win since 2003. *KENNETH HAWKINS JR./ THE REGISTER.*

Nationally, attention focused on domestic terrorism again as Rep. Gabrielle Giffords was one of 18 victims of a shooting in Arizona. She survived. April tornadoes killed 44 nationwide, including more than 20 in eastern North Carolina.[188] On the other side of the world, a deadly tsunami in Japan was followed by radiation leaks at a flooded nuclear power plant.[189]

Canisha Cierra Turner, a freshman agricultural business major, was named in the Janet Jackson 20 Under 20 program honoring young people for extraordinary contributions to the community.[190]

The New Academic Classroom Building was dedicated, housing the Center for Academic Excellence, which helps students succeed academically,

the Office of International Programs, and the Honors Program.[191] Shows sold out for "The Greatest Homecoming on Earth" (GHOE) and at least one, the gospel show, had to be moved to a larger venue.[192]

In a first, the new UNC system president Tom Ross chose to be installed at A&T.[193]

Two national events bracketed the news in 2012. The February shooting of Trayvon Martin, an unarmed 17-year-old African American, led to marches and debates. "It could have been me, I'm wearing a hoody today and I don't think I look threatening, but someone else may think I do," said Derrick Newkirk, a business management major from Fayetteville, North Carolina. Months of debate followed

Tom Ross is congratulated by Chancellor Martin at his inauguration as president of the UNC system in a ceremony at A&T.

Flags indicating the homelands of A&T students brighten the interior of the New Academic Classroom Building. *JESSIE GLADDEK/UNIVERSITY RELATIONS.*

the not-guilty verdict for perpetrator George Zimmerman.[194] At the end of October, Superstorm Sandy hit New Jersey, becoming the second-costliest hurricane in U.S. history with $68 billion in damage to the heavily populated northeast coast.[195]

Michelle Obama became the first African American first lady to give the commencement address,[196, 197] following a veteran Democratic political strategist, Donna Brazile, who spoke in the fall of 2011.[198]

Two Aggies were among the 20,000 Marines honored with Congressional Gold Medals as "Montford Point Marines," who took basic training at the separate facility of Camp Lejeune from 1942 to 1949. John Thompson and Fleetwood Howell were among those honored during the ceremony at the U.S. Capitol. Both served in the Pacific Theater and entered A&T after being discharged. Howell worked in the campus bookstore, while Thompson

First Lady of the United States Michelle Obama receives an honorary degree following her commencement address to the Class of 2012 in May. Also pictured are Interim Provost Winser Alexander (left) and Chancellor Harold L. Martin Sr. (rear). *CHARLES WATKINS/UNIVERSITY RELATIONS.*

Coach Patricia Cage-Bibbs talks to her team before they add to their lead over Savannah State University. *KENNETH HAWKINS JR./THE REGISTER.*

worked in the Greensboro Public Schools.[199]

Patricia Cage-Bibbs gained her 500th victory, becoming the second MEAC coach to join the NCAA Division I 500 Club.[200, 201] India Arie grooved in Harrison Auditorium,[202] and the Lyceum Series kicked off in the fall with legendary drummer and singer Sheila E.[203]

The A&T chapter of the NAACP hosted the program "What's Wrong With Us?" to raise awareness on societal issues. Fantasia Barrino, winner of *American Idol* Season 3, performed the national anthem at the football game against Morgan State.[204] Rachel Swarns, a *New York Times* reporter, came to discuss her book *American Tapestry: The Story of the Black, White and Multiracial Ancestors of Michelle Obama.*[205]

Alicia Keys backed early voting and President Obama, and students marched to the cast their ballots in October.[206]

India Arie greets and thanks the audience in Harrison Auditorium, April 2012. *KENNETH HAWKINS JR./THE REGISTER.*

Dr. Solomon Bililign, director of the Interdisciplinary Scientific Environmental Technology Center, meets with President Obama.

Aggies marked a dual celebration early in 2013 with the second inauguration of Barack Obama and the Martin Luther King Jr. birthday observance.[207] As President Obama

The new Student Health Center at dawn. *JESSIE GLADDEK/UNIVERSITY RELATIONS.*

began his second term, students were debating "Obamacare," the killing of Osama bin Laden in Pakistan, the end of a recession, and Obama's support of new guidelines for student loans.

A&T joined local residents at a town hall meeting to speak out against a plan by the city of Greensboro to extend Florida Street through the A&T farm. The Board of Trustees later tabled the plan.[208]

A $1.76 million grant from the North Carolina GlaxoSmithKline Foundation provided funding for the Science, Technology, Engineering and Mathematics (STEM) Center for Active Learning.[209]

Construction began on a new Sebastian Health Center on Benbow Road, replacing one built in 1953. A team from the STEM Early College at N.C. A&T was one of 17 nationwide to have an experiment selected for the Student Spaceflight Experiments Program.[210]

The Aggies basketball team, which made its 10th appearance in the "Big Dance," had tallied 16 MEAC championships as of 2013, more than any other conference member.[211] The Athletics Department announced a seven-year plan to add men's and women's golf, women's soccer, and men's tennis, while eliminating women's swimming.[212]

A three-day celebration concluded with a gathering at the Koury Center to say farewell to retiring dean

STEM Early College students are doing research that will go into space. *CHARLES WATKINS/UNIVERSITY RELATIONS.*

Quiester Craig, who had headed the School of Business and Economics since 1972.[213] Pulitzer Prize-winning reporter Michael Moss visited campus as part of Text-in-Community, which used his book *Salt Sugar Fat: How the Food Giants Hooked Us.* Richard Blanco, who wrote the poem for Obama's second inaugural, spoke to students.[214]

The long debate between Du Bois and Washington—classical education versus hands-on learning—took a new spin at the intersection of academics with applications. Emmanuel Johnson became the first A&T undergrad to receive the Fulbright Scholarship, allowing him to study robotics in the UK,[215] while Nadine Jansen, a junior math major, became the first A&T student to receive the Goldwater Scholarship.[216] Non-traditional ways of learning

were also making news. The Honors Program opened its Farmers' Market. Construction Management students gained firsthand knowledge by observing at the new Student Health Center construction site.[217] In 2013–14, the B.S. in Environmental Health and Safety degree was the first fully online program of its kind in the country. The School of Technology also offered online programs in Information Technology and Geomatics. The School of Agriculture and Environmental Sciences remains the largest agricultural school among the nation's HBCUs.[218]

The New Year of 2014 brought sadness and celebration. The campus mourned the passing of Franklin E. McCain Sr., one of the A&T Four and a highly recognized supporter of his alma mater.[219] The Blue and Gold

The memorial service for Greensboro Four/A&T Four icon Franklin E. McCain Sr. was held on the campus in Harrison Auditorium.

The Lady Aggies "Circle of Victory" after the MEAC 78-47 win over Norfolk. *Charles Watkins/ University Relations.*

Women's sports, such as Aggie softball, shown here, continued to grow—and a woman took over as athletic director.

ABOVE: The Aggies took on Louisville in 2013, returning to NCAA March Madness. *Charles Watkins/University Relations.*

RIGHT: Desmond Lawrence running the 100-meter at the 2014 NCAA track regionals hosted by A&T. *Charles Watkins/University Relations.*

The Campus Recreation Center helps athletes at all levels maintain their condition. *Jessie Gladdek/University Relations.*

Reginald Johnson was crowned Mr. HBCU at the 2013 HBCU Kings Leadership Conference and Competition, the first Aggie to take the title. Other Mr. A&Ts were Austin James in 2009, Todd Porter II in 2010, Jordan Brunson in 2011, Anthony Fitzhugh in 2013, and James Bowen II in 2014. *DERRICK STOWE.*

Marching Machine won the Honda Battle of the Bands.[220]

As North Carolina and other states grappled with budgetary issues, the African American community became aware of the lack of funding for HBCUs. The closing of St. Paul's College in Lawrenceville, Virginia, came as a wake-up call, as colleges formed in the days of segregation saw their role threatened.[221] The White House named two students as HBCU All-Stars to serve as ambassadors for the White House. By Executive Order 13532, President Obama promoted excellence, innovation, and sustainability at HBCUs,[222] but a sad truth is that a six-year plan has become the college norm.[223] Another blow to students came as the Supreme Court reversed affirmative action initiatives.[224]

The university launched doctoral degree programs in computer science and rehabilitation counseling, for a total of nine doctoral programs. A&T gained another national academic honor with its first recipient of the George J. Mitchell Scholarship, Destenie Nock.[225]

The 100th anniversary of the founding of Cooperative Extension was marked in 2014. A&T's long dedication to the small farmer was celebrated in March, as it had been for the previous 27 years, with the observance of Small Farms Week and announcement of the 2014 Small Farmer of the Year.[226]

Al Attles, an Aggies star from 1956 to 1960 and a legendary NBA player, received the 2014 John W. Bunn Lifetime Achievement Award by The Naismith Memorial Basketball Hall of Fame. He was honored for more than 50 years with the Golden State Warriors. He led them to an NBA Championship in 1975, when for the first time, two African American head coaches faced off in the finals.[227]

In the fall of 2014, A&T opened the Center for Outreach in Alzheimer's, Aging and Community Health, in a 10,000-square-foot space at the university-owned Yanceyville Center. "We have done extraordinary things in this arena," said Dr. Goldie Byrd, who has led the African-Americans & Alzheimer's Disease Project.[228]

Dr. Stephanie Luster-Teasley of the College of Engineering received the 2014 ASEE DuPont Minorities in Engineering Award. Luster-Teasley, a 1996 graduate, was the first female African American faculty member to be named inventor on a patent issued to A&T.[229]

The team of Mel Swann (left) and William Spencer Gwynn covered Aggie sports from 1974 until health problems led Swann to step down in 2011. Gwynn, the play-by-play radio voice of A&T football, went on to close out a 50-year career as a broadcaster in 2014 with the final football game between the Aggies and the Morgan State Bears.

A&T and community officials celebrate the opening of the Center for Outreach in Alzheimer's, Aging and Community Health in November 2014. CHARLES WATKINS/UNIVERSITY RELATIONS.

A&T entered a new era in service to the military with the opening of one of the nation's few standalone centers for veterans' services. The Aggie Student V.E.T.S. Center is located in the former chancellor's residence, The Oaks. Joshua Jones, director of Veterans and Disability Support Services and a retired lieutenant colonel, said that "V.E.T.S. is an acronym for Veteran's Educational Transition Support. We are creating a one-stop shop for the more than 500 students who are veterans and veteran dependents that we serve. We want to ensure they make the smooth transition from boots to books."[230]

Faculty accomplishments over the years were highlighted by the announcement that Dr. Karen Hornsby was named the 2014 North Carolina Professor of the Year by the Carnegie Foundation for the Advancement of Teaching and the Council for Advancement and Support of Education.[231]

A&T retained its ranking as the leading HBCU in North Carolina for the third consecutive year in the *U.S. News & World Report* rankings. A&T also was 15th in the Best Online Graduate Computer Information Technology Programs, in the top third of the High School Counselor Rankings, and in the top two-thirds of the Industrial/Manufacturing/Systems Engineering Concentration Rankings of the Best Engineering Schools on the graduate level. Chancellor Harold L. Martin Sr. said, "We will continue to aggressively assess our performance as we push toward the fulfillment of our strategic plan, A&T Preeminence 2020."[232] As the university heads toward its 125th anniversary, this new initiative represents a long-term plan for the future while preserving the core values of A&T's heritage.[233]

A&T achieved another first in 2014, becoming the largest four-year HBCU in the nation. "Florida A&M ... has for

Dr. Jianmei Yu of the School of Agriculture and Environmental Sciences, Department of Family and Consumer Sciences, is one of three Aggie researchers who came up with a patented process to reduce allergens in peanuts. *Jessie Gladdek/University Relations.*

The Richard Hunt sculpture, *Progress.* *Jessie Gladdek/ University Relations.*

years been the largest four-year historically black college and university in the nation. But a steep decline in enrollment has bumped Florida A&M to the No. 3 spot—and A&T to No. 1."[234]

Backing up Preeminence 2020 is a new brand identity, "Aggies Do!," launched in the summer of 2014: "We are better than yesterday, but never as good as tomorrow. Because our excellence has no boundaries—and because that's what Aggies DO!"[235] While the university responded to the national call for increased science, technology, engineering, and math (STEM) education with tougher curricula and new initiatives, the demand for the liberal and fine arts remained. Faculty and administrators structured programs that would address current and future job markets. Construction of facilities such as the bell tower, new health center, global village, and the sky box are indicators of what Aggies can do.

A&T started as an institution dedicated to farming and

technology. Alumni make certain that "Aggie Pride" remains the foundation of a historically black university anchored in tradition while stretching toward the future. As the history of this country is interwoven with the history of A&T, students search for new leaders and become leaders themselves. Booker T. Washington, W.E.B. Du Bois, Carter G. Woodson, Rosa Parks, Malcolm X, the Rev. Martin Luther King Jr., and the people of this university provide the inspiration, but the future of North Carolina A&T State University lies in the hands of those who are willing to shape it.

"I'd like to see our university have courage to dream and dream big, then have courage to face current reality to know what is and how and what to do about it, and have courage to confront and be confronted, to have courage to live and grow and then have courage to act," said Velma Speight-Buford. "If we do that I think we will be in good shape."[236]

## ENDNOTES

1. O'Neill, 383
2. February 5, 2001
3. Renick, "Annual," 8
4. February 19, 2001
5. March 19, 2001
6. March 26, 2001
7. April 2, 2001
8. April 9, 2001
9. Renick, "Annual," 10
10. "200 Years"
11. Huffman
12. May 7, 2001
13. September 17, 2001
14. "George W. Bush"
15. September 17, 2001
16. November 5, 2001
17. September 17, 2001
18. September 24, 2001
19. Jones et al., 47
20. February 4, 2002
21. January 28, 2002
22. Wesley et al., 2
23. January 28, 2002
24. April 29, 2002
25. March 25, 2002
26. January 28, 2002
27. October 21, 2002
28. April 1, 2002
29. September 30, 2002
30. September 9, 2002
31. September 16, 2002
32. "A&T History"
33. School of Business, 2
34. Harris, H.B.
35. March 17, 2003
36. January 27, 2003
37. November 20, 2003
38. Rowland
39. March 17, 2003
40. October 16, 2003
41. February 3, 2003
42. September 4, 2003
43. February 24, 2003
44. September 18, 2003
45. October 23, 2003
46. Ferguson
47. November 13, 2003
48. November 20, 2003
49. November 20, 2003
50. Jones et al., 49
51. Jones et al., 48
52. Jones et al., 48
53. Jones et al., 48
54. Jones et al., 49
55. Jones et al., 49
56. October 7, 2004
57. September 9, 2004
58. Dept. of Journalism and Mass Comm.
59. "Reagan Laid to Rest"
60. November 4, 2004
61. October 16, 2003
62. March 18, 2004

63. September 23, 2004
64. September 9, 2004
65. September 9, 2004
66. December 2, 2004
67. September 16, 2004
68. April 15, 2004
69. October 21, 2004
70. December 2, 2004
71. October 15, 2004
72. February 10, 2005
73. Sedghi
74. November 9, 2005
75. Hern
76. October 30, 2003
77. September 28, 2005
78. Cone
79. "Converge"
80. Jarboe
81. "Hurricane Katrina"
82. "Katrina"
83. September 7, 2005
84. September 14, 2005
85. Styles
86. March 17, 2005
87. October 5, 2005
88. January 20, 2005
89. Wesley et al., 2
90. January 18, 2006
91. April 14, 2005
92. April 28, 2005
93. August 17, 2005
94. September 28, 2005
95. April 28, 2005
96. October 19, 2005
97. November 2, 2005
98. September 21, 2005
99. October 19, 2005
100. January 11, 2006
101. September 27, 2006
102. Newell
103. January 25, 2006
104. January 25, 2006
105. February 8, 2006
106. April 5, 2006
107. April 12, 2006
108. April 28, 2006
109. February 26, 2004
110. April 12, 2006
111. November 1, 2006
112. February 1, 2006
113. February 8, 2006
114. Withers
115. September 27, 2006
116. October 25, 2006
117. September 20, 2006
118. January 25, 2006
119. October 15, 2004
120. Keller
121. "2009 Junior"
122. Wooten
123. November 15, 2006
124. October 31, 2007
125. November 7, 2006
126. January 24, 2007
127. "Campus Briefs: Richard"

128. Jones et al., 53
129. January 24, 2007
130. April 4, 2007
131. April 25, 2007
132. September 5, 2007
133. April 18, 2007
134. September 19, 2007
135. October 17, 2007
136. February 6, 2008
137. Jones et al., 54
138. January 9, 2008
139. Obama
140. April 9, 2008
141. February 27, 2008
142. February 6, 2008
143. March 12, 2008
144. March 19, 2008
145. March 26, 2008
146. April 30, 2008
147. April 2, 2008
148. September 24, 2008
149. April 16, 2008
150. October 1, 2008
151. April 16, 2008
152. Hargrove
153. August 27, 2008
154. October 1, 2008
155. March 15, 2006
156. February 27, 2008
157. October 28, 2008
158. November 5, 2008
159. Dowdy, E.E.S.
160. January 21, 2009
161. January 21, 2009
162. March 11, 2009
163. March 18, 2009
164. "2009 Year"
165. February 4, 2009
166. September 23, 2009
167. October 28, 2009
168. November 11, 2009
169. Jones et al., 54
170. "Distinguished"
171. Jones et al., 55
172. Jones et al., 56
173. November 10, 2010
174. January 20, 2010
175. February 3, 2010
176. April 14, 2010
177. November 3, 2010
178. Jones et al., 56
179. "The STEM"
180. "Middle"
181. October 26, 2011
182. February 2, 2011
183. August 24, 2011
184. January 26, 2011
185. February 16, 2011
186. October 19, 2011
187. November 2, 2011
188. April 20, 2011
189. Broomhall
190. April 20, 2011
191. September 21, 2011
192. October 19, 2011

193. October 12, 2011
194. March 28, 2012
195. "2012 Year"
196. "First and Foremost"
197. Nutting and Moore
198. November 30, 2011
199. Patterson, D.W.
200. Mills
201. February 29, 2012
202. May 2, 2012
203. October 24, 2012
204. September 26, 2012
205. October 17, 2012
206. October 24, 2012
207. January 23, 2013
208. February 13, 2013
209. February 20, 2013
210. February 27, 2013
211. March 20, 2013
212. August 28, 2013
213. April 24, 2013
214. October 16, 2013
215. April 17, 2013
216. May 1, 2013
217. September 18, 2013
218. "Points"
219. "A Legacy"
220. *Aggies Do!*, 9
221. February 12, 2014
222. February 26, 2014
223. March 19, 2014
224. March 26, 2014
225. "Campus Briefs: Students"
226. "Inside"
227. "Legendary"
228. Newsom
229. "Campus Briefs: Faculty"
230. "Veteran's"
231. "Hornsby Named"
232. "N.C. A&T Is Top"
233. Martin
234. "A&T Tops"
235. "New Branding"
236. Speight-Buford

The February One
Monument at night.
*Jessie Gladdek/
University Relations.*

# Student Government Association Presidents

| | | | |
|---|---|---|---|
| 1939 | Nelson V. Maconson | 1979 | Anthony Hines |
| 1940 | William H. Gilmore | 1980 | Kelvin L. Buncum |
| 1941 | Glenn Rankin | 1981 | Pamela McCorkle |
| 1942 | Francis H. Mebane | 1982 | Stephen S. Kirk |
| 1943 | Alvin V. Blount | 1983 | Bobby Hopkins |
| 1944 | Barbara Canada | 1984 | Christopher Onyemem |
| 1945 | Wilson York | 1985 | James France |
| 1946 | James A. Hill | 1986 | Rev. James P. Tharrington |
| 1947 | Charles R. Wallace | 1987 | Michael Brunson |
| 1948 | Eugene Marrow | 1988 | Karen Y. Mickens |
| 1949 | Samuel Hill | 1989 | Lee Christian |
| 1950 | John Tiller | 1990 | David Miller |
| 1951 | James E. Bryant | 1991 | Ponce D. Tidwell Jr. |
| 1952 | Sampson Buie | 1992 | Zanda Bryant |
| 1953 | Douglas Cromartie | 1993 | Erica Smith |
| 1954 | James Matthews | 1994 | Rodney Boone |
| 1955 | Charles D. Bussey | 1995 | Keith Bryant |
| 1956 | Herman Sutton | 1996 | Aquarius Moore |
| 1957 | William D. Mason Jr. | 1997 | Rasheed A. Cromwell |
| 1958 | Alexander Gardner | 1998 | Arthur Smith |
| 1959 | Edward Nesbitt | 1999 | Nathan Ingram |
| 1960 | Charles Debose | 2000 | Kendra J. Hill |
| 1961 | Walter T. Johnson | 2001 | Nikkita Mitchell |
| 1962 | Jack Ezell | 2002 | Gregory B. Drumwright |
| 1963 | Ezell Blair Jr. | 2003 | Nashett Chaunte Garrett |
| 1964 | Jesse Jackson | 2004 | Terrence Jenkins |
| 1965 | Rumsey Helms | 2005 | Calvin F. Williams Jr. |
| 1966 | George E. Stevens Jr. | 2006 | Justin D. Ramey |
| 1967 | Roy White | 2007 | Arnita F. Moody |
| 1968 | Marsh Campbell | 2008 | David N. Street |
| 1969 | Calvin Matthews | 2009 | Marcus R. Bass |
| 1970 | Vincent McCullough | 2010 | Syene Jasmin |
| 1971 | Matthew Simpson | 2011 | Wayne Kimball Jr. |
| 1972 | Ronald Ivey | 2012 | Christian Robinson |
| 1973 | Larry Stanwyck Hinton | 2013 | Allahquan Tate |
| 1974 | Marilyn Marshall | 2014 | Canisha Turner |
| 1975 | Bennie L. Glover | 2015 | Dorian Davis |
| 1976 | Ted L. Mangum | | |
| 1977 | Tony A. Tyson | | |
| 1978 | Tony Graham | | |

*Compiled from Student Affairs and University Archives.*

# Miss A&T

"According to Alumni who were students in the 1930s, the traditional Miss A&T had its beginning somewhere around 1934 or 1935 after the return of females to the campus (from 1902 to 1928 enrollment was restricted to males only) …. [A] group of students decided the school should have a campus wide queen, like many other colleges and universities, and she would be chosen by the entire student body …. The qualification required of candidates for Miss A&T was a good record in scholarship and deportment. An unwritten qualification was that she would be '*pretty*.' Over the years this qualification became less dominant. Candidates began presenting platforms of interest to students and the voters began to assess the candidates based upon their platforms and how well they presented themselves." —*The Effervescence of Aggie Essence*, written by Bridgett Herring, edited and updated by Dr. Judy Rashid.

| | | | | | |
|---|---|---|---|---|---|
| 1935 | Kathryn Tynes | 1962 | Rosebud Richardson | 1987 | Stephanie Jones |
| 1936 | Ruth Green | 1963 | Peggy Hinson | 1988 | Moneé McGuire |
| 1937 | Izora Bradley | 1964 | Allegray White | 1989 | Michele Crawley |
| 1938 | Pearl Bradley | 1965 | Debra Austin | 1990 | Sharon Jenkins |
| 1939 | Doris Williams | 1966 | Nannie Kearney | 1991 | Pamela Askew |
| 1940 | Margaret Kiler | 1967 | Patricia Wallace | 1992 | Machelle Cato |
| 1941 | Ellen Dabney | 1968 | Shirley Watkins | 1993 | Tanglar Graves |
| 1942 | Gwendolyn Davis | 1969 | Lillian Campbell | 1994 | Jennifer Lee |
| 1943 | Rose Mallory | 1970 | Pearl Brown | 1995 | Taiwan Barksdale |
| 1944 | Angline Roberts | 1971 | Patricia Thompson | 1996 | Joetta Patrick |
| 1945 | Katrina Watson | 1972 | Arlene Price | 1997 | Bridgett Herring |
| 1946 | Claracee Schnell | 1973 | Delores Tuiloss | 1998 | Donyelle Shorter |
| 1947 | Felecia Rowe | 1974 | A. Michelle Burney | 1999 | Gabrielle Hurtt |
| 1948 | Jessie Johnson | 1975 | Christal Pereira | 2000 | Nicole Watlington |
| 1949 | Jessye Smith | 1976 | Vivelisa Perry | 2001 | Jeannelle Feimster |
| 1950 | Nina Williams | 1977 | Deborah Price | 2002 | Brooke Myatt |
| 1951 | Yvonne Marrow | 1978 | Paulette Petty | 2003 | Jocelyn Jacobs |
| 1952 | Clara Exum | 1979 | Joyce Walker | 2004 | Latiera Streeter |
| 1953 | Albertha Latimer | 1980 | Gretta Smith | 2005 | Anisah Rasheed |
| 1954 | Elizabeth Preston | 1981 | Tommye Brown | 2006 | Crystal Williams |
| 1955 | Shirley Page | 1982 | Robin Whitaker | 2007 | Candace Johnson |
| 1956 | Josephine Luck | 1983 | Brenda Cunningham | 2008 | TaNisha Fordham |
| 1957 | June Bumley | 1984 | Sybil Lynch | 2009 | Ngozi Opara |
| 1958 | Felecia Greenfield | 1985 | Debara Blackwell | 2010 | Carla J. Saunders |
| 1959 | Jacqueline Pyatt | 1986 | Stephanie Tidwell | 2011 | Jasmine Gurley |
| 1960 | Dorothy Richmond | | | 2012 | Catherin Hamilin |
| 1961 | Diane Bell | | | 2013 | Ambriya Neal |
| | | | | 2014 | Jordan Outing |

# Bibliography

When only a date is listed, endnotes refer to articles located in either:

Aggie Digital Archives. "The Register." In *NCAT Student Newspapers*, edited by F. D. Bluford Library Institutional Repository. Greensboro, NC: A&T, 1915-2009. http://cdm15116.contentdm.oclc.org/cdm/landingpage/collection/p15116coll1.

*The A&T Register.* Palo Alto, CA: ISSUU, 2009-2014. http://issuu.com/theatregister/docs.

———————

*50th Anniversary of the Class of 1964: 1964-2014.* Reunion and Induction Ceremony into the Society of Golden Aggies. Greensboro: A&T, May 9, 2014.

"200 Years of Famous Greensboro Visitors." *Greensboro News & Record*, February 17, 2008, A6.

"2009 Junior Olympics Go to N.C. A&T." *Greensboro News & Record*, July 10, 2008, C1.

"2009 Year in Review: News." *Chicago Tribune.* http://www.chicagotribune.com/sns-yir-2009-news-pg-photogallery.html.

"2012 Year in Review: Curiosity, Romney, Phelps, Sandy and More." *Los Angeles Times*, 2012. http://www.latimes.com/nation/nationnow/la-na-nn-year-in-review-major-news-photos-20121213-photogallery.html.

"A&T History: Information about the History of A&T, Including Significant Milestones by Year." F. D. Bluford Archives & Special Collections. http://www.library.ncat.edu/resources/archives/history.html.

"A&T Tops Student Enrollment in HBCU." *Greensboro News & Record*, September 29, 2014.

Abrams, Douglas Carl. "Works Progress Administration (WPA): One Failure to End the Great Depression." In *North Carolina History* Project. Raleigh: John Locke Foundation, 2014. http://www.northcarolinahistory.org/commentary/130/entry.

Abrams, Douglas Carl, H. Tyler Blethen, Michael Hill, Harley E. Jolley, David A. Norris, Randall E. Parker, and George W. Troxler. "Great Depression." In *Encyclopedia of North Carolina*. Raleigh: University of North Carolina Press, 2006. http://ncpedia.org/great-depression.

*Aggies Do!* Greensboro: A&T, 2014. http://www.ncat.edu/academics/schools-colleges1/grad/assets/gradimages/viewbook.pdf.

"Agricultural Colleges (Second Morrill Act of 1890)." Act of August 30, 1890, ch. 841; 26 Stat. 417; 7 U.S.C. 322 et seq. http://www.constitution.org/uslaw/sal/026_statutes_at_large.pdf.

"Agricultural Extension Work (Smith-Lever Act of 1914)." Act of May 8, 1914, ch. 79; 38 Stat. 372; 7 U.S.C. 341 et seq.; PL-95. http://www.constitution.org/uslaw/sal/038_statutes_at_large.pdf.

Albright, Alex. *The Forgotten First: B-1 and the Integration of the Modern Navy.* Fountain, NC: R.A. Fountain, 2013.

Alexander, Dr. Winser E. Interview, F. D. Bluford Library Archives and Department of Journalism and Mass Communication. *The North Carolina Agricultural and Technical State University Experience Through the Voices of Outstanding A&T Alumni* (June 16, 2013). Published electronically October 2, 2013. http://youtu.be/XsnYV8uXPQg.

"The American Federal Story: 25 Years 1959-1984." Edited by American Federal Savings & Loan Association. Greensboro: Sieber, Barnes-Sieber, Ltd., 1984.

*Armistice Day: North Carolina A&T College vs. U.S. Navy Under Sea Raiders.* Polo Grounds, NY: Associated Football Charities, November 11, 1946.

Armstrong, Elson, Jr. "NCCU to Honor an NFL Pioneer." *The Herald-Sun* (January 15, 1998): B1. http://nccueagles.yuku.com/topic/2957.

*The Ayantee.* Greensboro: The Senior Class of A&T, 1939. http://library.digitalnc.org/cdm/ref/collection/yearbooks/id/2044.

Barr, Candy M. "A&T Extensions Widens Its Horizons." *Greensboro News & Record: Supplement. NC A&T State University—Celebration and Challenge: A Second Century 1891-1991,* January 13, 1991, 6.

"The Bay of Pigs." John F. Kennedy Presidential Library and Museum, 2002. http://www.jfklibrary.org/JFK/JFK-in-History/The-Bay-of-Pigs.aspx.

Bedford, William L. "Professional Qualifications and Experience." Philadelphia: Electrical Power Systems Engineering, Inc., [1978].

"Bicentennial Minutes January-March." Greensboro Public Library and Greensboro Historical Museum. http://www.greensboro-nc.gov/index.aspx?page=986.

"Bicentennial Minutes July-September." Greensboro Public Library and Greensboro Historical Museum. http://www.greensboro-nc.gov/index.aspx?page=988.

"Bicentennial Minutes October-December." Greensboro Public Library and Greensboro Historical Museum. http://www.greensboro-nc.gov/index.aspx?page=989.

*Biennial Report, Agricultural & Mechanical College for the Colored Race, Greensboro, N.C.* Greensboro: The Record Job Office, 1910.

Biondi, Martha. *The Black Revolution on Campus.* Berkeley: University of California Press, 2012.

"Black Arts Festival and Symposium." Program. Greensboro: A&T, May 7, 1977.

Bluford, President F. D. "Annual Report." Greensboro: Agricultural and Technical College of North Carolina at Greensboro, May 1932.

———. "Annual Report." Greensboro: Agricultural and Technical College of North Carolina at Greensboro, May 1937.

———. "Annual Report." Greensboro: Agricultural and Technical College of North Carolina at Greensboro, May 1943.

———. "Annual Report." Greensboro: Agricultural and Technical College of North Carolina at Greensboro, May 1945.

———. "Annual Report." Greensboro: Agricultural and Technical College of North Carolina at Greensboro, May 1946.

———. "Annual Report." Greensboro: Agricultural and Technical College of North Carolina at Greensboro, May 1947.

———. "Annual Report." Greensboro: Agricultural and Technical College of North Carolina at Greensboro, May 1948.

———. "Annual Report." Greensboro: Agricultural and Technical College of North Carolina at Greensboro, May 1949.

———. "Annual Report." Greensboro: Agricultural and Technical College of North Carolina at Greensboro, May 1952.

———. "Annual Report." Greensboro: Agricultural and Technical College of North Carolina at Greensboro, May 1953.

———. "Annual Report." Greensboro: Agricultural and Technical College of North Carolina at Greensboro, May 1954.

———. "Quarterly Report." Greensboro: Agricultural and Technical College of North Carolina at Greensboro, January 1940.

———. "Quarterly Report." Greensboro: Agricultural and Technical College of North Carolina at Greensboro, September 1941.

———. "Quarterly Report." Greensboro: Agricultural and Technical College of North Carolina at Greensboro, September 1942.

Bost, Cecile. "Commendable Catawbans: A Transcript of an Interview Conducted on October 7, 1990." *Past Times: The Quarterly Newsletter of the Catawba County Historical Association* 24-25, no. 3-4 (July-December 2005): 14-22.

Branch, Taylor. *Parting the Waters: America in the King Years, 1954-1963*. New York, NY: Simon and Schuster, 1988.

Brandon, Lewis A., III. Interview, F. D. Bluford Library Archives and Department of Journalism and Mass Communication. *The North Carolina Agricultural and Technical State University Experience Through the Voices of Outstanding A&T Alumni* (May 17, 2011). Published electronically August 11, 2011. http://vimeo.com/27631372.

Broomhall, Kirsten. "2011 in Review: Your Top 10 Stories of 2011." *The Guardian*, January 3, 2012. http://www.theguardian.com/world/blog/2012/jan/03/your-top-10-stories-2011.

*Browder v. Gayle*. 142 F. Supp. 707 (M.D. Ala.), 352 U.S. 903 (1956). http://law.justia.com/cases/federal/district-courts/FSupp/142/707/2263463/.

*Brown v. Board of Education of Topeka*. 347 U.S. 483 (1954). https://supreme.justia. com/cases/federal/us/347/483/case.html.

*Brown v. Board of Education of Topeka*. 349 U.S. 294 (1955). https://supreme.justia. com/cases/federal/us/349/294/case.html.

"Campus Briefs: Faculty." *A&T Today* (Summer/Fall 2014): 13. http://relations. ncat.edu/pubs/attoday/attodaysummerfall-2014.pdf.

"Campus Briefs: Richard E. Moore Lecture Series." *A&T Today* 9, no. 4 (Summer 2006): 4. http://archive-staff.ncat.edu/univrel/publications/copy/attoday/ attodaysummer06.pdf.

"Campus Briefs: Students." *A&T Today* (Summer/Fall 2014): 17. http://relations. ncat.edu/pubs/attoday/attodaysummerfall-2014.pdf.

Carmichael, Stokely. "Power and Racism: What We Want." *The Black Scholar* 27, no. 3-4 (1998): 52-57, Reprinted from a pamphlet published by New England Free Press (Boston), 1966, Student Non-Violent Coordinating Committee.

Chafe, William Henry. *Civilities and Civil Rights: Greensboro, North Carolina, and the Black Struggle for Freedom*. New York, NY: Oxford University Press, 1980.

Chopra, N. M. Letter to Chancellor Harold L. Martin, Sr., March 28, 2014.

"Chronology." In *The Negro Caravan*, edited by Sterling Allen Brown, Arthur Paul Davis, and Ulysses Lee. The American Negro, His History and Literature, 1061-77. New York, NY: Arno Press, 1970.

"Civil Rights Act of 1964." The U.S. National Archives and Records Administration. http://www.ourdocuments.gov/doc.php?doc=97.

Clemetson, Lynette. "A Senator's Ambitious Path Through Race and Politics." *New York Times*, February 21, 2007. http://www.nytimes.com/2007/02/21/ books/21broo.html?_r=0.

Clemson University Libraries. "Harvey Gantt and the Desegregation of Clemson University." Exhibit, Clemson University: Office of Institutional Research, January 28, 2003. http://www.clemson.edu/oirweb1/FB/factBook/Historical% 20Enrollment/Integration.htm.

Clinton, William J. "PDD 39: U.S. Policy on Counterterrorism." *Presidential Decision Directive/NSC* (June 21, 1995; declassified January 27, 2007). http://www. clintonlibrary.gov/_previous/Documents/2010%20FOIA/Presidential% 20Directives/PDD-39.pdf.

Clinton, William J. "Timeline of Major Actions." The Clinton Presidency: Eight Years of Peace, Progress and Prosperity, January 2001. http://clinton5.nara. gov/media/pdf/eightyears.pdf.

Cobb, William Jelani. "Evolution of an Activist: 'Stokely: A Life,' by Peniel E. Joseph." *New York Times: Sunday Book Review*, March 23, 2014, BR14. Published electronically March 21, 2014. http://www.nytimes.com/2014/03/23/books/review/stokely-a-life-by-peniel-e-joseph.html?_r=0.

*Collection of Aggie Alumni and Faculty.* Greensboro: The Beloved Community Center of Greensboro, Inc., n.d.

College of Arts & Sciences. "Highlights and Milestones." Greensboro: A&T, August 25, 2004.

Cone, Edward. "An Invitation to the Future." *Greensboro News & Record*, September 25, 2005, H3.

"Conrad Laurel 'The Hawk' Raiford." February 20, 2012. http://www.findagrave.com/cgi-bin/fg.cgi?page=gr&GRid=85259004.

"Converge South." http://convergesouth.com/.

"Cortez W. Peters, Sr." (August 9, 2007). http://www.findagrave.com/cgi-bin/fg.cgi?page=gr&GSln=peters&GSfn=cortez&GSmn=w.&GSby=1906&GSbyrel=in&GSdyrel=all&GSob=n&GRid=20854973&df=all&.

"Cuban Missile Crisis." John F. Kennedy Presidential Library and Museum, 2002. http://www.jfklibrary.org/JFK/JFK-in-History/Cuban-Missile-Crisis.aspx.

DeLassus, David. "North Carolina A&T Bowl History." College Football Data Warehouse, 2014. http://www.cfbdatawarehouse.com/data/div_iaa/mideastern/north_carolina_a&t/bowl_history.php.

Department of Journalism and Mass Communication. *A Community Forum: The 2004 Political Election and Its Impact on North Carolina.* Program. Greensboro: A&T, July 17, 2004.

"Distinguished Nanoscientist to Lead A&T, UNCG Joint School." *A&T Today* 11, no. 3/4 (Spring/Summer 2008): 9. http://archive-staff.ncat.edu/univrel/publications/copy/attoday/attodaysummer08.pdf.

Dowdy, Chancellor Lewis C. "[Can Black College Survive?]." *Greensboro Record*, June 1, 1979.

———. "An Epoch of Excellence, 1964-1979: Chancellor's Report." Greensboro: A&T, May 1979.

Dowdy, Elizabeth Etolia Smith. Interview, F. D. Bluford Library Archives and Department of Journalism and Mass Communication. *The North Carolina Agricultural and Technical State University Experience Through the Voices of Outstanding A&T Alumni* (November 13, 2008). Published electronically December 30, 2010. http://vimeo.com/19832361.

Dowdy, President Lewis C. "Annual Report." Greensboro: A&T, May 1970.

———. "Annual Report." Greensboro: A&T, May 1971.

Du Bois, W.E.B. "African American Photographs Assembled for 1900 Paris Exposition: Search Results." Washington, D.C.: Library of Congress Prints and Photographs Division. http://www.loc.gov/pictures/search/?q=greensboro&co=anedub.

———. "Of Mr. Booker T. Washington and Others." Chap. 3 in *The Souls of Black Folk: Essays and Sketches*, 41-59. Chicago: A.C. McClurg, 1903.

———. "Of Our Spiritual Strivings." Chap. 1 in *The Souls of Black Folk: Essays and Sketches*, 1-12. Chicago: A.C. McClurg, 1903.

Edmond, Alfred, Jr. "Off My Chest: I'm Proud to Be Part of the Legacy of Reginald F. Lewis." *Wealth for Life* (blog), *Black Enterprise*, November 30, 2012. http://www.blackenterprise.com/blogs/im-proud-to-be-part-of-the-legacy-of-reginald-f-lewis/.

———. "Reginald Lewis Cuts the Big Deal." *Black Enterprise*, November 1987, 42.

"Equal Employment Opportunity Act of 1972." Act of March 24, 1972; 86 Stat. 103; PL-92-261. http://www.gpo.gov/fdsys/pkg/STATUTE-86/pdf/STATUTE-86-Pg103.pdf.

"Equal Employment Opportunity Act of 1972 (Act of March 24, 1972; 86 Stat. 103; Pl-92-261)." U.S. Equal Employment Opportunity Commission (EEOC). http://www.eeoc.gov/eeoc/history/35th/thelaw/eeo_1972.html.

Eum, Jennifer. "How Oprah Went from Talk Show Host to First African-American Woman Billionaire." *Forbes: Media & Entertainment*, September 29, 2014, 2. http://www.forbes.com/sites/jennifereum/2014/09/29/how-oprah-went-from-talk-show-host-to-first-african-american-woman-billionaire/.

"The Family and Medical Leave Act of 1993, as Amended (February 5, 1993; December 21, 2009, Public Law 103-3)." U.S. Department of Department of Labor. Wage and Hour Division. http://www.dol.gov/whd/fmla/fmlaAmended.htm.

Feggins, Jeffrey C. Letter, 2014.

Ferguson, Stephen C. Rev. Dr. Wayman Bernard McLaughlin Sr., email, 2014.

"First and Foremost: First Lady Michelle Obama Captivates Grads with History and Hope." *A&T Today* (Fall/Winter 2012): 14-17. http://archive-staff.ncat.edu/univrel/publications/copy/attoday/attodaywinter13.pdf.

Folkerts, Jean, Dwight L. Teeter, and Keith Kincaid. *Voices of a Nation: A History of Mass Media in the United States*. 4th ed. Boston: Allyn and Bacon, 2002.

Franklin, John Hope. *From Slavery to Freedom: A History of American Negroes*. 2nd ed. New York, NY: Knopf, 1956.

Frye, Henry, Retired Chief Justice of North Carolina. Interview, F. D. Bluford Library Archives and Department of Journalism and Mass Communication. *The North Carolina Agricultural and Technical State University Experience Through the Voices of Outstanding A&T Alumni* (February 16, 2007). Published electronically December 30, 2010. http://vimeo.com/18434514.

Frye, Shirley Taylor. Interview, F. D. Bluford Library Archives and Department of Journalism and Mass Communication. *The North Carolina Agricultural and Technical State University Experience Through the Voices of Outstanding A&T Alumni* (October 28, 2006). Published electronically December 30, 2010. http://vimeo.com/18435670.

Fullinwider, Robert. "Affirmative Action." In *The Stanford Encyclopedia of Philosophy*, edited by Edward N. Zalta. Stanford University: Center for the Study of Language and Information (CSLI). The Metaphysics Research Lab, Dec 28, 2001; substantive revision September 17, 2013. http://plato.stanford.edu/entries/affirmative-action/.

Garvin, Glenn. "The African Americans of D-Day." *Miami Herald*, February 23, 2007, 5E. http://www.military.com/NewsContent/0,13319,126337,00.html.

"George W. Bush, 43." In *The Presidents of the United States of America,* edited by Frank Freidel and Hugh Sidey. Washington, D.C.: White House Historical Association, 2006. http://www.whitehouse.gov/about/presidents/georgewbush.

"G.I. Bill (1944): S. 1767 Servicemen's Readjustment Act." The U.S. National Archives and Records Administration. http://www.ourdocuments.gov/doc.php?flash=true&doc=76.

Gibbs, President Warmoth T. "Annual Report." Greensboro: Agricultural and Technical College of North Carolina at Greensboro, May 1956.

———. "Annual Report." Greensboro: Agricultural and Technical College of North Carolina at Greensboro, May 1960.

Gibbs, Warmoth T. *History of the North Carolina Agricultural and Technical College, Greensboro, North Carolina*. Dubuque: W.C. Brown, 1966.

"Greensboro: History." Cities of the United States: The South. City-Data.com, 2009. http://www.city-data.com/us-cities/The-South/Greensboro-History.html.

Haire, Kevlin. "Black History Month: Football Player Had Higher Calling Than Just 'Phys Ed'." In *From Woody's Couch: Our Playbook on OSU History*, edited by University Libraries. Columbus, OH: The Ohio State University, February 27, 2013. http://library.osu.edu/blogs/archives/2013/02/27/black-history-month-football-player-had-higher-calling-than-just-phys-ed/.

Hargrove, Samantha V. "Leadership Program Awards First Doctorates." *A&T Today* 11, no. 3/4 (Spring/Summer 2008): 12-13. http://archive-staff.ncat.edu/univrel/publications/copy/attoday/attodaysummer08.pdf.

"Harlem Renaissance." In *Encyclopædia Britannica Online,* 2014. http://academic. eb.com/EBchecked/topic/255397/Harlem-Renaissance.

Harris, Harry B., Jr., and United States, Department of Defense, Joint Task Force Guantánamo. *Combatant Status Review Tribunal Input and Recommendation for Continued Detention under DOD Control (CD) for Guantánamo Detainee, Isn: Us9sa-010011dp.* U.S. Naval Station, Guantanamo Bay, Cuba, December 8, 2006. http://doc.wrlc.org/handle/2041/85667.

Harris, John. "These Men Changed Baseball: Tom Alston." *The Sports PhD: Bringing Analytical Rigor to Discussions of Sports* (blog), March 25, 2010. http:// sportsphd.wordpress.com/2010/03/25/these-men-changed-baseball-tom-alston/.

Harry Ransom Center, The University of Texas at Austin. "The Woodward and Bernstein Watergate Papers." Exhibitions, 2007. http://www.hrc.utexas.edu/ exhibitions/web/woodstein/.

Hauser, Thelma. "Just a Note!" Letter, March 6, 2014.

Hawkins, Karen. "Dudley High School/NC A&T University Disturbances, May 1969." Civil Rights Greensboro, 2014. http://libcdm1.uncg.edu/cdm/ essay1969/collection/CivilRights.

Hawkins, Karen, and Cat McDowell. "Desegregation and Integration of Greensboro's Public Schools, 1954-1974." Civil Rights Greensboro, 2014. http:// libcdm1.uncg.edu/cdm/essaygreensboroschools/collection/CivilRights.

"Haywood Webb's Sons Perpetuate Excellence." *A&T Today: A&T State University Alumni Magazine, Annual Report* 68, no. 3 (July 1977): 7.

Hern, Alex. "Twitter Turns Eight: What Was Your First Tweet?" *The Guardian*, March 20, 2014. http://www.theguardian.com/technology/2014/mar/20/ twitter-turns-eight-what-first-tweet-social-networking.

Hevesi, Dennis. "Eunice Johnson Dies at 93; Gave Ebony Its Name." *New York Times*, January 10, 2010, A30. Published electronically January 9, 2010. http:// www.nytimes.com/2010/01/10/business/media/10johnson.html.

Hill, Michael. "Federal Writers' Project." In *Encyclopedia of North Carolina*. Raleigh: University of North Carolina Press, 2006. http://ncpedia.org/federal-writers-project.

Hine, Darlene Clark, William C. Hine, and Stanley Harrold. *The African-American Odyssey.* Combined 2nd ed. Upper Saddle River, NJ: Prentice Hall, 2003.

"Historical Timeline and Map." Civil Rights Greensboro, 2014. http://libcdm1. uncg.edu/cdm/timeline/collection/CivilRights.

"The History of UNCG." The University of North Carolina at Greensboro, 2013. http://www.uncg.edu/inside-uncg/inside-history.htm.

"History of UNCP." The University of North Carolina at Pembroke, 2014. http://www2.uncp.edu/uncp/about/history.htm.

History.com. "New Deal." A+E Networks. http://www.history.com/topics/new-deal.

———. "The Roaring Twenties." A+E Networks. http://www.history.com/topics/roaring-twenties.

Hodges, Samuel J., III. "Willie Edward Jenkins." In *African American Architects: A Biographical Dictionary, 1865-1945*, edited by Dreck Spurlock Wilson, 231-33. New York, NY: Routledge, 2004.

"Honors Program." Greensboro: A&T, [2014].

"Hornsby Named N.C. Professor of the Year." Greensboro: A&T, 2014. http://www.ncat.edu/news/2014/11/karen-hornsby.html.

Hornsby, Alton. *Chronology of African American History: From 1492 to the Present.* 2nd ed. Detroit: Gale Research, 1997.

House, Lee, Jr. "Black Power? A Slogan, a Threat, a Poor Choice of Words." *The A.&T. College Register* 38, no. 3 (September 30, 1966): 2. http://cdm15116.contentdm.oclc.org/cdm/compoundobject/collection/p15116coll1/id/22154/rec/1.

Huffman, Eddie. "Remembering an Unforgettable Lunch with Godfather of Soul." *Greensboro News & Record: Go, Triad*, July 31, 2014, 7.

"Hurricane Floyd: Event Review." In *National Weather Service,* U.S. Dept. of Commerce. National Oceanic and Atmospheric Administration, 1999. http://www.weather.gov/mhx/Sep161999EventReview.

"Hurricane Katrina." *The Guardian*, August 29, 2014. http://www.theguardian.com/world/hurricanekatrina.

Ifill, Sherrilyn A. "A Reflection from Sherrilyn Ifill." Brown at 60: Reflections, 2014. NAACP Legal Defense Fund. http://www.naacpldf.org/brown-at-60-reflections.

"Inside Aggieland: Millennials the Focus of 2014 Small Farms Week." *A&T Today* (Winter/Spring 2014). http://relations.ncat.edu/pubs/attoday/attodaywntrsprng13-14.pdf.

"Insurance Covers Heavy Fire Loss: Administration Building at A. and T. College Will Be Restored." F. D. Bluford Library Archives. Vertical File. Physical Plant. Dudley Building, January 27, 1930, see also Stroud Scrapbook 3.34.

"Invitation and Commencement Exercises." Greensboro: Agricultural and Technical College, May 21-25, 1922.

"Invites All North." *The Chicago Defender*, February 10, 1917, 3.

Jackson, Rev. Jesse Louis. "Address by the Reverend Jesse Louis Jackson." *FRONTLINE*, July 19, 1988. http://www.pbs.org/wgbh/pages/frontline/jesse/speeches/jesse88speech.html.

Jacobs, Laura. "Lean In, Lead On." *Vanity Fair* 56, no. 4 (April 2014): 112. http://www.vanityfair.com/style/2014/04/hillary-clinton-sheryl-sandberg-female-leaders-photos.

Jarboe, Michelle. "Conference Raises Awareness about Online Communities." *Greensboro News & Record*, October 8, 2005, B1-B2.

Johnson, Daniel M., and Rex R. Campbell. *Black Migration in America: A Social Demographic History*. Studies in Social and Economic Demography 4. Durham: Duke University Press, 1981.

Johnson, James Weldon. *Along This Way: The Autobiography of James Weldon Johnson*. New York, NY: Da Capo Press, 1933.

Johnson, Thomas A. "Fannie Lou Hamer Dies; Left Farm to Lead Struggle for Civil Rights." *New York Times*, March 15, 1977, 40.

Johnston, David. "In Justice Dept. of the 90's, Focus Shifts from Rights: In Justice Dept. of 90's, Rights Slips on the Agenda." *New York Times*, March 26, 1991, A1, A20.

"A Joint Resolution Honoring the Life and Memory of Warmoth Thomas Gibbs." North Carolina General Assembly: Resolution 20; Senate Joint Resolution 1252 (June 30, 1993). http://www.ncleg.net/Sessions/1993/Bills/Senate/PDF/S1252v2.pdf.

Jones, Cathy V., Bernice Bennett, Cindia Hairston, Gerard Clements, and Marvin H. Watkins. "Division of Research and Economic Development." Greensboro: A&T, November 30, 2010.

*Jubilee Institute Jazz Hall of Fame, 1900-1960*. Greensboro: The Beloved Community Center of Greensboro, Inc., October 2002.

"Katrina: The Storm We Always Feared." NOLA.com with *The Times-Picayune*, August 29, 2005. http://www.nola.com/katrina/archive.ssf.

Kearns, Francis E., ed. *The Black Experience: An Anthology of American Literature for the 1970s*. New York, NY: Viking Press, 1970.

Keller, Tom. "NCAA Track and Field at N.C. A&T." *Greensboro News & Record*, May 25, 2006, C1.

Kelley, Carrye Hill. *Profiles of Five Administrators: The Agricultural and Technical College History-Digest*. Bulletin of the Agricultural and Technical College [of North Carolina] Vol. 55, No. 5. Greensboro: Agricultural and Technical College of North Carolina, 1964.

Kerner, Otto, and United States National Advisory Commission on Civil Disorders. *Report of the National Advisory Commission on Civil Disorders*. Washington, D.C.: Supt. of Docs., U.S. GPO, March 1, 1968. http://www.eisenhowerfoundation.org/docs/kerner.pdf.

Kinard, Lee. A&T's 125th Anniversary, email, March 17, 2014.

King, Dr. Martin Luther, Jr. "I've Been to the Mountaintop." American Federation of State, County and Municipal Employees (AFL-CIO). http://www.afscme.org/union/history/mlk/ive-been-to-the-mountaintop-by-dr-martin-luther-king-jr.

King, Desmond S. *Separate and Unequal: Black Americans and the US Federal Government*. New York, NY: Oxford University Press, 1995.

"LBJ: Biography." LBJ Presidential Library. http://www.lbjlibrary.org/lyndon-baines-johnson/lbj-biography.

"A Legacy of Courage: Franklin Eugene McCain Sr. '64." *A&T Today* (Winter/Spring 2014): 22-27. http://relations.ncat.edu/pubs/attoday/attodaywntrsprng13-14.pdf.

"Legendary NBA Player Receives Lifetime Award at Basketball Hall of Fame." *The Alumni Times*, August 28, 2014. http://relations.ncat.edu/pubs/alumnitimes/2014/aug28/NBAPlayer-Al%20Attles.html.

Lewis, David L. *W.E.B. Du Bois: Biography of a Race, 1868-1919*. 1st ed. 2 vols. Vol. 1, New York, NY: H. Holt, 1993.

Lohr, Kathy. "50 Years Later, a Civil Rights Tribute … and Apology." *NPR*, April 16, 2010. http://www.npr.org/2010/04/16/126051007/50-years-later-a-civil-rights-tribute-and-apology.

"Malcolm X (1925-1965)." In *King Encyclopedia*, Stanford: The Martin Luther King, Jr. Research and Education Institute, n.d. http://mlk-kpp01.stanford.edu/kingweb/about_king/encyclopedia/x_malcolm.htm.

Martin, Chancellor Harold L., Sr. *A&T Preeminence 2020: Embracing Our Past, Creating Our Future. Strategic Plan 2011-2020*. Greensboro: A&T, 2010. http://www.ncat.edu/about/forms-pdf/strategicplan-preeminence2020.pdf.

McCracken, Harry. "Microsoft: A Brief History of Windows Sales Figures, 1985-Present." *Time: Technologizer*, May 7, 2013. http://techland.time.com/2013/05/07/a-brief-history-of-windows-sales-figures-1985-present/.

"Middle College at N.C. A&T." Greensboro: Guilford County Schools. http://ncat.gcsnc.com/pages/Middle_College_at_N_C__A_T.

Mills, Jeff. "A&T Coach in a League of Her Own." *Greensboro News & Record*, February 28, 2012, B1.

*Missouri Ex Rel. Gaines v. Canada*. 305 U.S. 337 (1938). https://supreme.justia.com/cases/federal/us/305/337/case.html.

*Mitchell v. United States*. 313 U.S. 80 (1941). https://supreme.justia.com/cases/federal/us/313/80/case.html.

Moore, Richard E. "Military Leaders Come from A&T ROTC." *Greensboro News & Record: Supplement. NC A&T State University—Celebration and Challenge: A Second Century 1891-1991*, January 13, 1991, 18.

———. "A&T First to Commission Black Female Officer through Air Force Program." *A&T Today* 65, no. 1 (February 1973): 3.

———. "A&T Hails Many Successful Alumni." *Greensboro News & Record: Supplement. NC A&T State University—Celebration and Challenge: A Second Century 1891-1991*, January 13, 1991, 4.

———. "A&T Sports Strong Athletic Tradition." *Greensboro News & Record: Supplement. NC A&T State University—Celebration and Challenge: A Second Century 1891-1991*, January 13, 1991, 8-9.

*Morgan v. Virginia*. 328 U.S. 373 (1946). https://supreme.justia.com/cases/federal/us/328/373/case.html.

Moss, George. *America in the Twentieth Century*. 4th ed. Upper Saddle River, NJ: Prentice Hall, 2000.

*The National Save Black Schools Project Report on the National Conference, April 6-8, 1973*. National Save and Change Black Schools, National Conference Proceedings. Greensboro: A&T, August 1973.

Naval History & Heritage Command. "Japan Capitulates, August-September 1945." Online Library of Selected Images: Events—World War II Diplomacy, 2014. http://www.history.navy.mil/photos/events/wwii-pac/japansur/japansur.htm.

———. "The Potsdam Conference, July-August 1945." Online Library of Selected Images: Events—World War II Diplomacy, 2014. http://www.history.navy.mil/photos/events/wwii-dpl/hd-state/potsdam.htm.

"N.C. A&T Is Top HBCU in North Carolina." *The Aggie Report* 16, no. 3 (September 12, 2014). http://relations.ncat.edu/pubs/aggiereport/2014/sept/sept12a.html#third.

"New Branding Campaign Begins." *A&T Today* (Summer/Fall 2014): 7. http://relations.ncat.edu/pubs/attoday/attodaysummerfall-2014.pdf.

Newell, Glenn C. *Annual Security & Fire Safety Report*. University Police Department. Greensboro: A&T, 2014. http://www.ncat.edu/divisions/business-and-finance/upd2/clery/2014%20NCAT%20Annual%20Security%20and%20Fire%20Safety%20Report.pdf.

Newsom, John. "A&T Finds More Room for Study of Alzheimer's." *Greensboro News & Record*, November 22, 2014, A2.

Nixon, Richard. "Statement about Signing the Equal Employment Opportunity Act of 1972." In *The American Presidency Project*, edited by Gerhard Peters and John T. Woolley. March 25, 1972. http://www.presidency.ucsb.edu/ws/?pid=3358.

North Carolina Advisory Committee on Civil Rights. "Trouble in Greensboro: A Report of an Open Meeting Concerning Disturbances at Dudley High School and North Carolina A&T State University." Civil Rights Greensboro, March 1970. http://libcdm1.uncg.edu/cdm/ref/collection/CivilRights/id/218.

*North Carolina Agricultural & Technical State University Historical Timeline*. Greensboro: A&T, [2005]. Adapted and amended from Founders Day and Honors Day Convocation Program, March 23, 2000.

North Carolina Freedom Monument Project. "North Carolina in the New South: 8. 1898 and White Supremacy, 8.3 the Wilmington Race Riot." In *North Carolina History: A Digital Textbook*, edited by UNC School of Education. Chapel Hill, NC: LEARN NC, 2009. http://www.learnnc.org/lp/editions/nchist-newsouth/4360.

North Carolina Museum of History, Division of State History Museums, Office of Archives and History, and North Carolina Department of Cultural Resources. "North Carolina Civil Rights Time Line, Reprinted by Permission." *Tar Heel Junior Historian* 44 (Fall 2004). http://www.king-raleigh.org/history/NCcivilRightsTimeLine.htm.

Nutting, Stefanie, and Francene Moore. "Michelle Obama: May 2012 Commencement Speaker." F. D. Bluford Library. Greensboro: A&T. http://libguides.library.ncat.edu/michelleobama.

Obama, Barack. *The Audacity of Hope: Thoughts on Reclaiming the American Dream.* 1st ed. New York, NY: Crown, 2006.

O'Keefe, Patrick, ed. *Greensboro: A Pictorial History.* Virginia Beach, VA: Donning Company Publishers, 1977.

O'Neill, William L. *A Bubble in Time: America During the Interwar Years, 1989-2001.* Chicago: Ivan R. Dee, 2009.

Page, Larry, and Sergey Brin. "Company." Google, 1998. https://www.google.com/intl/en/about/company/.

Patterson, Donald W. "Black Marines Get the Gold." *Greensboro News & Record*, June 21, 2012, A1.

Patterson, James T. *America since 1941: A History.* 2nd ed. Fort Worth: Harcourt Brace College, 2000.

PBS and Educational Broadcasting Corporation. "Timeline: Building Democracy (1866-1953)." *African American World*, 2002: 4 of 4. http://www.pbs.org/wnet/aaworld/timeline/building_04.html.

———. "Timeline: Civil Rights Era (1954-1971)." *African American World*, 2002:1-4 of 4. http://www.pbs.org/wnet/aaworld/timeline/civil_01.html. http://www.pbs.org/wnet/aaworld/timeline/civil_02.html. http://www.pbs.org/wnet/aaworld/timeline/civil_03.html. http://www.pbs.org/wnet/aaworld/timeline/civil_04.html.

———. "Timeline: Modern Times (1972 - Present)." *African American World*, 2002:1-4 of 4. http://www.pbs.org/wnet/aaworld/timeline/modern_01.html. http://www.pbs.org/wnet/aaworld/timeline/modern_02.html. http://www.pbs.org/wnet/aaworld/timeline/modern_03.html. http://www.pbs.org/wnet/aaworld/timeline/modern_04.html.

PBS and WGBH Educational Foundation. "The Decision to Run for President in 1984." *FRONTLINE*, 1995. http://www.pbs.org/wgbh/pages/frontline/jesse/impressions/decision84.html.

"Phairlever Pearson." Memorial Service Program. Newton, NC: St. Paul's United Methodist Church, March 22, 1999.

Piggott, Dr. Lucille. Interview, F. D. Bluford Library Archives and Department of Journalism and Mass Communication. *The North Carolina Agricultural and Technical State University Experience Through the Voices of Outstanding A&T Alumni* (April 11, 2006). Published electronically December 30, 2010. http://vimeo.com/18429077.

*Plessy v. Ferguson.* 163 U.S. 537 (1896). https://supreme.justia.com/cases/federal/us/163/537/case.html.

"Points of Pride 2013-2014." Greensboro: A&T, 2014.

"Program Upgrades Mark Fort's Tenure." *Greensboro News & Record: Supplement. NC A&T State University—Celebration and Challenge: A Second Century 1891-1991,* January 13, 1991, 2, 17.

Rashid, Judy. "The National Black Alumni Hall of Fame Queens Competition at NCA&TSU, 1990-2010." Greensboro: A&T, [2010].

Reagan, Ronald. "Remarks on East-West Relations at the Brandenburg Gate in West Berlin." Ronald Reagan Presidential Foundation and Library, June 12, 1987. Published electronically 2010. http://www.reaganfoundation.org/tgcdetail.aspx?p=TG0923RRS&h1=0&h2=0&sw=&lm=reagan&args_a=cms&args_b=1&argsb=N&tx=1748.

———. "Remarks on Signing the Bill Making the Birthday of Martin Luther King, Jr., a National Holiday." In *The American Presidency Project,* edited by Gerhard Peters and John T. Woolley. November 2, 1983. http://www.presidency.ucsb.edu/ws/?pid=40708.

"Reagan Laid to Rest after Final Tributes." NPR, June 12, 2004. http://www.npr.org/news/specials/obits/reagan/.

Redd, Kenneth E. "Historically Black Colleges and Universities: Making a Comeback." *New Directions for Higher Education,* no. 102 (1998): 33-43. http://dx.doi.org/10.1002/he.10203.

*Regents of University of California v. Bakke.* 438 U.S. 265 (1978). https://supreme.justia.com/cases/federal/us/438/265/case.html.

Reimer, Jeremy. "Total Share: 30 Years of Personal Computer Market Share Figures." (Internet Archive: WayBackMachine), *ARS Technica: The Art of Technology,* December 14, 2005. http://web.archive.org/web/20080612013218/http://arstechnica.com/articles/culture/total-share.ars/5.

Renick, Chancellor James C. "Annual Report." Greensboro: A&T, May 2001.

*Report of the Agricultural and Mechanical College for the Colored Race at Greensboro, N.C.* Winston, NC: M.I. & J.C. Stewart, 1897.

"Riders in the Storm." Robert F. Kennedy Center for Justice & Human Rights, May 20, 2011. http://rfkcenter.org/riders-in-the-storm.

Risen, Clay. "The Unmaking of the President: Lyndon Johnson Believed That His Withdrawal from the 1968 Presidential Campaign Would Free Him to Solidify His Legacy." *Smithsonian Magazine*, April 2008. http://www.smithsonianmag.com/history/the-unmaking-of-the-president-31577203/?all&no-ist.

Roberts, Gene, and Hank Klibanoff. *The Race Beat: The Press, the Civil Rights Struggle, and the Awakening of a Nation.* New York, NY: Vintage, 2007.

Roosevelt, Franklin D. "Executive Order 8802: Prohibition of Discrimination in the Defense Industry." The U.S. National Archives and Records Administration. http://www.ourdocuments.gov/doc.php?doc=72.

———. "Executive Order 9346: Further Amending Executive Order No. 8802 by Establishing a New Committee on Fair Employment Practice and Defining Its Powers and Duties." In *Federal Register*, 8 FR 7183, May 27, 1943.

Rowland, Nettie C. "Aggie in the Hall." *A&T Today* 7, no. 2 (Winter 2004): 12-15. http://archive-staff.ncat.edu/univrel/publications/copy/attoday/attodaywinter04.pdf.

Scheckner, Jesse. "Tuskegee Airman Lt. Colonel Eldridge Williams Honored on 97th Birthday." *Pinecrest Tribune* (December 6, 2014): 1. http://www.communitynewspapers.com/pinecrest/tuskegee-airman-lt-colonel-eldridge-williams-honored-97th-birthday/.

Schlosser, Jim. "Noted Athlete, 1926 Graduate of A&T Dies—N.C. A&T Sports Hall of Famer Conrad Raiford was among Greensboro's First Six Black Police Officers." *Greensboro News & Record*, May 22, 2002, B1.

School of Business. *Cause for Celebration.* Dedication Program. Greensboro: A&T, April 14-15, 2004.

School of Technology. "Brief History: The Evolution of the School of Technology." [1-3]. Greensboro: A&T, n.d.

"Second Morrill Act of 1890 (August 30, 1890, Ch. 841; 7 U.S.C. 322 Et Seq.; 26 Stat. 417)." U.S. Department of Agriculture (USDA). National Institute of Food and Agriculture (NIFA). http://www.nifa.usda.gov/about/offices/legis/secondmorrill.html.

Sedghi, Ami. "Facebook: 10 Years of Social Networking, in Numbers." *The Guardian*, February 4, 2014. http://www.theguardian.com/news/datablog/2014/feb/04/facebook-in-numbers-statistics.

Simkins, Dr. George, Jr., *Inventory of the Dr. George Simkins, Jr. Collection.* Greensboro: F. D. Bluford Archives & Special Collections. http://www.library.ncat.edu/resources/archives/finding-simkins.html.

Sloan, W. David, James Glen Stovall, and James D. Startt. *The Media in America: A History (Supplemental Material)*. Worthington, OH: Publishing Horizons, 1989.

Speight-Buford, Dr. Velma. Interview, F. D. Bluford Library Archives and Department of Journalism and Mass Communication. *The North Carolina Agricultural and Technical State University Experience Through the Voices of Outstanding A&T Alumni* (May 4, 2006). Published electronically December 30, 2010. http://vimeo.com/18433465.

Spivak, Michelle. "Women's History Month: Remembering Their Contributions." In *The Flagship Wire*. Washington, D.C.: Veterans Affairs Medical Center, March 2011.

Spruill, Albert W. *Great Recollections from Aggieland: A Human Interest Account of the Development of the Agricultural and Technical College of North Carolina from 1893-1960*. Wilmington, NC: Whitehead, 1964.

"The STEM Early College at N.C. A&T." Greensboro: Guilford County Schools. http://stemec.gcsnc.com/pages/STEM_Early_College_at_N_C__A_T.

Stockley, Grif. "Daisy Lee Gatson Bates (1913?–1999)." *The Encyclopedia of Arkansas History and Culture* (2013). http://www.encyclopediaofarkansas.net/encyclopedia/entry-detail.aspx?entryID=591.

Styles, Teresa. Accreditation status of the Department of Journalism and Mass Communication, email, May 10, 2005.

"Telegram from King to President Eisenhower Urging Action in Little Rock." Martin Luther King, Jr. and the Global Freedom Struggle, September 9, 1957. http://mlk-kpp01.stanford.edu/index.php/encyclopedia/documentsentry/telegram_from_king_to_president_eisenhower_urging_action_in_little_rock.

Thompson, Charles H. "The Education of the Negro in the United States." In *The Negro Caravan*, edited by Sterling Allen Brown, Arthur Paul Davis, and Ulysses Lee. The American Negro, His History and Literature, 936-47. New York, NY: Arno Press, 1970.

Thompson, James G. "Should I Sacrifice to Live 'Half-American'?" *Pittsburgh Courier*, January 31, 1942. Reprinted in Part. In *A Question of Sedition: The Federal Government's Investigation of the Black Press During World War II*, edited by Patrick S. Washburn, 54-56. New York, NY: Oxford University Press, 1986.

"Time Line of African American History, 1901-1925." In *African American Perspectives: Pamphlets from the Daniel A.P. Murray Collection, 1818-1907,* edited by Rare Book and Special Collections Division. Washington, D.C.: Library of Congress, October 19, 1998. http://memory.loc.gov/ammem/aap/timelin3.html.

"Timeline of World War II." In *The War: At War,* edited by Ken Burns and Lynn Novick. Washington, D.C.: WETA, PBS, and American Lives II Film Project, 2007. http://www.pbs.org/thewar/at_war_timeline_1939.htm.

Truman, Harry S. "Executive Order 9980: Regulations Governing Fair Employment Practices within the Federal Establishment." The U.S. National Archives and Records Administration. http://research.archives.gov/description/7873508.

———. "Executive Order 9981: Desegregation of the Armed Forces." The U.S. National Archives and Records Administration. http://www.ourdocuments. gov/doc.php?doc=84.

"Veteran's Educational Transition Support Center to Open Soon." *The Aggie Report* 16, no. 3 (September 12, 2014). http://relations.ncat.edu/pubs/ aggiereport/2014/sept/sept12a.html#third.

"Vocational Education (Smith-Hughes Act of 1917)." Act of February 23, 1917, ch. 114; 39 Stat. 929; PL-347. http://www.constitution.org/uslaw/sal/039_ statutes_at_large.pdf.

"Voting Rights Act of 1965." The U.S. National Archives and Records Administration. http://www.ourdocuments.gov/doc.php?doc=100.

"Walker, Madam C. J. (1867-1919)." In *Guide to People, Organizations, and Topics in Prosperity and Thrift: The Coolidge Era and the Consumer Economy, 1921-1929*. Library of Congress, 1999. http://memory.loc.gov/ammem/coolhtml/ coolensz.html#dtwalker.

Weinberg, Arthur, and Lila Shaffer Weinberg. *The Muckrakers: The Era in Journalism That Moved America to Reform, the Most Significant Magazine Articles of 1902-1912*. New York, NY: Simon and Schuster, 1961.

Wesley, Joy, Sherry Poole Clark, Charles E. Watkins, and Gloria Pitts. "The Journey Continues: The North Carolina A&T University Foundation at 60." Greensboro: A&T, 2006.

"William J. Clinton, 42." In *The Presidents of the United States of America,* edited by Frank Freidel and Hugh Sidey. Washington, D.C.: White House Historical Association, 2006. http://www.whitehouse.gov/about/presidents/williamjclinton.

Williams, Andre. "Art Statum Figures He has much More Work to be Done." *The Morning Call*, May 21, 1995. http://articles.mcall.com/1995-05-21/ sports/3034409_1_phys-ed-physical-education-recreation-specialist.

Wilson, Woodrow. "Wilson's War Message to Congress." *WWI: The World War I Document Archive*, April 2, 1917. http://wwi.lib.byu.edu/index.php/ Wilson%27s_War_Message_to_Congress.

Withers, Lanita. "Veteran Educator Appointed A&T Interim Chancellor." *Greensboro News & Record*, May 2, 2006, A1.

Wolff, Miles. *Lunch at the Five and Ten, the Greensboro Sit-Ins: A Contemporary History*. New York, NY: Stein and Day, 1970.

Wooten, Eddie. "A&T's Fast Track Draws Top Athletes." *Greensboro News & Record*, July 28, 2009, B6.

# Index

# About the Authors

**Teresa Jo Styles** is a retired professor and former chair of the Department of Journalism and Mass Communication at North Carolina Agricultural and Technical State University. Following an extensive career as an award-winning journalist with CBS News in New York, she has taught, presented, and published nationally and internationally in the areas of broadcast journalism, media history, and media management. Styles is the recipient of the 2012 University of North Carolina Board of Governors Teaching Award. A native of Atlanta, she received a B.A. from Spelman College, an M.A. from Northwestern University, and a Ph.D. from the University of North Carolina at Chapel Hill.

**Professor Valerie Nieman** teaches creative writing at North Carolina Agricultural and Technical State University. An award-winning newspaper reporter and editor, she came to A&T in 2000 to teach journalism and work with the student newspaper before moving to English. She is the author of three novels, the most recent being *Blood Clay*, 2012 winner of the Eric Hoffer Award in General Fiction. She also has published two poetry collections, with *Hotel Worthy* appearing in 2015, and a collection of short stories. In addition to numerous newspaper awards, she has held writing fellowships from the National Endowment for the Arts and the North Carolina Arts Council. A native of western New York, she holds a B.S. in Journalism from West Virginia University and an MFA from Queens University of Charlotte.